www.wadsworth.com

www.wadsworth.com is the World Wide Web site for Thomson Wadsworth and is your direct source to dozens of online resources.

At *www.wadsworth.com* you can find out about supplements, demonstration software, and student resources. You can also send email to many of our authors and preview new publications and exciting new technologies.

www.wadsworth.com
Changing the way the world learns®

The Ghosts of Iceland

The Ghosts
of Iceland

ROBERT ANDERSON
Mills College

THOMSON
™
WADSWORTH

Australia • Canada • Mexico • Singapore • Spain
United Kingdom • United States

THOMSON

WADSWORTH

Senior Acquisitions Editor: *Lin Marshall*
Assistant Editor: *Nicole Root*
Editorial Assistant: *Kelly McMahon*
Technology Project Manager: *Dee Dee Zobian*
Marketing Manager: *Matthew Wright*
Marketing Assistant: *Tara Pierson*
Advertising Project Manager: *Linda Yip*
Project Manager, Editorial Production: *Catherine Morris*

Art Director: *Maria Epes*
Print/Media Buyer: *Karen Hunt*
Permissions Editor: *Kiely Sexton*
Production Service: *Mary Deeg, Buuji, Inc.*
Copy Editor: *Cheryl Hauser*
Cover Designer: *Scott Ratinoff*
Cover Image: *Martin Barraud/Getty Images*
Compositor: *Buuji, Inc.*
Text and Cover Printer: *Malloy Incorporated*

For more information about our products, contact us at:
Thomson Learning Academic Resource Center
1-800-423-0563
For permission to use material from this text or product, submit a request online at
http://www.thomsonrights.com.
Any additional questions about permissions can be submitted by email to
thomsonrights@thomson.com.

Library of Congress Control Number: 2004102460

ISBN 0-534-61052-8

Thomson Wadsworth
10 Davis Drive
Belmont, CA 94002-3098
USA

Asia
Thomson Learning
5 Shenton Way #01-01
UIC Building
Singapore 068808

Australia/New Zealand
Thomson Learning
102 Dodds Street
Southbank, Victoria 3006
Australia

Canada
Nelson
1120 Birchmount Road
Toronto, Ontario M1K 5G4
Canada

Europe/Middle East/Africa
Thomson Learning
High Holborn House
50/51 Bedford Row
London WC1R 4LR
United Kingdom

Latin America
Thomson Learning
Seneca, 53
Colonia Polanco
11560 Mexico D.F.
Mexico

Spain/Portugal
Paraninfo
Calle Magallanes, 25
28015 Madrid, Spain

For Stanley Victor Anderson,
My lifelong friend and professional colleague,
  my brother,
And in memory of our parents, Victor and Stella

Contents

Chapter 4

Dimensions of Mediumship   44

Chapter 5

Daily Life in the Spirit World   67

Chapter 6

Ghosts and Children   89

Chapter 7

Priests versus Mediums   **108**

Chapter 8

Socializing to Access Spirits   **129**

Chapter 9

New Age Elves and Fairies   **153**

Preface

THE REASON THINGS HAPPEN

A couple of years ago I got to know an English clairvoyant medium when she was conducting séances in Iceland. I was present at a sitting with her in Reykjavík when the spirit of a woman who died of cancer was said to be in the room with us along with other visitors from the spirit world. Speaking directly to a young woman in our group the medium said, *So, what they are saying to you is can you just accept more as things happen? Because they happen for a reason.*

In the United States, John Edward, a medium who claims to "talk with the dead," says exactly the same thing. "I believe everything happens for a reason" (2001: xiii, 22). It is also what I was taught by my mother who challenged all adversity by saying, "All things work together for good" (from Romans 8:28).

In a contradictory way, however, at this very moment as I write my daughter Debby is under anesthetic in a nearby hospital where she is in surgery for breast cancer that was revealed by routine mammography. She has a difficult year ahead of her as she anticipates radiation and chemotherapy. I am a skeptic. I find it hard to believe that everything that happens to people, no matter how awful, is for their own good. What good can there possibly be in having breast cancer that makes it better than not having cancer at all? I profoundly wish that Debby could have lived her entire life without it.

I am a skeptic, but I think I am open-minded. As a professional anthropologist, my job is to learn about other social worlds, other ways of being human, and to write about what I have learned. I have been trained as much as it is humanly possible to avoid ethnocentric closed-mindedness and to try as skillfully as I can to understand how alternative ways of thinking, acting, desiring, and believing can make good sense where they occur, no matter how different they may be from my own ways.

I also try to be flexible, to "go with the flow," as a professional necessity. I would not have done the research reported on here had it not been for serendipity, which is about something good or useful happening that was unexpected and unplanned for. This book is a product of serendipity. I was doing research in Iceland on how low back pain is diagnosed and treated (Anderson 2000). It sometimes happens that while doing fieldwork an anthropologist will discover a fruitful line of inquiry that he or she did not anticipate. That is exactly what happened to me.

In conversations with Icelanders who were seeking relief from pain I began to hear stories about ghost doctors who continued to practice medicine after they died. Those invisible doctors seemed to be widely known and appreciated. They even make house calls at night. Without hesitation, I added an investigation of deceased doctors to a list that had already escaped the confines of conventional medicine to include Reiki practitioners and Pentecostal prayer "warriors."

But, as part of the holistic approach favored by anthropologists, I needed to place my research on ghost doctors in the larger context of how living people make contact with the dead in other ways as well. As explained in Chapter 1, I ended up exploring a universe of pervasive nationwide beliefs about the many ways in which living people interact with spirits of the dead. I was deeply touched as Icelanders spoke to me of how loved ones remain a part of the family after they die and as they introduced me to a nameless, minimally institutionalized spirituality that thrives independently of the formalities of the state Lutheran church to which every Icelander belongs, almost without exception.

In probing deeper, I also learned about guardian angels, space aliens, elves, and other invisible humanoids that some people encounter and that a few can even see. As described in Chapter 2, they are part of an array of possibilities, a cultural menu, from which people can choose, perhaps without conscious reflection, as they learn to rely on certain selected paranormal relationships and to reject or disregard others.

In Chapter 3, I zero in on ghosts and poltergeists, by which I mean spirits of the dead who were neither family members nor friends. Ghosts can be horribly dangerous, and I retell some old Viking stories from the Icelandic sagas to illustrate just how deadly they were in the past. On the whole, however, contemporary ghosts are quite refined and harmless. Many, especially ghost doctors, are thought of as generous benefactors of the living.

I also learned how mediums are selected for their craft. As I point out in Chapter 4, the selection process differs from that of the clergy, who become Lutheran pastors only after finishing a university education and being formally ordained by a bishop. Mediums emerge out of an informal process that begins early in life when they display an uncommon openness to the spirit world that is fine-tuned later by apprenticeship and confirmed when they demonstrate an ability to convey messages from the spirit world.

In Chapter 4 I also record what I was taught along with what I was able to figure out about different kinds of mediums. I was told that clairvoyant mediums converse with spirits of the dead but do so without using language in the normal sense. They communicate directly mind to mind and visualize the bodily appearance of the spirit in their mind's eye. Most mediums perform in that way. Possession mediums are rare in Iceland, but a possession séance allows the spirit to bypass mind-to-mind transmission by using the medium's voice to carry on vocal conversations that everyone can hear. A transfiguration medium, rarer still, takes the process one step further by seeming to take on the physical appearance of the spirit in addition to using ordinary speech. The most dramatic of all, and the least common, is the physical medium whose spirits move objects around in apparent defiance of the normal laws of gravity and inertia. These different kinds of mediums, along with psychic healers, can be distinguished from one another and ranked in a hierarchy of skill and status.

Using mediums as informants I put together an ethnography that describes daily life after death, as set forth in Chapter 5. The afterworld is always characterized as a utopia in which spirits possess supernatural powers and knowledge. Mediums generally agree that food is smelled rather than eaten, but they disagree on whether the dead enjoy active sex lives.

Chapter 6 arose out of numerous accounts of encounters with ghosts by children and adolescents. For the most part, the ghosts seen by smaller children are benign and taken for granted, although in a few cases these ghosts have been troublesome. The most intriguing encounters for adolescents occur in the use of a Ouija board to address questions to a ghost. The game frequently frightens participants, which may be the very reason for playing it in the first place.

In Chapter 7 I report on my interviews with representatives of various Christian churches, including the national Lutheran church and churches with a small presence in Iceland, including the only Catholic church in Reykjavík. My question was can a Christian be a spiritist? Responses ranged from "absolutely not!" to "How can a Christian not be a spiritist!"

Spiritism is fluid and minimally organized in Iceland, especially in contrast to Christian churches. Yet, to some degree it is institutionalized, as pointed out in Chapter 8. However, as befits a population that can be characterized as secular rather than devout, spiritist social institutions in Iceland are called schools and meditation circles rather than churches and chapels.

Some of these institutions attach more importance to elves and fairies than to spirits of the dead, whom they merely acknowledge and then ignore, as narrated in Chapter 9. The emphasis on elves and fairies is accompanied by global New Age beliefs and practices such as channeling and shamanism.

I was struck with the extent to which mediumship in Iceland at times can be staged as a kind of theater that resembles vaudeville in being humorous and entertaining. I refer to these theatrical appearances of spirits of the dead in Chapter 10 as staged illusions.

In Chapter 11, I provide transcripts of two occasions when mediums facilitated supposed conversations between my deceased father and me. Based on those and other personal experiences, I have to conclude that spirits of the dead do not truly communicate with the living and I question whether they can be said to exist at all.

I want to emphasize that I do not assume that mediums consciously misrepresent themselves. I prefer to believe that they are self-deceived. I also freely acknowledge that while I found no evidence that the dead survive the grave, it is always possible that someone else will, because I can only deny the specific claims that came to my attention. Note, too, in Chapter 11 and in the concluding epilogue, that I ended up being deeply appreciative of the beauty and value of spirit beliefs that center on the ultimate importance of loving and serving others, the cosmic lesson useful to everyone.

But who is likely to find this book worth reading? Above all, of course, I have tried to give university students and other readers a sense of how one professional anthropologist works and thinks. To that end, in each chapter I explicitly discuss how I have applied research methods and built on ethnological theory. I need hardly add that other anthropologists might well have proceeded differently. An important part of the dynamism of the discipline is that anthropologists are very tolerant of diversity, including variety in methodological techniques and differences in theoretical orientations.

However, I wrote *The Ghosts of Iceland* with the expectation that it might attract a much wider range of readers simply because it investigates the way many people cope with knowing that in the end each person must die. The meaning that spiritists attach to death can function as a way to find meaning in being alive. One can be thoroughly unbelieving about spirits of the dead and still be uplifted by an emphasis on the personal and social values of love and compassion. Spirituality has meaning independent of spiritism.

Because this book is about the ultimate meaning of life, I think it may prove stimulating to students taking courses in anthropology, religious studies, the sociology of religion, the history of Christianity, and the philosophy of religion. For religious studies I offer this as a case study in comparative religion in which the popular religion of a society is not the politically prominent institutionalized Christian church, but a congeries of beliefs and practices that deviate from Bible-based theology. For the sociology of religion, *The Ghosts of Iceland* provides an example of how individuals interact within social institutions, and how religious groups organize socially and differentiate or imitate one another culturally in symbolic power plays. For courses on the history of Christianity, and specifically the history of heaven and of hell, the reader will find apocryphal beliefs about the afterlife in spiritist and New Age thinking that have persisted in the interstices of popular culture at least since they were articulated in ancient Greece and the Renaissance. But perhaps the most provocative potential of this study will be for students in courses on the philosophy of religion, because this ethnography provides students with a pragmatic basis for challenging or making sense of truth claims relating to the immortality of the soul and life after death.

ACKNOWLEDGMENTS

If I were to do no more than to list the names of people in Iceland who made my research possible this acknowledgment would look like a telephone book. Iceland is unexcelled as a nation of generous, helpful citizens. I must, however, single out some people on whom I relied heavily. At the University of Iceland, professors Gisli Pálsson (anthropology), Elendur Haraldsson (psychology), Terry Gunnell (folkloristics), and Jón Hnevill Adelsstensson (folkloristics). Many anthropology students pitched in to guide and assist me, but I came to rely especially on Krístin Erla Hardardóttir and Gudrun Hulda Eythorsdóttir. Jón Boásson on the nonacademic staff was an unfailing friend and helper.

My hosts, guides, respondents, and teachers on the esoterica of communicating with deceased loved ones and other spirits of the dead are described and quoted throughout the following pages. Unfortunately, following a convention of scholarship and the recommendation of an anonymous anthropologist, all but Magnus Skarphedinsson, Erla Stefánsdóttir,

Gudrun Bergman, and Thorsteinn Gudjónsson are identified by pseudonyms in order to protect their privacy. When the others read the book they will recognize themselves, and I want each of them to know that I love, respect, and appreciate them all, including Tobba Jónsdóttir and Anna Einarsdóttir, whom I feel I should identify here by real names.

This project was an offshoot of medical research on the diagnosis and treatment of low back pain in Iceland. Jósep Blöndal, physician and surgeon, was not only my colleague and mentor in that undertaking but continued to be equally so when my investigation branched out from back pain patients to spirits and ghosts. He also introduced me to Sturla Kristjánsson and Ingi Gerdur Snorradóttir who were so helpful to me in Akureyri.

My work in Iceland was made possible in part by a sabbatical leave from Mills College, for which I thank the faculty research committee and the president of the college, Janet Holmgren. Edna Mitchell, professor, was especially supportive academically and in other ways. In addition, my work was supported by a Fulbright grant. Local representatives of the Fulbright Commission and the U.S. embassy included William Douglas and Stella P. Hálfdánardóttir.

During the critical and challenging transition that transformed the manuscript I originally submitted into the book you now have before you, I benefited enormously from my association with the Wadsworth publishing team. As senior acquisitions editor for anthropology, Lin Marshall arranged for feedback from professors Raymond A. Bucko, Paul Durrenberger, Norman Kline, Kathryn S. Oths, and two anonymous anthropologists, all of which led to major revisions that greatly improved the presentation. More than anyone else, based on her own training as an anthropologist, Lin worked side by side with me to reorganize and fine-tune the final product. As I look back now on the submitted manuscript, I marvel that she was able to see its potential, and to the extent that it now has value, I am especially grateful to her.

ABOUT THE AUTHOR

Robert (Bob) Anderson, professor and head of the Department of Sociology and Anthropology at Mills College, is a physician as well as an anthropologist. For two decades, early in his career, he specialized in documenting culture change and the ethnology of Europe. His earlier books include *Traditional Europe: A Study in Anthropology and History*, *The Vanishing Village: A Danish Maritime Community* (with Barbara Anderson), and *Denmark: Success of a Developing Nation*. In 1998, fol-

Edna Mitchell

Robert Anderson, M.D.

lowing a long interlude in other parts of the world, he returned to undertake ethnographic fieldwork in two of the Nordic countries where his ethnographic career began. He returned to Denmark to document the theory and practice of a small number of surviving traditional healers known as *kloge folk,* "wise people" (2005, a chapter in *Manipulating the Body: Bonesetting and Manual Medicine in Global Perspective,* edited by K. Oths and S. Hinojosa), and he returned to Iceland, where his findings as a medical anthropologist were recently published as *Alternative and Conventional Medicine in Iceland: The Diagnosis and Treatment of Low Back Pain.* A long-standing interest in the anthropology of religion took him in the past to China, Nepal, Bali, Brazil, Mexico, and Zimbabwe, but most recently he indulged that interest in Iceland where he carried out the investigation that led to this study of ghosts, deceased ancestors, elves, and aliens from outer space.

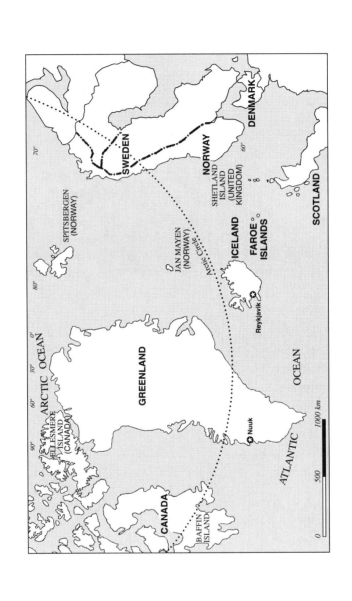

TO TALK WITH THE DEAD

HOW CURIOSITY LED TO THIS RESEARCH

On a beautiful sunny morning while driving to work and listening to National Public Radio, I heard about a man from Bulgaria or Romania who plans to write a book about the last 72 days in the life of Vincent van Gogh. In that book he will challenge the common assumption that the painter bled to death, based on new evidence about how he actually passed away. The nature of the evidence he offers is unconventional. He learned "the true story" directly from the dead man himself in a conversation they had in Arles, France, where the spirit of the painter was sitting on the roof of his former home and was agreeable to talking about his demise.

At about the same time, Wayan Lidawati, a Mills College student from Bali, joined me over coffee to explain that in Balinese belief reincarnation always takes place within the family. Wayan herself is said to be the reincarnation of her great-grandmother on her father's side. *They say my character is like hers. My grandmother told me that.* Until the reincarnation takes place, however, a deceased loved one lives on as a spirit who watches over the family. *My mother's father died before my mother was born,* Wayan continued. *As a small girl, until I was 9 years old, or maybe it was 12, I could feel someone big behind me, but I couldn't see him. I felt protected. I would wander alone—to the river—without fear. When I was 5 I traveled from Bali to Java, alone. I had no fear. I'm not sure if it was him or another spirit, or just my imagination. I always said it was my grandfather, because people told me that. They said it was because I was the first granddaughter and therefore was closer to him.*

For years and from all over the world I have heard stories about encounters with spirits of the dead, but above all I was told of such events while I was a Fulbright lecturer at the University of Iceland. That small

1

northerly nation took me by surprise. I thought at first that Icelanders were quite unreligious. As in Denmark and Sweden, their official, state-supported Lutheran churches are beautifully maintained and impressive architecturally, but generally nearly empty on Sundays (Tomasson 2002: 61). Almost without exception, the people I spoke with told me that they are officially members of the national church, but they also acknowl-edged that they rarely attend church services.

Independently of the official institutional church, however, super-natural beliefs and practices thrive as an unnamed, unpretentious, and quiet, nearly silent, spiritual movement that impacts most of the popula-tion either directly or indirectly in deeply personal ways. They practice a religion that is minimally institutionalized and almost never thought of as somehow equivalent to Christianity. Yet, although nearly invisible in the public arena, it is of profound importance in their lives. This book is about spiritism, the practice of communicating with spirits of the dead, which, to a surprising extent, I would characterize as the unofficial but widely influential people's religion of Iceland.

Iceland is one of the Nordic nations, along with Denmark, the Faeroe Islands, Finland, Norway, and Sweden. It stands out geographi-cally in that it is not directly attached to Europe, although it has always had close ties with Scandinavia and was a Danish political dependency until World War II. Located almost entirely on a single large island at the very edge of the Arctic Circle, and seemingly under constant threat from the stormy North Atlantic, it is understandable that the country was called "ice-land" and remained almost entirely uninhabited until the early Middle Ages, when it was finally settled by hardy Vikings who spoke the language of western Norway (Karlsson 2000: 9–15).

Icelanders were originally devotees of a pantheon of Nordic gods such as Odin and Thor, but they chose Christianity as their official reli-gion in a national plebiscite just over a thousand years ago. For most of their history they lived in isolated farmsteads dispersed across a rugged terrain of volcanoes, lava beds, glaciers, and fjords, each family feeding itself by growing a few hardy crops, especially hay for their livestock, and by bird netting and fishing. During the last half of the 20th century their total population remained small. Even today it only counts about 280,000. But in that last half century, Icelanders totally abandoned the old parochial way of life. Most now live in cities, especially in and around Reykjavík, where their economy and political system resembles that of the rest of Europe and North America, although still with a heavy depen-dence on the fishing industry. By means of modern air transportation, radio, television, and universal literacy, Icelanders have become highly cosmopolitan and are completely up-to-date on the latest in social and cultural trends worldwide.

Old-style fishing boats and postmodern church architecture

Coming from an interest in the anthropology of religion and being highly intrigued that many educated and thoroughly sophisticated people in this modern and supposedly secular society believe they have been or could be in contact with spirits of the dead, I eagerly devoted as much of my time in Iceland as I could to applying my field research experience and training, that is to say, my ethnographic skills, to learn about this nearly invisible religion.

On Doing Field Research

I write as an anthropologist, and readers will catch a glimpse of why anthropologists refer to their signature research methodology, ethnographic fieldwork, as doing participant observation. While living and working in Reykjavík, many friends, acquaintances, students, and colleagues talked with me about their experiences of contact with spirits of the dead. Field research relies heavily on conversations and interviews, but in addition I did what many Icelanders themselves do. I spent time with spirit mediums who attempted to put me in touch with spirits of the dead. I also joined in group séances, observing and recording conversations between the living and the dead and arranging for spirit doctors to treat sick friends. I sat in on lectures at spiritist schools and attended spirit society coffee klatches.

I hope you will not be put off by the extent to which I write about myself. It is rather self-centered, I confess, but not because I feel self-important. It is just that I have been influenced by postmodernist theorizing to believe that for readers to evaluate the integrity of what I report they need to know how I was involved and what I was thinking (Eriksen & Nielsen 2001: 135–156; e.g., Rabinow 1977). James Clifford (1986) seemed to have this approach in mind some years ago when he stated that anthropologists were writing in a new self-reflexive way that he characterized as "variously sophisticated and naive, confessional and analytic" (p. 14).

Michael Jackson (1989) speaks of the anthropological approach I employ here as radical empiricism, which he describes as doing fieldwork based on "the ethnographer's *interactions* with those he or she lives with and studies," so that what we end up writing about is, as he put it, "grounded in our practical, personal, and participatory experience" (p. 3). It is notable that this kind of research can impact the fieldworker in deeply personal ways.

These involvements certainly touched me in deeply personal ways. I found spiritual warmth in the intimacies of group séances and in supportive friendships, especially since I was living away from my wife and family at the time. I also found myself unexpectedly reaching into my own Nordic ancestry. From beginning to end my Danish American father, Victor Anderson (born Viggo Andersen in 1887) and my Danish mother, Stella (born Hansen in 1900), both now long deceased, were key players in this research on the ghosts of Iceland, along with other Danish ancestors, because they "came through" in séances, or so I was told.

I remain a complete skeptic about the reality of God, angels, spirits of the dead, life after death, and conversations with my dead father and mother. However, séances in which my parents appeared activated a latent awareness of how love does survive the grave and that it is important to pass that on. Perhaps my most important finding, although not at all original, is that God, spirits of the dead, and other supranormal beings need not actually exist in order to help people survive and find joy in a chaotic and dangerous world.

This method for documenting the daily realities of a society and culture is intensely personal, and readers need to be alert to the possibility that the anthropologist has succumbed to personal bias in distortive ways. To that end, I have done two things. For one, almost all interviews and observations, with permission, were videotaped to ensure accurate reporting, using a small, pocket-size digital camcorder. Second, I give voice to the people who instructed me, using their narratives as data by eliciting and listening to their stories, employing what folklorist David Hufford (1982) refers to as an experienced-centered method that allows people to speak for themselves, interlacing their narratives with my own, as I just did with Wayan Lidawati.

Ideally, anthropologists learn to speak the language of the people they are studying. Yet, almost without exception, the language of the narratives I elicited in Iceland are in English, and that requires explanation. Because I speak Danish and Danish is a required subject in Icelandic schools, I made two false assumptions. First, I assumed that I would rapidly learn to converse in Icelandic, because many decades ago I discovered that it wasn't very difficult to get by in Swedish and Norwegian based on linguistic similarities with Danish and a few months of self-study. Icelandic is an offshoot of Norwegian as it was spoken a thousand years ago, but what I didn't realize was that Icelandic today is totally different from present-day Norwegian, and impossible to learn in half a year, so that didn't work out at all. Second, I also assumed that I might speak Danish with Icelanders, since children still study Danish in the public schools, but that proved unnecessary, because those who spoke Danish usually also spoke English. That, in itself, is a measure of how cosmopolitan Icelanders now are. For perhaps the one out of twenty of my informants who did not speak English or Danish I used a translator, mostly Kristín Hardardóttir, an anthropology graduate student whom the university employed to serve as my research assistant.

QUANTITATIVE RESEARCH

Further on the subject of research methods, anthropologists can be said to employ two basic strategies in their efforts to understand human diversity. One is to study a single society in breadth and depth and the other is to narrow the subject of interest but to search for similarities and differences in cross-cultural surveys. My strategy in Iceland was the former. I attempted to learn as much as I could about Iceland alone in order to produce what Clifford Geertz (1973) refers to as a thick description. The method is qualitative in the sense that I describe named individuals whom I observed up close and whose stories I was told in the context of their lives.[1] But on that basis alone I could not know the extent to which Icelanders resemble other peoples or are different from them.

---

[1] It is customary in Iceland under ordinary circumstances to use first names as terms of reference and address. Although last names and titles exist, they are sparingly invoked, so for the most part I will refer to the people I got to know by their first names. However, just to be sure that nobody is embarrassed or inconvenienced, I used pseudonyms for all respondents, except for four who are so well known that anonymity would be impossible, namely Erla Stefánsdóttir, Gudrun Bergman, Magnus Skarphedinsson, and Thorsteinn Gudjonsson. Professional colleagues, of course, are identified by their real names.

Robert Anderson

The University of Iceland campus

Fortunately, I was able to draw on cross-cultural surveys carried out by my University of Iceland colleague, Elendur Haraldsson, because he specifically gives a global perspective to the Icelandic experience that I record. To that end he extends his gaze widely, but as an inevitable trade-off, thinly. By including brief summaries of his findings in this chapter, I hope to guide readers through both the thick and the thin of how Icelanders experience the afterlife.

Haraldsson carried out a well-designed and precisely executed national mail survey relating to spirits of the dead in 1974. Reporting on that carefully selected random sample of 1,132 Icelandic adults (with an 80 percent response rate yielding 902 respondents), he found that 31 percent answered yes to the question, have you ever been "really in touch with someone who had died?" On a gender basis, the answer was affirmative for 36 percent of the women and 24 percent of the men.

In a later study, Haraldsson (1988: 105; see also Swatos & Gíssurarson 1997: 226) identified an increase to 41 percent of respondents reporting contact with the dead, which represents a marked trend upward, although he cautions that the change could reflect a difference in how the question was phrased rather than a true increase in prevalence. In that survey he asked, "Have you ever perceived or felt the nearness of a deceased person?"

Prevalence rates at such high levels, although uncommon, are not without precedent elsewhere in Europe. W. D. Rees (1971) concluded from his investigation in Wales that it is normal for 46 percent of widows and 50 percent of widowers to report in a clearly waking state seeing their dead spouses. Why it should be slightly more common among men than women is not clear.

My own findings suggest that the apparent trend from 1974 to 1983 in Iceland has continued to grow, although I hasten to acknowledge that the results of my questionnaire are somewhat impressionistic, since it was administered to a small, opportunistic sample. Ninety university students, out of a total of 93 enrolled in my courses on medical and biological anthropology, completed the questionnaire I distributed in class. Of that number, 47 percent—nearly half—said yes, they had "experienced contact with the spirit of someone who had died." A striking gender difference was evident. Whereas 29 percent of the men responded in the affirmative, an even greater number of the women did so, an impressive 51 percent. The social life of half of these young women included dead people, if I may put it in that admittedly melodramatic way. Further, it is highly suggestive that nearly all of the student sample, 80 percent of them, reported that if they had not themselves been in touch with a dead person they did know someone who could claim that experience. On reviewing these survey findings I became convinced that spiritism did, indeed, constitute a very meaningful cultural pattern on the national level.

Haraldsson and I both documented fewer claims of contact among men than among women. Why fewer men? In one-on-one interviews with students I often asked that question. The responses of both men and women almost always stressed that while it was not embarrassing for a woman to acknowledge encounters with spirits, to do so might impugn a masculine ideal of being tough-minded. Men are supposed to be pragmatic and objective. They are not supposed to demonstrate softhearted emotions or spiritual vulnerabilities. A less common alternative explanation was that men were less in tune with themselves and less intimate with others and less able, therefore, to make contact with the beyond.

But those explanations were not completely convincing. I interviewed a few women as well as a few men who insisted that they were completely skeptical about the reality of spirits. Women seem to be fully as tough-minded as men. What a couple of interviews brought out, however, was that several of the skeptical men and women who denied having had contact with the dead simply read the question in a more restrictive way than others. On probing, they usually acknowledged an experience that simply did not seem definitive enough to justify an affirmative answer.

Haukur, for example, wrote that no, he had never had such an experience himself. Yet, he told me his girlfriend was frightened one dark and wintry night on a wilderness road when a ghost unexpectedly sat next to her in her car. As we talked more, he also told me that once he himself had encountered a ghost along that same lonely road. He saw a man skiing down the mountainside at midnight in bad weather when it could not possibly have been a living person. He was shaken at the time, but later came to distrust the accuracy of his memory.

Among students who had experienced contact with a dead person, it was most common for it to be with a departed relative. In my survey, 76 percent of all reported contacts were with family members, usually grandparents (constituting 63 percent of all contacts with relatives). This was not surprising, since the average age of these students was only 23.5 years. Most of them were too young to have dead parents or deceased spouses. And, encounters with relatives were routinely recalled as being pleasant.

So, Iceland turned out to be an ideal place to look for family continuity beyond the grave, as I found out from Halldór, whose story is more dramatic than most. When he was about 30 years old, he was driving across the vast, lonely wilderness and winter darkness of Iceland, mesmerized by the lonely road, slippery ice, and ghostly white snow. Miles from the nearest farmhouse, he saw a man at the edge of the road, so he stopped to offer a ride. As he pulled over the man disappeared. Getting out of the car and looking around he saw no one and no place that might have concealed somebody. Strange. On a quirky impulse Halldór opened the door on the passenger side and said, "Come on in." But nobody was there to respond. He shook his head, closed the door, and drove on.

Five minutes later he noticed that someone had materialized in the passenger seat, clearly visible, and quite responsive. They talked all the way from Akureyri in the north to Reykjavík in the south. Who was it? *It was my father.* What did you talk about? *Everything about my life. What I was doing. The calm weather. Like that. The same as when he was alive.*

Did he seem to know about your life subsequent to his death? *Yes, he seemed to know what I was doing, and a few times told me to do it another way.* Can you elaborate a bit? *Well, for example, I had been working too hard for a long time. He said I needed to ease off. My [deceased] grandfather has said the same to me.*

When is the last time your grandfather came to you? *About 10 months ago. I had a very serious accident. At work I fell from a roof, landing on the frozen ground below and getting all broken up. So I was told I could no longer work as a carpenter or fisherman. The recommendation was for me to train as a teacher, but I was reluctant, and that's when Granddad came. He said, "Don't be so stubborn. Just make the change." Also, I had an old car I had been working on for years. He said, "Drop it. Get rid of it." That was good advice.*

Halldór then explained that he had only encountered his father that one time on the road. Otherwise, it was always his grandfather who looked after him, and he gave two dramatic examples. Once, many years ago, he was working alone, late at night, building a house for his family, when a stack of heavy timber fell on him. Trapped, he pushed with all his might, but completely failed to budge the timber.

I was thinking, I'm stuck here until tomorrow, when the fishing boat has to leave and they will look for me—6 or 8 hours. I can't hold out in this freezing weather. An hour went by. I thought, I don't know how, but I must get free. All of a sudden I was able to lift the timbers and slip out from underneath. I don't know how I did it, but **I know I was not alone; I had help** [emphasis added].

Another time Halldór was at sea on a fishing boat. Fishing is a very dangerous occupation. People drown on stormy seas every year, especially in bad weather, and the weather that day was foul. *A huge wave washed two of us overboard.* **I wasn't afraid** [emphasis added]. *The first thing I thought of when I found myself in the water was that the other guy was from a farm, so he surely can swim, because he was raised on a farm. But he was drowning, so I swam close enough to grab him by the hair and pull him to the boat, where he was hauled aboard. But he slipped away again, so I followed, hoping to get hold of him again, but he drowned. I drifted in the waves for another 10 minutes, but* **I was never afraid I would die** [emphasis added]. *The skipper was doing the only thing he could, sailing so I would drift toward the boat, where they pulled me aboard. Through that whole affair* **I felt I am not alone** [emphasis added]. "I wasn't afraid." "I am not alone." Now about 60 years old, Halldór still faces life's dangers with that reassurance.

But Halldór is only one among many who told me of ongoing relations with dead loved ones. As a young woman, Jóhanna attended a large group séance in which her grandmother came to her through the medium. Her grandmother said nothing, but patted her on the cheek and on the back of her hand in a special way, just as she had when she was alive. It was a loving touch.

Jóhanna was also one of several who mentioned that while she and I were in a room together, spirits of the dead were also present. It happened once when we were chatting in her living room on the outskirts of Reykjavík. While we talked, her deceased grandparents were also there, listening in on the conversation but not interrupting. Jóhanna explained: *Sometimes we detect smells, my grandfather's tobacco, for example,* pointing to a portrait photo on the living room wall in which he is standing next to his wife. *My* [paternal] *grandfather and grandmother were very close to me. They always come together.*

Sometimes I see them with my eyes closed, she added. *Last night when I was going to sleep, my* [maternal] *grandmother came. She said, "Yes, I*

The deceased grandparents who were in the room with us in spirit form

---

know what you are doing now." Jóhanna smiled at that recollection. *She is in this room with us right now, following us.* How do you know she is here now? *I have the feeling that comes over me like this,* moving her hands along the sides and top of her head. *Sometimes I feel warm over my heart. That means they come with love. That's how they tell me, "We are here and we love you." I love them very much.*

Most encounters with deceased loved ones are dramatic only in the first instance and become rather prosaic as time passes. For example, Gudmundur, who was president of the Spirit Research Society of Iceland when I first met him, told me that he has contacted his father many times through mediums, but it has become a kind of taken-for-granted relationship.

What does he say to you? I asked. *He says almost the same thing to me as when he was alive. Nothing special or new. Maybe he will describe how he feels and what he is doing, but in the same old way. There is nothing new.* Is your father involved in your life now? *He just tells me he follows me, so he knows what's happening. He may say, "What you are doing is difficult."* Does your father protect you in any way? *I believe so, but I have no concrete proof. He says, "I'm looking after you all the time."*

Magnus Skarphedinsson captured both the transformative impact of a first encounter and the mundane acceptance of follow-up encounters when I first met him and asked, have you ever had contact with a loved one? *Yes,* was his instant reply. *It was with my Grandfather Magnus, whom I'm named after.* When was the last time he came to you? *Oh, that was some years ago. I did it* [contacted him] *many times at first but in recent years, it's just, "Here's Granddad." He says, "Hello." That's all.* When is the last time you had contact? *Several years ago. I don't need that anymore. That need was fulfilled.*

Yet you say that those early visits were helpful to you. *Oh, my, yes. They took away the grief of his loss, which moved me greatly. But what was equally important, knowing he is still around changed my attitude toward life.*

With an involuntary start I said, Wow! Do you mean it gave your life a new or different meaning? *Oh, yes, exactly so. Those encounters with my grandfather totally and fundamentally changed my understanding. They made me realize that I should live my life knowing that I will live on in an afterlife. Knowing that life goes on after death is a reality with enormous implications for how one should live this life in an earthly body.* He then told me that it aimed him at a career that included becoming the founder and director of the Spirit Research School, which maintains an active program of documenting encounters with those who have passed over, as spiritists often put it.

Conclusion

Many years ago, it seemed that the main job of an anthropologist was to report back from distant, seemingly exotic places the way Margaret Mead did from the South Seas during the 1920s. But it is notable that in subsequent decades, Mead also wrote extensively about American culture, and in recent decades, when every nation has its own indigenous anthropologists, more and more of us in North America and Europe interrogate our own societies and describe our own ways of being human. However, the research methods used in far-off parts of the world are applicable as well to the complex urban-industrial Western societies that gave birth to the profession of anthropology. It is not a break in the history of the discipline that we carry out both qualitative and quantitative research in places like Iceland.

The religious culture of Iceland, a thoroughly Western society, can be described using the same concepts and methods ethnographers use for other parts of the world where beliefs and practices are quite different and, to the uninformed, seemingly exotic and difficult to understand. In Iceland I encountered conservative Lutheran Protestantism as the official state religion and found that it was perfectly appropriate for cultural analysis. The national church coexists with non-Christian beliefs and practices relating to a form of modern spiritism that originated in upstate New York in the 1840s as well as to eclectic New Age forms of spirituality associated with the emergence of the counterculture of the 1960s. Lutheranism, spiritism, and New Age spirituality are at home in the urban-industrial West, but I investigated them through intense personal involvement just as Mead (1966) did when she documented how practitioners of magic and sorcery on Manus Island in Melanesia interacted with natives who by then had become ordained ministers in the Anglican church.

THE MENU OF
HUMANOID POSSIBILITIES

THE CONCEPT OF CULTURE AS A THEORY

In the past, when anthropologists wrote about how people lived their lives, they usually organized their findings in terms of a theory of culture that implied considerable uniformity or homogeneity within any one society. The way cultures were described implied that everyone in a society more or less conformed to a clearly definable lifestyle. Some mid-century anthropologists referred to cultures as "designs for living" (Kluckhohn & Kelly 1945: 9). In the early 1930s Ruth Benedict (1934) described characteristic "patterns of culture" for each of the societies she described implying that all Kwakiutl Indians in the Pacific Northwest, for example, or all Dobuans in Melanesia, or all who live in a tribal community in some other part of the world shared basic values, beliefs, and habits that characterized their society and made behavior largely predictable as a result. I wrote books based on that kind of theorizing myself earlier in my career (Anderson & Anderson 1964, 1965), and even to this day anthropologists typically define culture as "learned and shared human behaviors and ideas" (Miller 2002: 388). Lawrence Hirschfeld (2002) refers to this anthropological penchant as "theories that cast cultures as bounded, relatively stable, and homogeneous environments, populated with actors who consistently share interests and knowledge" (p. 616).

But most anthropologists theorize culture differently now. We still identify learned and shared ideas relating to ways of interacting with kin, establishing friendships, getting educated, finding work, giving time to recreation, committing to personal goals, claiming identity vis-à-vis others, finding meaning and purpose in life, and adopting beliefs about death and the hereafter, but we no longer see what is learned and shared as a lifestyle of conformity. On the contrary, we theorize cultural traits as

13

options that one may activate or ignore, as constraints that one may conform to or resist. "At any given moment," Hirschfeld (2002) writes, "the cultural environment which an individual inhabits is fragmented, fluid, noisy, and negotiable . . . comprised of multiple, contesting, competing subcultural environments" (p. 615).

Taking my lead from Ann Swidler (1986), I find it helpful to think of "culture as a 'tool kit' of symbols, stories, rituals, and world-views, which people may use in varying configurations to solve different kinds of problems" (p. 273). From that perspective, one might say that insofar as Icelanders attempt to cope with personal or existential problems by establishing relationships with non-ordinary beings, their culture provides them with a range of options, a tool kit of beliefs, which is not limited to spirits of the dead. It also includes angels, space aliens, and elves.

ANGELS IN ICELANDIC LIFE

As a general rule, in societies where spirits of the dead are thought to socialize with living people, so too do spirits with no ancestry as human beings. In the Christian world the most familiar nonhuman spirits are angels.

Angels are well known to Icelanders from accounts of their activities in the Bible, the teachings of pastors, confirmation classes, Christian art, passing references in ordinary conversations, and in literature and movies. The general consensus would undoubtedly be that angels are a lot like human beings. According to the Bible, they run errands and do other chores for God. They make mistakes, sometimes sin, and may even become quite evil, for which they will be judged and punished. Satan, after all, is a fallen angel. Unlike living people, however, they do not marry or have babies. Being inexperienced in sex, they are like eunuchs, human-like, but not fulfilled as human beings. They are, on the other hand, very much like spirits of the dead, because they are able to cover great distances with ease, show up unexpectedly anywhere they choose, and at times hang out with living people, usually but not always while remaining invisible.

As part of my curiosity about contact with spirits, I talked with people about angels at times, but never got much of a response. It seems that in Iceland they are rarely thought about, even by those who strongly believe that they really do exist and are important. Hafsteinn, a pastor assigned to the National Cathedral, told me that God protects those who believe in him by sending angels to watch over them, but Hafsteinn had nothing more to say about angels except to warn me that the supposed

A church in downtown Reykjavík

spirit of a deceased loved one might well be none other than an evil angel, the devil in disguise.

Erla Stefánsdóttir, with a gift for seeing invisible humanoids, including occasional angels, refers to the latter only in passing, but when she told me that she was a Christian, even though she usually attends church only at Christmas and Easter, she did mention them. In that conversation I asked, do you pray? Her answer was, *Every day.* To Jesus? *No. To God.* But later she amplified that statement to say that she prays to God and the angels. In my experience it is almost unheard of for Lutherans to pray to angels, so I was intrigued. Later, however, when we discussed invisible beings, angels proved to be distinctly peripheral to her life world.

The oldest person I spoke with, a retired teacher and not-for-profit healer in his eighties who lives part of each year in Germany, was describing his spiritual healing methods when the subject of angels intruded. For some reason he commented, *A German patient came to me for a fourth visit and said, "Do you believe in angels?" I was silent for a moment,* he told me, *after which I said, yes.* Looking directly at me he explained, *When I was 2 or 3 years old my mother used to sing a lullaby—"Be well behaved because God and all his angels are awake,"* after which he added, *so I believe in angels.* He finished that story by saying, *The patient was silent then.* Feeling at loose ends when the story ended without resolution I asked, Why did he ask? *I don't know,* and that was all he had to say about angels. They simply do not figure prominently in his cosmology, although spirits of the dead do.

The same was true of a clerical worker in her sixties. When Adalbjörg was giving me, as it were, one of my first lessons about spirits of the dead, she made a passing reference to angels one afternoon, just after saying, *Yes, I'm a Christian.* She was explaining, *You don't go to heaven right away when you die.* She did not have in mind that the Christian dead will lie slumbering in their graves for a long, long time until they are to be resurrected at the second coming of Christ (Revelation 20:5). On the contrary, her belief offers an example of how folk Christianity is often greatly at variance with priestly theology. *Before that,* she explained, *you come back to be with your loved ones.* I nodded my head to acknowledge that I was paying attention, which led her to say, *It's kind of like coming back as an angel.* Again, that was the only reference to an angel in any of our several conversations about spirits.

A much younger woman, a student at the university, was telling me how she had been informed that her dead grandfather protected her, making sure that as the future unfolds, *everything will be okay.* She was told that by a woman she dreamed about, she said. Probing in response I asked, was the woman in your dream an angel? Apparently surprised that my question came at a significant moment in her awareness of angels, she answered, *I was just reading about angels. Angels are the highest beings. Those around me,* and she paused without finishing that thought, detouring from her dream to explain that she had been told she is surrounded by *lower people* and that she herself is a *higher* person. Her next words were, *One time this man,* whom she took to be an angel, *was on the same scale as me. The same level.* So, once again, talking about angels led to a matter-of-fact acknowledgment that they exist and sometimes contact people, but only in occasional, remote, and unemotional ways. For her as for many others, spirits of the dead were the important protagonists in occult relationships.

I asked Helga, also in her twenties, do you think there's an angel who watches over you as distinct from spirits of the dead? *Yes,* she said, *a guardian angel, but she has no wings.* Who is it? *I don't know. I don't know if my grandmother is a guardian angel, or a guide, or what is she? I don't know how to separate these, although there is also one woman that I dream* [about] *sometimes. She has a beard,* and that was the end of her comment on angels.

In short, Icelanders I spoke with appear to know about angels as part of their cultural repertoire, as possibilities to draw on for explanations of the inexplicable or for hope in the face of hopelessness. However, that part of the repertoire is inert and largely unexploited by the people with whom I spoke. Just as the institutional church is rarely resorted to except for weddings, funerals, Easter, and Christmas, powerful biblical beings such as angels and the Holy Spirit are distant and subconscious. Even Hafsteinn, the high-ranking Lutheran pastor, seemed not actually to resort to angels, apparently because he had God and Jesus more immediately at hand to meet his spiritual needs.

Furthermore, no one I spoke with ever referred to certain other non-human spirits who are well described in the Bible: cherubim (Hebrews 9:5), seraphim (Isaiah 6:2), and, at the side of God's throne, a living creature with the face of a man, six wings, and multiple eyes both front and back (Revelation 4:6–8). Unlike angels, they simply are not part of the cultural tool kit people access as nonhuman guardians.

ALIENS FROM OUTER SPACE

Many of the Icelanders I spoke with have clearly been influenced by spiritual concepts that are New Age in inspiration. Among them is an openness to the possibility that space ships and voyagers from other galaxies are in touch with Planet Earth. Galactic aliens have been added to the cultural inventory during the last half century. Their reality is disputed, to be sure, but unquestioned by some whom I got to know.

Interplanetary space travelers are quite real to some Icelanders, perhaps many, but they seem not to be invoked for help in times of need nor for protection in times of fear. They are not New Age angels who protect and salvage vulnerable people troubled with personal or interpersonal concerns. However, they may be seen as messengers of salvation, bringing hope to a terrestrial generation that lives in fear of nuclear annihilation, environmental wipeout, or a global Armageddon. They offer hope because they promise to bring knowledge from more advanced civilizations that have learned to live peaceably under utopian conditions of sustainable splendor.

I queried Magnus Skarphedinsson about interplanetary tourism because he is president of the Icelandic UFO Society and custodian of the society's collection of books and videotapes. Who are the aliens, I asked one evening, and what do they do for us? In his somewhat professorial style he responded with a summary of *all we know about aliens.* He began by saying, *There are good and bad aliens that visit Earth regularly. Lots of humans have talked with them, and we have lots of information from those meetings. When they come they leave a "calling card" that in one way or another instructs us to use the force of the universe to benefit our planet. They use phrases such as "charity force," or "care force."* I asked, Do they speak of a universal intelligence? *Yes.*

Continuing his impromptu private lecture he added, *They experiment on individual humans in both good and bad ways.* I was not sure what he meant by that, because he rushed right on to say, *They have brought a lot of messages.* What, for example? *Most concern conservation. Protect the atmosphere. Behave better to animals.* Magnus is personally, socially, and politically very committed to these goals. He is president of the Icelandic Friends of the Mouse Society. Primarily at his initiative, the Mouse Society imports and distributes a trap that captures mice without harming them. It is built with an escape hatch that makes it possible to take captured mice to an empty field where they can be released in a mouse-friendly place (if such exists). Magnus is also president of the Save the Whale Society and is a vegetarian, not for health reasons, but because he is opposed to killing animals for food. *I'm an ethical vegetarian,* is the way he put it. Also important in alien messages, he told me, are two moral injunctions: *Believe in God,* and *Behave! Behave! Behave!*

Because I am a fan of the *Star Wars* and *Star Trek* series, and because I noticed some video cassettes in the society's library, I asked, Is there any truth in movies about outer space? Magnus thought for a moment before responding. *Seven or eight people have seen space ships land and creatures come out, so that much is true. But films exaggerate, misunderstand, and misuse. Yet basically their portrayals are true.* To that he added, *But most of these beings are invisible. Psychic people see them much more often than non-psychics.* Do you have UFO movies in your library? *Not many. We have a Roscoe film.*

The last time I attended one of the séances Magnus regularly organizes, a participant friend gave him a key ring to which was attached a brass image of E.T., the space alien made famous in a fantasy movie that was a big box-office attraction in the 1980s. Pulling on the chain made its red eyes light up, and we all shared his amusement as Magnus demonstrated this new toy, not an idol to be revered, but an icon of the interest Magnus and others have in unidentified flying objects.

I wondered if accepting the reality of spirits of the dead made people more open to other supernatural beliefs when Deborah, the English medium who conducts séances in Iceland every fall, told me how open-minded she is. *You see, I'm into many things. I'm also into UFOs.* Thinking I had misunderstood her I repeated, UFOs? *Oh, yes. I've had experiences with that.*

Tell me about one, I asked, adhering to the ethnographic ideal of urging people to talk about specifics rather than to offer generalizations. *The last time I stayed with Ragnheidr here in Iceland I had a beautiful experience in her home.* (Ragnheidr is employed by the Icelandic Society for Spirit Research and hosts Deborah every year.) *And the next day it was all on the television and on the news. Over the years—over the last 14 or 15 years—I've been seeing beings, okay?* That other people are not seeing? I asked. *Yes.*

She eventually told me about her encounter in Ragnheidr's home, but it took a while to get to that. Deborah is a talented raconteur and she wanted to prepare me for the Ragnheidr story by telling another as her preface. *The first time I saw somebody from other worlds,* she said, *was when I was with a friend who used to visit me on Sundays. On that particular Sunday in England we were sitting in my kitchen and my friend had just told me he needed some help from the spirit world. So we were sitting talking, and all of a sudden I saw this gentleman appear back of him. So I said to him, somebody quite high up, very holy looking, is standing behind you. And all of a sudden I hear this voice say to me, "I am no spirit."*

She said she was overwhelmed by the experience. *It was such a shock to me, and I said, "What are you doing here?" And he said, "I am not here." And I said to him, "But I can see you, you are standing here." "No I'm not. What I am doing, I am projecting my image to you."* Hearing her say that I immediately flashed back to *Star Wars* in which people are shown projecting themselves across light-years of space as shimmering images. She seemed to have the same imagery in mind as she continued, *And he was kind of shimmering. So I says, "What are you doing here?" And he says, "And I am not of your universe." And I says to my friend, "Oh, I've flipped. I've gone mad."*

But that, of course, was just a bit of hyperbole. Her tale continued in a very matter-of-fact way. *I said, "What are you doing here?" He said, "We're already here upon your Earth." I says, "Why?"* The alien's answer resonates well with what Magnus told me about messages to Earthlings. *He said, "Because we are concerned of the state of the Earth. If anything happened to the Earth it would affect the whole solar system." So I said, "I'll go along with that." So he says to me, "And I am not of your universe." And he says, "And where I come from we have two moons." And he says, "And we travel a hundred times faster than the speed of light." And I went, "That's going some." Okay? So I says, "Well, why are you here?" He said, "It's not time for you to know yet." And then he disappeared.*

Apparently Deborah's friend neither saw the alien shimmering in the room nor heard the conversation, because his presence in her kitchen is not referred to again, nor is he described as a witness to these unusual events. As she continued her story, the next episode began when she went to bed that evening. *So I sat up, when I went to bed, I sat up in bed, and*

I said or prayed, "Right. Now, it's either a very good figment of your imagination OR it was real. Now if it's real, then prove it to me." Okay? "Because I don't accept what I've heard and what I've seen. So, if it's not a figment of my imagination you can hear my thoughts and you must prove it to me. "

Well, she told me as she continued to narrate her adventure, in the space of two weeks I had so many people turn up at my door who were connected to UFOs. They were coming out of the woodwork. I didn't know where they were all coming from. I sat there. I just couldn't believe what was happening.

Were they Earthlings? I asked, not realizing until later when I reviewed the video recording of our conversation that I had slipped quite easily into using imagery I absorbed as a boy in the 1930s when I was an addicted reader of the adventures of a comic strip interstellar pilot known as Buck Rogers. Yeah, she answered. Come in for private readings, and they were all connected with UFOs.

A young woman who came as a client had mentioned that her father was a lecturer on UFOs. So I decided I would go to a UFO meeting where this young woman's father was giving a talk. I went with some friends and I listened to his lecture, and all of a sudden—he had all this information, all these documents, all from America and everything—and then all of a sudden he said, "Where some of them come from they have two moons." Well, I nearly fell off my chair, because, I thought, Hey, he said that to me.

As part of his documentation he showed some photographs, and among them was a picture of a man who looked very much like the man she had seen. So I went and spoke with this gentleman, and he said to me, "My dear young woman, if you can speak to the so-called dead, surely you can speak to the living." Her response was, Well, okay, and she laughed.

She then segued into yet another story. So the next time I came to Iceland, and my last day in Iceland, my last couple—[I was] doing this private reading to a man and wife—and all of a sudden, here's this gentleman stood at the back of this couple. So I said to this couple, "You wouldn't have anything to do with UFOs, would you?" "Yes," he says, "me and my wife had an experience years ago." So I explained what I was seeing [standing behind them]. At any rate, [the client] was a healer and had psychic powers of his own. The next time I came back to Iceland he said, "I've seen you with that gentleman." "You have?" "Yeah."

At that moment she reached for her purse as she continued talking about this episode. So I'm doing a demonstration in a hall here in Iceland and I'm waiting to come on, and I'm sitting quiet, and all of a sudden I hear this voice saying to me, "Tell him the answer is yes." Then here is this young man in front of me. I says to him, "Did you ask the spirit world a question?" He says, "No, but I asked your alien friend a question." So I said, "Well, I don't know what you asked, but all I heard was a voice saying, "Tell him the answer was yes." So I said, "What have you asked?" Well, he said, "I've never seen the spirit and I asked him would they allow me the energy to see the spirit."

Referring, then, to the group séance she had convened, she continued, *That gentleman sat behind me while I was working and he saw every one of my spirit contacts as I worked. So before I left Iceland he came to see me. He said, "I've got something for you,"* and with that she reached into her purse to take something out as she said, *I always carry it with me,* adding without pause, *He said, "Your friend appeared," and I have to give you something." He said, "And I have to tell you, it has been charged up with energy for you from him." And that's what I was given,* whereupon she displayed a smooth piece of crystal in the size and shape of a small bar of bathroom soap. *I've had it many years. When I need energy it just fits in my hand. And it gets very, very hot. Only for certain people.* Whatever she meant by that was unclear.

Then, after just one more verbal proscenium, she was ready to pick up where she had left off when she started to tell me about encountering space aliens in Ragnheidr's home. *So, anyway, I've had quite a few experiences over the years, but the last time I was here I stayed with Ragnheidr. Before coming to Iceland, on a Friday with a different group, listening to what they were saying, and they said, they know everything about us when they visit us. I said to myself, "Right. Okay. You're visiting when I am asleep and I want to know that the visit truly took place and was not just the fantasy of a dream. So I want a mark on me so I know you have visited me. Leave a mark on me."*

I came to Iceland Sunday. Monday I did a transfiguration, meaning that her face took on the physical appearance of a spirit who possessed her. *After, I sat with Gudmundur and Ragnheidr in there,* nodding toward a room next to the one we were in. *Talking. I looked down. "What the hell's that?"* There, pointing to her left elbow, *I had this big black round thing stood on my arm. No pain,* she added before I could say a word. *During the next 3 weeks people said, what's that on your arm. I had no idea, so I said, laughing, and I am only joking at the time, "Well, I asked for them to leave a mark and that's what they have left me."*

Tuesday of last week I went to bed early but couldn't fall asleep. All of a sudden everything seemed magnified. I was in bed 2 hours. All of a sudden I hear the tap dripping very loud. I had to get up and turn it off. As I'm coming back, there's somebody walking about in the lounge. I open the door, walked in, couldn't see anybody, shut the door, got back in bed. Then I thought, there's somebody here in the bedroom. I could hear them.

As I turned around, three lights appeared, one from either side of the room, and these three lights came to the side of me bed. I'm sitting up in bed leaning on me pillow.

There was three small people. From her description I decided they must have been about the size of E.T., the enigmatic extraterrestrial who is well known throughout the world. *And I'm looking at these three people and I start to talk to them. But before that happened, as I was laying there, all of a sudden, clairvoyantly, I sees a whale in front of me. I nearly fell out of bed with shock. All of a sudden I've got my head up against a whale, and I thought, what am I seeing a whale for? But I'm picking up all these sub-thoughts: What mankind do to things they don't understand. How they kill things and hurt things that they don't understand. I was getting upset.*

All of a sudden these lights appeared and these three people, finishing her sentence by gesturing with her hands towards the floor to indicate about 3 feet tall. *And they started to talk to me about the earth, the planet, again how mankind was destroying things that they didn't understand and what damage they were doing to the Earth. And they talked to me for over an hour.*

And all of a sudden one of them said, "You have to go to sleep now. But when you get up, you will ask Ragnheidr what she heard." I turned over, looked at the clock, and an hour had passed. I turned over, looked at them, and just pulled the bedclothes up and went fast asleep. They still stood there, as though it was quite normal to do that. Went to sleep. I woke up, lay there, thought I'd had a funny dream. They had said, You'll wake up before 6 o'clock. I turned over and looked at the clock. It was 10 to 6:00. I gets up, goes to the shower, looks, and that big black thing on my arm was gone. It had been there for 3 weeks. It can't possibly disappear overnight.

I asks Ragnheidr, "Did anything happen last night?" She said, "It's funny you should say that. I heard somebody walking around." So I told her what had happened. So we went to the society. A woman there said, "Have you heard the TV news this morning?" I said, "No, Why?" She said, "There was three UFOs spotted over Iceland last night. Three lights. Ragnheidr looked at me. She said, "We know where they came, don't we."

One was spotted over the sea by a plane. Radioed the coast guard. Coast guard seen it coming out of the water. The other two were over Iceland. We were interrupted by a knock on the door. Her next client had arrived and it was time for me to go. As I stood ready to leave I asked, Are you able to see the elves? *I have seen them,* was her reply. *Only once. Driving. I looked out. It was raining. There was this little man running alongside of the bus.*

ELVES AND FAIRIES ON THE CULTURAL MENU

Although Iceland was settled by Nordic adventurers who imported the medieval culture of Western Norway, many of them did not sail directly from Scandinavia. On earlier migrations they had occupied other islands in the North Atlantic, and as a result, when they moved on to Iceland they brought along quite a few Irish folk and other Celts who were attached to them as wives, servants, and slaves (Karlsson 2000: 14). As a result, their transplanted culture included beliefs about elves, fairies, and other human-like beings, mostly quite small and invisible, who defy scholarly efforts to tease apart old Scandinavian beliefs and practices from similar traditions that are Celtic in origin. What is clear is that even after the passing of a thousand years, such beliefs are still quite common on the island, enough so that Deborah, influenced by her Icelandic friends and clients, on one occasion, thought she saw an elf running alongside of her bus on an isolated stretch of road.

Because elves are still prominent on the Icelandic cultural menu, I absolutely must write about them. However, I will wait to do so until we get to Chapter 9, because there is a lot I need to tell you about first.

CONCLUSION

The worldview of 21st-century Icelanders is in no way constricted by their remote Atlantic location at the edge of the Arctic Circle. It incorporates cultural traits from the distant past, such as angel and elf lore, as well as others that are current in a global present, such as aliens from outer space and encounters with spirits of the dead (spiritism).

Especially since the end of World War II, the United Kingdom has exerted a massive influence on the beliefs and practices of spiritism in Iceland. Deborah is just one of many English mediums who are scheduled, often on an annual basis, to meet local clients and conduct group séances, most often at the headquarters of the Icelandic Society for Spirit Research. As a consequence, the Icelandic culture of the occult includes much that originated abroad, especially in England, but it is equally true that this culture is now thoroughly at home in Iceland.

To grasp these realities anthropologists need a theory of culture that is more flexible than the one we worked with at the mid-20th century, when it was taken as a largely unexamined given that every society was characterized by a more or less universally shared and transmitted way of life—a culture. Following contemporary revisions of how culture has been refined or redefined, I find it helpful here to think of angels, aliens, elves, and spirits as items on a cultural menu. Individuals choose or are served up options they can exercise. I believe that's what Lawrence Hirschfeld has in mind when he speaks of multiple cultural traits that contest and compete with one another. It is consistent with what Ann Swidler refers to as "a 'tool kit' of symbols, stories, rituals, and world-views, which people may use in varying configurations."

Yet, even though it is no longer acceptable to assume that a society such as Iceland is characterized by cultural uniformity, it is still realistic to observe that some items on the menu are more popular than others. Certainly, as concerns beliefs about immortality, most Icelanders will avow that individuals do survive physical death, and almost as many will insist that the living can communicate with departed souls. It is contact with the dead in its various manifestations that I will explore in Chapter 3.

GHOSTS PAST AND PRESENT

ANTHROPOLOGY AS HISTORY

In Chapter 1, I discussed two basic anthropological methods: fieldwork based on participant observation and quantified survey research using precision sampling procedures and carefully designed questionnaires. Those methods refer to how ethnographers are trained both to describe the lives of living people in their local social context (qualitative methods), but also how to search for similarities and differences by designing and administering questionnaires (quantitative methods). A third methodological approach—historical research—can be either qualitative or quantitative. Anthropologists may, when circumstances permit, incorporate historical and archeological perspectives that document how cultural characteristics have persisted or changed over time.

History demonstrates the extent to which a culture has systemic characteristics. While from an individual point of view one may well pick and choose from a menu of cultural options, from a societal point of view anthropologists encounter shared patterns of behavior. These patterns of behavior are striking because they tend on the whole to combine cultural and social traits consistent with one another.

Local ethnographies, surveys, and historical research offer complementary perspectives on how cultural menus can vary. The historical antecedent of a culture will be both similar to and different from its living descendent. In the case of Iceland, the medieval seafaring adventurers who first settled the island were ancestral to those living there today, but their culture was very different. How Icelanders then were like those of today, and how they differed, is one way to deepen one's understanding, in this case, of religion and beliefs about the afterlife.

The methods for doing historical research depend on the nature of the problem. When the time depth is thousands and even millions of years, anthropologists use the techniques of prehistoric archeology to study excavated structures and artifacts or they apply the related techniques of paleoanthropology to find and interpret ancient skeletal material (Willey & Sabloff 1993; Spencer 1982). The past of Iceland is not prehistoric, however, because a lot of information has survived in written form. Much of what can be known about the past of this society therefore requires the skills of specialists who practice historical archeology. Intellectual adventurers of this sort must feel as much at home doing archival research indoors as doing field excavations in the great outdoors.

Archeology and paleoanthropology have nothing to offer for my own research on spiritism, but I was able to draw on publications by historians and folklorists to reconstruct the background of contemporary beliefs and practices. There have been ghosts in Iceland for as long as there have been people there to encounter them.

MURDER IN THE NIGHT

You can define a word any way you want, letting Webster gather dust on your bookshelf if you so choose. The measure of a definition is not whether it is right or wrong but whether it is useful or not. Of course, if we define words according to Webster they will be quite useful because we will be less likely to misunderstand one another. Nonetheless, I choose to escape the constraints of a dictionary by using the term *ghost* in a special way that is more helpful for my purposes.

According to my copy of *Webster's New Collegiate Dictionary*, no longer truly new, since I bought it 25 years ago, a ghost is "a disembodied soul," or, more precisely, "the soul of a dead person believed to be an inhabitant of the unseen world or to appear to the living in bodily likeness."

I prefer to constrict the openness of that definition by limiting the term *ghost* to mean the soul of a stranger as its primary reference, and not usually to indicate the spirit of a deceased relative or friend. Restricting the term that way is consistent with the way most people use it. In my experience, at least, when people speak of ghosts they have in mind spirits of the dead who were never loved ones, not ancestors or departed friends, but strangers who in some cases may be intent on causing grievous harm.

Medieval Icelandic sagas and contemporary folktales include horrific ghost stories of this sort that have persisted in the Icelandic collective unconscious for at least a thousand years. Every contemporary Icelander knows stories of ghosts who could materialize in strong, muscular bodies and threaten to overwhelm ordinary mortals.

One from *The Saga of the People of Laxardal,* an oral legend that was committed to writing in the mid-1200s, tells of a nasty man named Hrapp, who while alive was feared and hated by neighbors he bullied and attacked. Just before his death he arranged to be buried standing upright on his farm so he could see and brutalize people just as he had during his lifetime.

According to the saga author, old Hrapp was worse dead than alive. He killed his workers, harassed his neighbors, and frightened his wife, forcing the living to abandon what otherwise was a fine productive farm. In the end, local farmers persuaded a powerful man named Hoskuld to dig up the cadaver and move it far away. Reburial helped, but even so, when Hrapp's son Sumarlidi reoccupied the homestead he was soon driven crazy and died, presumably by Hrapp, who was so evil that he even caused harm to his own wife and son (Hreinsson et al., 1997: V, 19).

Another ghastly story of brutality and danger from the saga age is included in an early 14th-century version of *The Saga of the People of Floi.* It tells of a Viking named Thorgils who was attacked by a powerful phantom. Bravely raising his ax against the hideous giant, Thorgils chased him back toward the burial mound he had come from. When they arrived at the grave site, the ghost turned on him again. Stunned by the sudden reversal, Thorgils let his ax fall to the ground, which allowed the ghost to grab him and wrestle. At times it looked as though the good man was doomed, but in the end the ghost fell on his back with Thorgils firmly astride. After taking a moment to catch his breath, the Viking reached out, retrieved his ax, and chopped off the head of the monster. He then uttered a magical spell to bind it forever. The ghost has not been heard of since (Hreinsson et al., 1997: III, 281).

Of all of the saga ghosts, however, none is more hideous or better known than the ghost named Glam, from *The Saga of Grettir the Strong* (written on parchment around 1400). The hero of the story, Grettir, arrived at a farm known as Thorhallsstadir where he was made welcome by the terrorized farmer, who was especially happy when Grettir agreed to stay for what was to be the first of three nights.

Nothing happened on the first night, so Grettir said he would stay on. During the second night, while everyone slept, the ghostly Glam quietly abducted Grettir's horse from the barn and broke every bone in its body. Grettir decided he would stay a third night, even though the farmer warned him, "You're a dead man if you wait for Glam."

That night, Grettir slept in his clothes, completely hidden under a large fur cloak. In the middle of the night the ghost climbed on top of the great hall of the farm where he kicked the roof timbers long and hard, causing the whole building to shake as if in an earthquake. Climbing down, Glam squeaked open the door, stuck his head inside, and looked around. Grettir was horrified at the sight of the revenant, who looked as fierce as the devil himself, but he kept his cool.

Unexpectedly, Glam spotted the cloak and decided he would take hold of it. Grettir resisted, bracing his feet against a timber. Glam pulled again, suddenly aware that some living creature was tugging against him. Again he failed to take the cloak. On the third tug, Grettir was pulled into a sitting position, and Glam was astonished that a mere man could be that strong. As they pulled against each other, the cloak ripped down the center, leaving each with half.

In that moment of distraction, Grettir bravely slipped behind the giant, grabbed him around the waist, and squeezed as hard as he could. But Glam broke free and attempted to drag him outside where it would be easier to finish him off. Grettir resisted by bracing himself against benches and doorposts, but the ghost kept pulling with enormous force. Suddenly, Grettir changed his tactic from resisting to pushing. Caught off guard, the combatants tumbled outside to the ground, Glam on his back with Grettir on top, just the way Thorgils gained advantage over his ghost adversary.

Glam, however, possessed great magical power. With a mere glance of his evil eyes, he unnerved and paralyzed his opponent, who found himself unable to draw his sword. Then Glam put a curse on him that would force him to live for the rest of his life as an outlaw, alone in the rugged outdoors with its inhospitable subarctic climate. To Icelanders who rely on shelter and companionship for survival, Grettir's banishment was a cruel sentence to social and physical death.

Fortunately, just as Glam completed his curse, Grettir got back his strength, grabbed his short sword, and cut off the giant's head, which he placed against its buttocks. Almost immediately, the grateful farmer approached to give thanks to God and to Grettir for freeing his family from the evil spirit. Glam was burned to ashes, which were buried far away from the house, barns, pathways, and fields. That ghost never caused trouble again.

After recovering at the farm, Grettir moved on. He was given many gifts, including a good horse and fine new clothes. But for the rest of his life he was forced to trudge from place to place, homeless and exposed, never able to escape Glam's curse (Hreinsson et al., 1997: II, 105–107).

Stories about wrestling with ghosts are as old as the sagas, but they have also been collected by folklorists in recent times, especially in the culturally conservative northwestern fjords. The details of ghost stories vary from one teller to another. Sometimes they include stories of wrestling with a ghost. According to the narrator of one exemplar of this genre, two country lads, Rosinkar and Bjarni, got into a fight in 1892 at a small fishing hamlet. Rosinkar wrestled Bjarni to the ground in a way that both hurt and humiliated him. Outraged, Bjarni swore revenge, shouting, "I will get you down, if not during my lifetime, then after death."

In a December shipwreck not long after, Bjarni drowned. The night after his death, his ghost found its way to Rosinkar's farm, where it grabbed its unsuspecting enemy from behind as he walked between farm buildings in the dark. Rosinkar was appalled to find himself wrestling with a spirit whose face was missing and whose body had an unnatural, spongy feel.

Limp and faceless, the ghost of Bjarni inflicted pain. In one episode collected by folklorist Arngrimur Bjarnarson, Rosinkar reputedly said that it grabbed his muffler. "We tugged at it in the passage-way until the muffler tore apart [like Grettir's cloak at least 500 years earlier], or he lost hold of it, I don't know which." According to local storytellers, the attacks continued over Christmas and New Year's Eve. Prostrate with terror, Rosinkar took to his bed, where he slept with the window tightly sealed and a light that burned throughout the night. He died prematurely around the end of January (Adalsteinsson 1987).

WHEN ICELAND BECAME CHRISTIAN

Medieval ghosts such as Hrapp and Glam antedate Christianity. Iceland was settled in or around the year 874 by devotees of the Nordic gods. In subsequent decades, the islanders were exposed to Christians while abroad on Viking expeditions. Many converted, but most remained pagan until they officially accepted Christianity as a nationwide decision a millennium ago. As the story is narrated in the sagas, the king of Norway threatened the death of high-ranking Icelanders if they refused to become Christians. Influential men from all over the island gathered in 1000 (or more likely, 999) at the annual assembly known as the Althing to decide how to respond. Strong voices spoke out on both sides of the debate. At last the dispute was put to Thorgeir, a respected arbitrator known as the Lawspeaker. His name reveals a family dedication to the god Thor.

According to Jón Hnefill Adalsteinsson (1978), Thorgeir was probably a shaman who had been trained either directly or indirectly by a Sámi (Lapp) magician from northern Norway. Following shamanic custom, he crawled under a horsehide where he apparently lay in a trance for a day and a night, communing, no doubt, with powerful spirits. On throwing off the horsehide he recommended in favor of Christianity. The leadership agreed and Iceland officially became a Christian nation. That pacified the Norwegian king, but Thorgeir's recommendation also pacified reluctant heathens, because they also agreed that any man who wanted to continue worshipping the old gods was free to do so, as long as it was done in the privacy of his farmstead. Since every one of them lived on his own isolated holding, the only time one had to practice Christian rites was for a week or two at the annual Althing. With that compromise, the old ghosts were also free to hang around the way they always had.

By a generation or two later, holdouts for the Nordic gods had died out and everybody had become Christian in their private as well as public lives. Without a pause since the pagan Middle Ages, however, many Icelandic Christians continued to believe that encounters with the living dead took place. Saga-style ghosts with physical bodies, the kind the resurrected Jesus must have had when he ate a fish dinner, continued to materialize until well into the 20th century.

THE NEW SPIRITISM

If an openness to communication with spirits of the dead by members of the Christian church simmered on for a thousand years, it bubbled up anew around the turn of the 20th century when a new spiritism became widely popular throughout Europe and North America. It appeared in Iceland when the so-called New Theology was imported from Copenhagen by recent graduates of the University of Copenhagen (Swatos & Gíssurarson 1997: 163–168). According to these well-educated "modernists," the Bible as a text should be evaluated the way one would evaluate any historical document, weeding out mistakes, identifying internal contradictions, and acknowledging exaggerations. The Bible was subject to a "higher criticism" based on historiographic research, literary analysis, and scientific reason (Anderson 2003a).

In Iceland, the New Theology prepared the ground for a generation of young priests who saw spiritism as a way to salvage the wonder of the scriptures. Spiritist experiences provided direct scientific evidence that people survived death and that biblical miracles such as Saul's meeting with the ghost of Samuel and encounters after the resurrection of Jesus were not miracles at all, but merely the natural activities of spirits of the dead.

Two men brought these iconoclastic beliefs from Copenhagen to Iceland. One was a son of the dean of the theological seminary in Reykjavík who eventually succeeded to his father's post and the other was a nephew of the Bishop of Iceland. Close family ties within the church hierarchy and their own advancement to positions of rank and privilege helped them override orthodoxy with their imported revisionist beliefs. One could be a spiritist and still be a Christian because the scriptures were fallible and spirit claims and predictions could be verified by checking what was said by spirits against what was known to be fact. Two prominent Lutheran pastors, Stefán and Hjörtur survive from that generation, but the tide has turned. Fearful that the Bible was losing its authority, and the church its scriptural rationale, the official position of the national church reverted to an older more conservative theology that advocates strong biblical constraints against meeting with mediums and spirits of the dead.

Pastors in the national church actually do very little to directly oppose spiritist beliefs because to do so would offend many of their parishioners. I once said to Stefán, What do you say when a member of your congregation asks about believing in spirits of the dead? His answer could have been given by any pastor in Iceland: *They don't ask.* As a corollary, pastors don't bring the subject up in their conversations or counseling, although they may say something about it in sermons.

Sesselíus, pastor of the neighborhood church I attended, was very helpful as I tried to understand how clergy dealt with this issue. *There used to be a spiritist movement within the church,* he explained, *in which the vanguard persons were pastors. By mid-century there was a split. Now, most pastors disapprove of the spiritist movement.* Why? *These people are meddling in something they shouldn't be doing.*

How do you deal with it in your church? *My position as a counselor—for example, when someone dies—many pastors tend to take it on lightly as relates to spiritism.* What do you mean? *I mean, if it is a funeral, and they have ideas about the afterlife, we tend to go rather smoothly. In that state of trauma, they are not ready for any discussion. In that situation, you do not confront them. But in a regular service—or sermon— pastors tend to confront them.*

THE FIRST SPIRITIST MEDIUM

Indridi Indridasson grew up on a remote farm where he achieved literacy and numeracy through home study, there being no school in his neighborhood because farmsteads in rural areas were widely dispersed. As a youth he moved to Reykjavík, which in those days was just a small town located in a remote Danish colony. He arrived carrying his modest possessions in a small chest that he stored in his room, where his landlady could rummage through it and see that he owned no magician's equipment. It is extremely unlikely that as a country lad he had ever traveled abroad where he might have seen a medium in action or been taught what to do, and there were no mediums in Iceland at that time. He could not have seen moving pictures at that early date nor have listened to the radio, but he undoubtedly heard some talk of spiritism after he arrived in Reykjavík, just a short time before he suddenly demonstrated psychokinetic powers that astonished everyone.

In town, the 22-year-old literate but unschooled country boy found a place to live at a time when spiritism had recently attracted attention among some of the town folk, including the family with whom he lived. Just as he was settling in, the people who rented him a room were naïvely experimenting with techniques for contacting the dead, stimulated by newspaper and traveler reports of a growing fad in Denmark and England.

One evening Indridi happened to walk by the room where an effort at table tilting was under way. With a wave of her hand his landlady beckoned him to pull up a chair. Almost as soon as he took his seat the table began to tremble, a startling event, since nothing at all had happened until then.

In subsequent days, he and his friends discovered that his mere presence could cause tables to bump around the room. Then, quite unexpectedly, he began to produce automatic writing whereby he found himself recording statements without conscious intent. Word of these mysterious events were rapidly noised around, the way gossip does in what was then just a small town. Indridi immediately found himself lionized by leading members of the local elite, who themselves were caught up in the excitement. Einar Kvaran, a university-educated newspaper editor, invited him to join a small group that had repeatedly tried to establish contact with spirits and were discouraged by their complete lack of success. The group was about to abandon all efforts when Indridi happened along and turned the enterprise around.

He soon became the central figure in a program of clairvoyant experimentation that attracted considerable public attention for the next several years. Indridi's brief but active professional career lasted only from 1905 to 1909, cut short by typhoid fever and tuberculosis. Fortunately, Swatos and Gíssurarson recently published the results of their research on him and his time in *Icelandic Spiritualism* (1997). I will, of necessity, draw heavily on their work.

From the start, the goal was to ensure that Indridi's demonstrations were in no way fraudulent. By meticulously eliminating every conceivable possibility of trickery, the trials seemed to add up to scientific verification of the spiritist theory that the dead live on and are able to communicate with the living.

Precautions against fraud were both minute and elaborate. Not all experiments were well controlled, but the most convincing were conducted in a small building constructed from the ground up to serve as a laboratory. Great care was taken to ensure that neither Indridi nor anyone else could possibly install deceptive devices or conceal collaborators in the structure. No cellar was built under the floor, which itself was covered with a seamless carpet of linoleum. A flat roof, lacking an attic, provided no crawl space. A strong fishing net stretching from ceiling to floor and from wall to wall partitioned the experimental room into two sections, one without windows for the medium, and the other with two firmly shuttered windows for the audience. A slit through the middle of the mesh allowed people to move from the audience area into the experimental space, but the edges were securely sewn together and sealed before each trial, and the mesh was too small to permit a hand to reach through. Every part of the room was carefully examined before each séance to verify that no tampering had occurred. Most importantly, a member of the experimental team, the so-called watchman, sat next to Indridi and held his hands in order to know that he remained in his seat and was not actively manipulating objects while they sat in darkness. The biggest impediment to scientific verification was that séances were conducted in complete darkness, except for certain brief moments when observers were told they might strike a match.

In private homes, in his own small apartment attached to the laboratory, and in the laboratory itself, Indridi produced a remarkable variety of spectacular phenomena. For a chronological account of these extraordinary events I refer the reader to Swatos and Gíssurarson (1997), whose findings I summarize here.

Psychokinesis   From a worldwide perspective, the most common expression of psychic powers in the physical realm is to make objects move by concentrating the mind and wishing movement to happen. After his first clumsy and apparently unintended success in moving a table, Indridi became quite adept at moving objects in this way. On one occasion, in the dim light of evening, some friends asked him to make a table rise up from the floor. He agreeably caused the table to lift itself until it struck the faces of the men standing around it. They tried to push it back down, but failed. It seems that by the end of that evening he and his friends had learned to work together so that they were able to move the table simply by holding their hands just above it and then lifting without touching. One of the most entertaining demonstrations of psychokinesis occurred when a 50-pound music box seemed to wind itself up and move around the room while playing a tune high up under the ceiling.

Flying Trumpets   For the sake of greater clarity, I decided to mention one form of psychokinesis as a separate category simply because it constitutes the only form of psychokinesis I encountered in contemporary Iceland. The objects involved are referred to in the spiritist literature and in current parlance as trumpets, but that use of the term is archaic and the objects are more accurately described as megaphones.

In some of Indridi's séances, a trumpet materialized and was used by spirits for voice amplification. On one occasion it was described as moving around the room at great speed. On another, a spirit spoke through it while it swayed from one end of the room to the other, a distance of 24 feet. It could also be heard striking the ceiling, which was 12 feet high, far beyond the reach of Indridi or anyone else known to be present. On still other occasions, a spirit placed the wide opening of the megaphone directly against the ear of a sitter and shouted through it, moving it so rapidly from one person to another that it seemed almost to be simultaneously covering two ears at once.

Materialized Spirits   It was one thing for Indridi to report that he could see a spirit, but quite another when people with him also could see the spirit. On one memorable evening, a deceased Dane named Jensen materialized in the home of Einar Kvaran. At his first appearance he asked in Danish, which was widely understood in Iceland, "Can you see me?" Luminous enough to be visible in the dark, although only for a few seconds at a time, he was said to be garbed in a white robe and to appear in different parts of the room, often in unusual poses. Once they saw him standing on the sofa. Another time he sat with Indridi on his lap. Several attendees managed to touch him, confirming that he had a material body, but no one ever got a clear look at his face.

Pummeled by Spirits   During one experiment, Professor Hannesson of the University of Iceland was hit hard by an invisible spirit. Professor Hannesson had slipped through the slit in the net in order to retrieve the chairs Indridi and the watchman had been sitting on before a spirit had pulled them away and cast them into a corner. In debriefing, the professor recalled that the watchman invited him to come into the experimental area, but when he reached out to pick up the chairs he was hit very hard on the back by what felt like a clenched fist (Hannesson in Swatos & Gíssurarson 1997: 129).

Extraordinary Sounds   Within days of the first psychokinetic demonstration, wall knocking was heard in different parts of the room, even high up near the ceiling. When sitters asked the spirit to knock at a particular place it was done. Sitters also learned that by agreeing on how knocks would be interpreted, they could ask questions that would elicit yes or no answers. Observers mentioned that these knocking interactions took place while Indridi was busy either with automatic writing or with speaking as the voice of a spirit.

Extraordinary Lights   Dozens of lights flashed on and off against the walls or in the air. They could be quite small or quite large and somewhat variable in color. At times a whole wall became mysteriously lit up. At other times visitors spoke of a pillar of light, sometimes described as being white with a blue tinge. A pillar could be bright enough to illuminate the medium who was close to it, but not sufficiently bright to light up the entire room.

Gusts of Wind   A wind blowing with enough force to ruffle hair and move paper was sometimes felt, even though there were no open windows. At other times sitters reported relief from a cool breeze spontaneously blowing in a hot, airless room.

A Poltergeist   About halfway through his brief career, while taking a walk in the outdoors with some young women, Indridi claimed to see the spirit of a man in shirtsleeves whose name, he said, was Jón. The apparition was invisible to his companions but offensive to Indridi, who let loose with some profanity when the man appeared.

Back in the small apartment he shared with a student named Thordur Oddgeirsson, strange things began to happen after dark. A plate inexplicably flew off its shelf in the sitting room and landed on the floor of their bedroom. The student's slipper sailed across the room and into a wash-up basin. The other slipper also flew across the room, after which the beds began to shake and move. Indridi cried out in alarm because the ghost was dragging him out of bed. Then a pair of boots flew out from under the bed to knock over the lamp (Haraldur Níelsson quoted in Swatos & Gíssurarson, 1997: 98).

Levitation   In a vain effort to stop the poltergeist assault, Indridi and his companions lit candles and a lamp. As they attempted to escape, Indridi's friend Brynjólfur Tórdarson suddenly turned to see Indridi floating in a horizontal position about 4 feet above the floor. Grabbing hold, he thought he would pull him down but instead he found himself pulled up with Indridi. In a terror, he screamed for Thordur to rescue them, and with that the three managed to escape (Brynjólfur Tórdarson in Swatos & Gíssurarson, 1997: 100).

Spirit Possession   Early on Indridi was possessed by a spirit who said he was Indridi's great-uncle Konrad Gislason. Serving as a spirit guide, Konrad announced that the experimenters should organize nightly séances in a darkened room. After meeting a few times as instructed, Indridi's handlers experimented with lighting a red lamp in the hope of being able to see, but the spirits objected, so they returned to total darkness (Swatos & Gíssurarson 1997: 110).

Spirit Surgery   At one point in his career something happened to Indridi's left arm. Just what is not clear, but sitters could hear crackling sounds when he moved it. Surgical treatment was decided on by the spirits, who took three sessions in a private home to complete their work. Observers reported that Indridi was taken into a cabinet, and that when he emerged from it his left arm seemed to have disappeared. All they could feel was an empty sleeve and no sign that the arm was somehow concealed against his body. Striking matches was permitted, but unfortunately they were forbidden by the spirit guide to remove his clothes in order to directly examine his shoulder. The arm seemed to have dematerialized until the end of each session, after which it materialized again. Apparently surgery resulted in a cure since no one reported hearing crepitations after that and he never complained of pain or limited movement.

THE HARMLESS GHOSTS OF OUR TIME

During my visits to Iceland, I was told many stories of ghosts who just seemed to want companionship, sharply in contrast to the ghosts of earlier years and centuries. Living people may be frightened, but not because the ghost behaves in a menacing manner. Or, they may not be frightened at all, as in the case of Hledis, a bank clerk in her mid-thirties who is also a part-time student at the university. She told me that people at the bank talk about three people who died in that building, including one who lived in a flat on the top floor. They say that the building is haunted by the ghost of the former tenant, as Hledis found out for herself about 3 years before our conversation.

One morning I climbed the creaky stairway to work on some of the records we keep on the third floor, where the flat now serves only for the storage of files. I entered the room on the right side of the hall, and when I was finished I started to leave. As I was coming out of the room I happened to look across the corridor where, to my surprise, a man was standing in the doorway. His appearance wasn't a trick of the light, because it was quite bright out-of-doors.

Old buildings in central Reykjavík

I was puzzled. It would have been impossible for anyone to come up after me, because you can always hear anyone who might climb those old rickety stairs. I also thought it was strange because I had never seen that man before. He was tall, in a dark suit that made me think, "how old-fashioned." In that moment, he vaporized in front of my eyes. She concluded her ghost story with a lighthearted laugh.

Hledis also spoke of a ghost who seems to be living with her. *This may sound a bit strange, but I believe a presence is with me almost every day in my apartment. I'm absolutely sure of it because I have felt someone looking over my shoulder. When I turn to look I see someone from the corner of my eye. I can see a shape. I can't figure out whether it is a man or a woman, old or young, but someone is there. It's a sort of presence you feel. I mean, there have been occasions when I have felt these classical things that are supposed to happen, like the room temperature changing or something.*

As if wanting to offer more proof, she went on to say, *and I am not the only one who has felt it. It was a bit weird this summer. My sister was in Reykjavík for 10 or 15 days just before she had her baby. She and her husband were staying with me. When she came home from the hospital with her baby she said, "It was really weird, but when we were living with you before the baby was born it was as though someone was always in the hallway. Now this someone is in the room with us."*

Edna Mitchell

The coastline of Iceland

Is that good or bad, I asked. *We take it as a good omen. She said this presence didn't go home with her when she returned to the Westmann Islands where they live. But before the baby was born and she was at my place, this presence was always somewhere in the vicinity of her room. After the baby was brought to the flat, it was in the room itself. She said it was as though someone was watching over us. It didn't make her uncomfortable or anything like that.* And is it still there? *Yes. Someone is there, but now it is a new person.*

Sigurdur is an elderly laborer who told me about living with a ghost in his room for 7 years. It began when he was about 18 years old in rural north Iceland. He grew up on a farm, but moved to a coastal hamlet to find work. The time was World War II. A British ship sank, and the body of a British sailor floated ashore, eventually to be buried.

He knew that the spirit of that sailor became his roommate, even though he never actually saw him. He knew because he could feel his presence and see evidence that he was around. Lights turned on when no one visible was in the room, and they switched off sometimes when he seemed to be completely alone. He sensed, somehow, that the ghost slept in his room and that he liked to read books in the middle of the night.

He was not uncomfortable about the presence of his ghostly roommate. The spirit never troubled him, and there were times when it prevented accidents at the last moment. For example, once he was moving sand on a barge. A dangerous storm was brewing, but, being stubborn, as he put it, he kept going until inexplicably, something turned the barge back. The turnabout probably saved his life.

How did you know it was an English sailor? *It was a rule of war, when bodies washed up on shore, locals were not allowed to touch them. We were supposed to secure the body from floating back out to sea and then report it to the authorities so that Icelandic soldiers could come to transport it. The soldiers said it was an English sailor.* How did the experience end? *The ghost didn't follow when I moved to the south of Iceland.* Do you miss him? *Yes, I do. He never bothered me, he looked out for my well-being, and I liked his company.*

GHOSTS CAN BE SOMEWHAT FRIGHTENING

Less commonly, ghosts are still occasionally perceived as dangerous. Every Western nation has its stories of haunted theaters, including Iceland. Hlíf, who belongs to an amateur acting company, told me of a ghost who frequents the theater in greater Reykjavík where she is involved. That ghost does not seem to be angry or dangerous at all, but its very strangeness causes apprehension, and on one occasion, startled fear. Different people guess differently at who the phantom is. At first I was told that it is probably the spirit of someone who used to work in the harbor fish factory that was demolished to provide space for the theater. Others say it is the spirit of a carpenter who was killed while working on construction of the new building. The most widely believed story is that it is the spirit of a fisherman who drowned in the harbor and who haunts the theater because it used to be a movie house and he loved movies. Now he just likes to be around where people are creating something. *Actually,* Hlíf told me, *we don't talk much about who the ghost might be.* Clearly, as an inquiring ethnographer, I was causing members of the troop to reify the ghost in an unaccustomed way.

Hlíf did tell me, though, that it can be scary to work there at night. Theirs is an amateur theatrical company, so they often work into the small hours of the morning. *It is very scary to be there alone, because we always hear some noises. Although I don't really care if there are ghosts or not, I have actually heard some noises. It doesn't feel very good. The guy who takes care of the lights up in the attic area is always there at night, and sometimes he's very scared, even though he has been in this for several years.*

Do you think it is a ghost? *Yes, sometimes I believe so. But I think it's not a house ghost. I think it's like—in drama clubs—some people say that ghosts want to be where people are creating something."* Is anybody afraid of the ghost? *I don't think so.*

But another time she told me that a few years ago at the end of a midnight rehearsal they were standing around in the entrance getting ready to leave when a young woman went back into the theater and up a ladder to the rigging above. She was going to make a last-minute adjustment to the lights. Suddenly she saw the ghost. Screaming, she scrambled back to the others and out onto the street. So there is some fear of this ghost, even though nobody believes it intends to do harm.

The Ghosts of Humanitarian Doctors

I was rarely told of contemporary ghosts who were frightening. Perhaps some Icelanders still tell saga-like stories of wrestling with a ghost or other such horrors, but if they do, their anecdotes never got to me. On the contrary. The first story told to me, within days of my arrival in Reykjavík, was about the spirit of a nonrelative, a deceased doctor who took the trouble to provide medical care for a boy severely injured in an automobile accident. Not mayhem, but altruism characterizes many of the ghosts of Iceland in our time.

Lára, who is a yoga instructor, gave me this example. *This is a story about a woman who lived in a rural area and was related to me by marriage,* she explained. *When she was around 50 years old, she became extremely ill and was taken to a hospital where they examined her and took X-rays. They discovered that one of her kidneys was poisoning her and would have to be removed. She went home to prepare herself for surgery. One night as she slept she had the feeling that people were coming into the room wearing white clinic jackets and doing something. She woke up and, since this was out in the countryside, used a chamber pot to pee. It filled with pus, which was disgusting and frightening, but her health changed after that. She began to feel better and eventually was completely well.*

When she returned to the hospital where the operation was supposed to happen they took another X-ray that showed only one kidney, the healthy one. Although Lára insists she is skeptical of these things, the only explanation that makes sense is that spirit doctors performed surgery and cured her. I asked if I could see the before and after radiographs. Unfortunately, they were gone. *I asked my brother-in-law recently if his mother had the X-rays, and he said yes, but I have not seen them myself.*

That spectral surgeon assisted the patient's living doctors who were quite unaware that they were getting this form of back up. Other physicians count on it, including Hannes, who is well known for combining the practice of medicine with unorthodox techniques, such as diagnosing by means of iridology, that is, by looking at color patterns in the iris of the eye. He told me he is always assisted in his medical practice by ghost specialists. I also interviewed a woman who practices a form of alternative medicine known as craniosacral therapy. She told me that a ghost always assists her whenever she is with a patient. I asked who it was, but she couldn't tell. *I don't know who it is, I am just thankful.* **I am never alone when I am working** [emphasis added].

In one group séance I attended, the voice of the medium, Sesselja, became that of a deceased physician who had possessed her. The convenor of that séance, Magnus Skarphedinsson, asked him to tell us about his medical activities that day. *Well, I had several cases—especially an operation in the national pediatric medical center—a small child—a severe case. I was present there while the [living] physicians and surgeons did their work.*

From that conversation I conclude that the ghost doctor provides care as a service to living people to whom he is referred. But how does he get directed to particular patients? Well, in the case of these group séances, a spectral doctor was called in every week when we met. All present were given an opportunity to talk directly with the doctor, who spoke with us through the medium. He always agreed to make house calls later that same night. To that end, each of us in turn provided the names and addresses of those we wished to have visited. It was not customary to indicate what the sickness might be. A deceased doctor can manage quite well without that information.

As an example of how participants feel about the spirits of dead doctors making home visits, one evening when Sesselja was possessed by a doctor, my merchant marine friend Eyjólfur made several requests. Later we talked about them. *I always ask the doctor to make calls. Mostly I ask him to visit the same people. They have all been sick for a long time. For example, one of my friends has an incurable disease of the liver and other organs. I also ask for my mother, who is old with heart disease and depression. I believe this works.*

Did the doctor visit your friend the last time? *Yes.* And was your friend better the next day? *I'm not sure about that. I said to the doctor, please visit the person I asked for before. The doctor asked, "what's your name." I answered, "my name's Eyjólfur." Then the doctor said, "Oh yes, yes, yes. We're still working on that one." Sometimes he says, "He's going to get better." So you can see the proof in some cases."* How is your mother since the last visit? *She seems a little bit better.*

Very commonly, ghost doctors just show up on their own accord. Jóna, a student at the university, told me about a time when her mother was very sick in her bedroom. Jóna was only about 13 years old then and recalls sitting in the room adjacent to the sickroom when she saw the ghost doctor in a white clinic coat walk by and enter her mother's room. She didn't see him leave, but her mother got better. Jóna also told me that when she was about a year old she became so sick with kidney failure that she was expected to live only a few more hours. Her mother prayed, after which she saw several ghost doctors standing over the crib. Jóna is still with us, more than half a century later.

CONCLUSION

Swatos and Gíssurarson (1997) describe those early decades when physical mediumship predominated as "the golden age of spiritualism," which they date from 1848 to the end of the 1920s. "By 1920," they conclude, "physical manifestations were already rare, and they had by and large disappeared by 1950" (p. 116).

Physical mediums were rare when I carried out my recent fieldwork in Iceland. Consistent with their near demise by the end of the golden age, I encountered only one physical medium, a visiting Englishman, and he could not match the startling demonstrations recorded for Indridi.

One can only speculate on the reason for this shift. In part it may be that audiences are less impressed with technological feats than they were before the electronic age, or that they find them less believable, but I am more inclined to favor a psychological explanation. What people want from spirits of the dead is reassurance on a personal level. They want to know that a loved one "is okay," as I was frequently told. They also want reassurance that they themselves will survive death. In any event, the difference between then and now is profound.

Ghosts themselves have changed. It is perhaps understandable that Icelandic ghosts were fearsome and murderous in that period of history when the defining occupation of Icelanders was to venture out as ruthless marauding Vikings. The nation now is wonderfully civilized in the sense that crime is minimal for a complex society and violence is uncommon. Icelanders on the whole are remarkably peaceable and tolerant, so it should come as no surprise that their ghosts are equally unthreatening and kindly.

Finally, the national church has dramatically changed its policy relating to mediums and contact with the dead. It was very receptive and supportive around 1900 when the new spiritism was introduced from Denmark with the claim that it would put Christian belief on a solid, scientific footing. By the last third of the century, however, the national church reversed itself to take a strong stand against it, ostensibly for sound scholarly reasons but also, I suspect, because spiritism was in effect a competitor for popular allegiance. In all events, consistent with being a nation highly tolerant of individual freedoms, church opposition finds expression mainly in theological discussions and occasional Sunday sermons where pastors preach to the choir. The Christianity of ordinary people is accepting of spirit communication, giving virtually no thought to the dispute.

In all, what a historical investigation demonstrates is the extent to which a culture tends to be functionally integrated. It is not surprising that Viking ghosts were fearsome in a violent and dangerous era while contemporary ghosts are not, that physical mediums are now less important to ordinary folk than are mediums who emphasize contact with loved ones, that ghost doctors are almost routinely called on to make house calls for seriously ill people, and that the church is tolerant of spiritists, even though orthodoxy insists that contacting spirits of the dead is dangerous and forbidden on the authority of the Bible.

DIMENSIONS OF MEDIUMSHIP

USEFUL ANALYTICAL CONCEPTS

Anthropologists and sociologists find it useful to distinguish status (an individual's social position) from role (the behavior that is expected or required by someone occupying a given status in society). A priest or a spirit medium, for example, can be characterized as occupying a certain status and as fulfilling associated role expectations. The status characteristics of Icelandic Lutheran pastors emphasize their qualifications as university graduates who have been ordained by the bishop. Their role as ordained ministers requires that they officiate as ritual leaders in church services, but also that they visit the sick, teach confirmation classes, and counsel parishioners. As a rule, the status and role of an Icelandic pastor is what Ralph Linton (1937) would term an achieved status, rather than one that is ascribed (Eriksen & Nielsen 2001: 93). In principle, at least, Icelandic pastors earn (that is, achieve) their position in the church hierarchy by virtue of education, experience, and vocational ambition. It is not ascribed to them in the sense of being a privilege of birth or temperament.

The status of a medium is different from that of a pastor in the basic way it is ascribed. A future medium is said to be born with an innate ability to communicate with the dead and in some cases to see the dead in their spirit bodies. These abilities usually manifest early in childhood. Of course, there is also an achieved component, insofar as aspiring mediums almost always are identified and even coached by established practitioners. Ultimately, status must be confirmed (achieved) by acknowledged success in mediating conversations between the living and the dead. Unlike the pastor who must study at the university to attain needed knowledge and skills, the medium is born with inborn psychic gifts that merely require polishing and recognition.

Recruitment to the role of medium offers one way to understand the profession. Ministers attend seminaries, physicians go to medical school, but how are mediums selected and trained? Some years ago David Landy (1977) reviewed the anthropological literature on recruitment to the healer's role. His findings apply to the role of medium, who usually is also a healer. Mediums achieve their status in a variety of ways that include self-selection, selection by others, undergoing a profound emotional experience, and exceptional personal traits. Thirty years earlier, Max Weber (1947) contrasted priests, who are recruited as bureaucratic functionaries, with prophets, who are self-selected through supernatural revelation and personal charisma. Curious about how one became a medium in Iceland, I found that they were self-selected on the basis of early contacts with spirits of the dead, instruction by established mediums, a willingness to serve others, and not the least, through acceptance by a public that responded to that quality of charisma that Weber identified for prophets, shamans, and magicians.

Not all mediums perform their roles in identical ways. Anthropologists find it useful to identify classification systems that are indigenous, or emic, which is to say, specific to one culture, rather than international, or etic, in that they apply to societies everywhere. Kenneth Pike (1954), a linguist anthropologist, coined the terms *emic* and *etic,* which have found wide usage within anthropology. Emic description is what an ethnographer identifies when doing participant observation, while etic terminologies are the categories used in carrying out quantitative cross-cultural surveys (Perry 2003: 64–65).

Within a culture, persistent inquiry reveals ways in which people define or classify phenomena in their own, culturally specific (emic) ways. Anthropologists identify these so-called folk taxonomies, sometimes based on a very precise method of inquiry known as ethnoscience (Tyler 2004). In Iceland I simply asked mediums to talk about different ways of practicing. I only encountered one, Deborah, who explicitly articulated how she ranks mediums according to the wonders they perform, as I will explain later in this chapter. Perhaps she speaks more openly because she is English. Such rankings are played down by Icelanders, who share a strong egalitarian ethic that makes people uneasy with status titles and privileges. Deborah's hierarchy resonates well with what Icelandic mediums told me, however, and also with the fact that some forms of contact with the dead are common while others, requiring greater skill, are rare.

The emic categories of small-scale preindustrial societies are not usually helpful for etic purposes. For example, the Merina people of Madagascar differentiate ghosts of the unknown dead from nature spirits that take the form of butterflies and moths, which in turn differ from the ghosts of known individuals (Bloch 1994: 124–125). To look for a wide-spread cognitive model that contrasts ghosts with butterflies would obviously be a waste of time.

In Iceland, however, the categories used locally (emic) are applicable as well when discussing spiritism on a worldwide basis (etic), because spiritism is an aspect of modern global culture. In making cross-cultural comparisons, sociologist James McClenon (1994: 78) found it convenient to differentiate mediums, spiritual healers, and psychics, which is similar to differences I will describe for Iceland. I am sure he would also agree the distinction is not always as neat and straightforward as those terms might suggest.

I certainly encountered inconsistencies and apparent uncertainties about how mediums and psychics can be differentiated in emic or eth-nosemantic terms. Yet, on the whole, psychics are differentiated because they work with auras and not with spirits.

As concerns healers, anthropologists have a long history of documenting the multiple ways in which cultures conceptualize the human body and its torments. Following Arthur Kleinman (1980), it can be useful for analytical purposes to distinguish sickness and curing from illness and healing. That fundamental framework for analysis is implicit in *Curing and Healing* by Andrew Strathern and Pamela Stewart (1999). Sickness implies the diagnosis of some form of physiologic-anatomic pathology. Curing refers to treatment of that pathology by means of medicine, surgery, or body work.

In contrast, illness is the experience of a disease that includes psychological, emotional, and life-world aspects of whatever is making a person unwell. It is possible to heal the suffering of an illness even if the disease is not mitigated. I find it is helpful to think of this distinction in a related way by distinguishing mind-oriented healers from body-oriented healers (Anderson, 1996: 344, 371). Body-oriented healers in Iceland would include physicians, surgeons, dentists, chiropractors, and massage therapists. I characterize the healers discussed in this chapter as mind-oriented. They often attempt to treat a disease and occasionally seem to effect a cure, but they are much more likely to be successful in the healing of an illness (Anderson, 2000: 85–88).

THE DEFINING QUALITIES OF A MEDIUM

Those who are involved in contacting spirits of the dead pick and choose from the cultural menu in deciding what to believe and what to do about death and the afterlife, unconstrained by theological dogma or the authority of a priesthood. Many otherwise quite ordinary people encounter spirits of the dead spontaneously and entirely on their own.

Yet functionaries do exist to systematize beliefs, energize voluntary associations, conduct rituals, and, as their signature responsibility, give voice to the dead. We call them spirit mediums because they mediate between the living and the dead. They not only interact with spirits and ghosts on their own behalf, but also on behalf of others. In that sense, they have a ritual function in some ways comparable to that of a priest or minister. But what does it take to become a spirit medium? I learned about what it takes from the following five people who resemble mediums in some ways but incompletely so, and from a sixth who enjoys high status in the profession.

(1) Magnus

Four of these individuals struck me as good candidates for the role of spirit medium, even though they did not see themselves that way. I begin with that iconoclastic individual in Iceland known as Magnus Skarphedinsson, president of the mouse society and so much else. When we first got to know each other, he struck me as an obvious candidate for mediumship, but I was quite wrong. Being wrong taught me what was right.

I thought Magnus must be a medium because he was enormously active as the founder and director of the Icelandic Spirit Research School. Still in his early forties, he has spent the last quarter of a century conversing with spirits of the dead once or twice a week every winter through the intercessions of mediums. These encounters take place in a room carefully wired to pick up and record the voices of the medium, of Magnus, and of others present. At each sitting he speaks with five, six, or more different spirits, resulting, he told me, in a collection of perhaps 300 recorded sessions and more than 2,000 spirits. He also teaches winter courses about the spirit world. Given his long-term, intense involvement, I asked, why are you not a medium? He answered, *because I'm not psychic. I have no skills in that way.*

That answer fits with what I learned from others. The first requirement to be a medium is to discover that you have a talent for seeing or sensing the presence of spirits and for communicating with them. However, many who are not mediums also have that ability.

(2) Klara

One who has some ability to communicate with the dead is Klara, who is 22 years old, a student at the university, and curious and anxious about the possibilities for spirituality in her life. A few days after unexpectedly encountering her at a public séance, we got together to talk. After we were well into our conversation I asked, why did you go to a medium the first time? *I don't know.* **Just to know if there is someone watching over me** [emphasis added]. Is somebody watching over you? *Yes, my grandmother is. Also, I went to the medium because some of them do Tarot cards to tell the future.* I didn't find that to be as common as her comment would seem to imply, but no matter.

Thinking back on my conversation with Halldór, who told me his deceased grandfather was always with him, I tried to draw Klara out on what she implied in sharing that her grandmother is watching over her. *I already knew, but I went to the medium because I had heard her voice sometimes.* You heard your grandmother's voice? *Yes, I didn't know her because I was only a year old when she died. But I knew it was her, because if I was late to school or something, she was always waking me up. I would awaken thinking, "what?" I was certain it had to be my grandmother, because she had a soft and good voice. So I knew.*

What else does she do for you? *I sometimes dream of her—and, yes— if I'm feeling sad, I just feel her presence.* She doesn't talk with you, you just feel she's there? *Yes. Also my grandfather. There is a special grand- mother/grandfather smell. I sense that smell sometimes when they are present. I don't hear her, except when I'm sleeping and she wakes me up.*

As we continued talking she told me about a recurrent dream in which future events were predicted. *There is a woman of whom I dream sometimes. She has a beard, so I said, "you have a beard." Since then she always puts something over her face to hide the beard, so she talks through it. She always says if something is going to happen.*

She tells you in advance? *Yes.* What, for example? *Once she said I should learn to do my Tarot cards and to learn things. She was talking to me about guys. She showed me some stuff that was going to happen with guys. I thought, hmmm, why am I knowing this? Then I woke up. It can be good to know stuff like that, but not too much, because then you will know exactly what's going to happen in the future. Then you start living differently.* Later Klara told me how she was told in advance that her aunt would soon die of cancer, and indeed, she did die of cancer as predicted.

Further on in the conversation I said, so, do you think you might become a medium some day? *No,* was her prompt reply. Why not? *I don't have the talent. But it has been said to me by some mediums that I'm going to be a fortune lady [laughing].* A fortune teller? *When I'm older. I don't know, but, no, I don't think I'll be a medium.* As I left that conver- sation, I wondered if Klara would do what the bearded lady said, and learn how to read Tarot cards as a way to foretell the future.

But what did she mean when she said she didn't have the talent to be a medium? Unlike Magnus, who said he lacked the talent, Klara was contacting spirits of the dead in her dreams, hearing her grandmother's voice when she was supposed to wake up, and aware of the presence of her grandparents when fully conscious. However, her talents were limited to those events and to those intimate members of her family. Perhaps that is not enough. And perhaps, too, it is significant that a medium said she should learn to read Tarot cards, but did not suggest that she become a medium. Is it important if one is to become a medium that a medium offer help or encouragement?

(3) Jóhanna

I encountered more clues in my meeting with Jóhanna. You will recall that when I was in her home she told me her grandparents were there with us, listening to what we were saying but not interrupting. She can smell the presence of her grandfather, and also, like Klara, Jóhanna lives with the spirits of her dead loved ones who tell her, **We are here** and **we love you** [emphasis added].

Beyond what Klara does, Jóhanna mediates between living and dead loved ones. About 6 weeks before I visited her, she hosted a gathering of her family. *On the morning of the reunion, at about 10 o'clock, we were all here in the living room and I was sitting like this,* she said as she leaned back on the sofa, *when our third daughter came, who is in spirit. She has been in spirit for 5 years. I told others at the reunion that she had come along with my grandmother and another [deceased] family member. They were so excited, just like little girls. "Oh, she saw her," they said.*

Did your daughter talk to you alone or to the whole family? *She came only to me. She said nothing.* **She just wanted to let me know she was there** [emphasis added], *and I understood her message, "Tell them I came." She didn't say anything. She just looked at me, smiling. Maybe I imagined it, but I think she wanted me to say "hello" to members of the family.* Can you actually see spirits? *Not always, but this time I could see with my eyes open, I could sense they were there. I didn't actually see them, but felt their presence. I knew who they were. I could see them like I see you, but not clearly.*

That explanation left me confused about her ability to see spirits of the dead. Later she gave a different example of her spirit vision. *My mother-in-law passed into spirit last January. I went to the hospital with my husband to see her and I knew she was close to passing away. A few hours after I left the hospital I was sitting here watching the sun setting around 2 o'clock in the afternoon.* (The winter sun in Iceland lies low in the sky for about 4 hours a day. Otherwise the sky is as dark as midnight both day and night.) *I was looking at it in the window, and then it stopped. Shortly after that my husband called and said his mother was dead. I said, "I know. Somebody showed me that in the window."* Turning to me she added, *Every time somebody is buried I see the person like they were alive. It helps me a lot when somebody whom I care for passes, because I can see they are happy and feeling well.*

Has your mother-in-law visited you since she died? *Yes. She has been here a couple of times.* What does she tell you? *Very little. She is very happy. I can see her. When they come to me they look very young. She was 74 when she passed away, but now she looks about 50 or younger. When the deceased come in a meeting with a medium it is sometimes like that. They come so young looking that sometimes people don't recognize them. So they usually come the way they were when they died, or with some behavior that is recognizable, like knitting.*

When Jóhanna told me she helps people by healing with her hands I asked, how did you learn to do that? *I went to the Spirit Research Society of Iceland. They were hosting an English medium . . . who was very good.* How did he teach you to heal with your hands? *He didn't "teach" me. He showed how to do it and how to come into communication with the spirits. An Icelandic medium told me nobody can teach that. You do as you feel moved and you feel that the gift comes.*

What do you feel in your hands when you do healing? *Sometimes heat and sometimes cold. Sometimes people need a cold touch—cold energy. Sometimes, hot energy. Bone and blood need cold.* How do you know whether to give heat or cold? *It just happens. You know they are there,* pointing to invisible spirits behind herself.

For clarification I asked, they are using your hands for healing, making them hot or cold? *Yes.* Are they ghost doctors? *Yes. They show me. Sometimes they give me the feel of where the sickness is. I can touch the sick person and say, for example, "you have a headache." If I touch her head, I can feel it, and I put my hands on her head. People sometimes then tell me, "Oh, I'm feeling better." But I don't do it. It's the spirits who do it. I'm their instrument.*

Given Jóhanna's daily involvement with healing, with spirits, and her ability to see and sense what spirits want to say, I asked, shouldn't you become a medium? *Yes, she said, people have told me that. But I would rather help people.* Doesn't a medium help people? *Yes, they do. But I like it the other way.*

That answer left me quite perplexed. We talked about some other things, and then I returned again to the issue of becoming a medium. If you became a medium, what would be different for you? *I think people want to know about people who passed away.*

By the end of our visit together I felt I understood why she is almost a medium, but not quite. Her visions of the dead are unclear. Their mes-

Gullfoss waterfall, south central Iceland

sages are limited to expressing emotions. Only well-known loved ones reveal themselves, never strangers. And although she has been told she should become a medium, it has never been by a medium. On these counts Thorunn is more advanced in every way.

(4) Thorunn

The last time I saw Thorunn was in a chance encounter during a private sitting for a dozen people that convened in May 2000. Nine months had elapsed since I had last seen her and in the interim she had been diagnosed with breast cancer, undergone surgery, and was scheduled for radiation treatment at the end of the month. She was 41 years old and convinced that with help from the spirit world she will live out the rest of a normal life span in good health.

Thorunn engages regularly in spirit-related activities. Once, some years earlier, when she was contributing to the planning of a radio program about spiritual matters, she was startled by a remarkable experience. *I woke up in the middle of the night with a strange feeling in my spine, a kind of burning. It was probably the opening of a chakra.* She fell asleep again and had a strange dream. *I was having a child. I was so surprised. I took the child and thought, what am I going to do with it? Then I was back in my home and I saw my son in bed in red pajamas. Then he was in the other room in blue pajamas. I woke up.*

What do you make of that dream? *It was telling me that you can be in two places at the same time. I also felt I had to write some messages down at once. I sat down, thinking I was going to be given a message for the radio program. I prepared myself to write what I would be told when suddenly my hand started moving involuntarily. I couldn't stop it. Without any initiative on my part it wrote, **"Don't be afraid"*** [emphasis added]. *"It's okay. God is with you," and things like that. I couldn't stop it. I woke my husband, "Something very, very strange is happening to me, come to the kitchen."*

The next day I called this medium who was in Norway at the time. I said, "I don't know what's happening to me. I'm just writing and writing, in all kinds of handwriting styles. What can I do?" She just laughed and said, "It's all right. It's just automatic writing. You will find yourself doing it every day, but just relax and say your prayers. If you want it to stop, just say, 'It's enough,' and it will go away."

It has continued now for 3 years, she told me in 1998. *After 6 months it seemed to have opened up totally. In fact, I can't help it. I wake up in the middle of the night and just have to write, in all kinds of scripts.* You just wake up and start writing? *I just sit down and concentrate for a few minutes and it starts. The first message is always from a doorkeeper who comes in between the spirits and me. He's a monk from Tibet. He watches me, I know that. He always leaves his signature and his special picture. Then my grandfather starts. Then the monk, and then my grandmother or someone else.*

Sometimes a spirit comes saying it's my grandfather, but I recognize immediately that it is not, because the power is different and it doesn't speak to me the way my grandfather does. It is important not to be afraid when that happens, to just relax, and I know my doorkeeper will take care of it. He says, "Don't take notice of that. It was an interruption." It hasn't happened often, but it can happen.

When the spirits of loved ones write, do they help you and your family? What do they tell you? *I get a lot of messages for my brother, who has been depressed. He gets a lot of encouragement. Once when my son was sick I was told to go to Hannes, a medical doctor who in part practices alternative medicine.* She did, and the treatment cured her son's skin condition. *They also tell me what they are doing, that they are learning a lot.* What are they learning? *My grandfather is learning about the future of humanity, but they are not allowed to tell us.*

Have you had written messages from any who are not members of your family? She said, *Yes, often,* and then told me about a famous man who corresponded with her. *He was a healing medium who died a long time ago, Einar Einarsson.* Oh, yes, I countered, Einar of Einarstadur was very famous in the mid-20th century. I have heard many stories of his miraculous cures. *Yes. I couldn't believe it at first. I went to a Lutheran minister who worked with Einar for many years, and he recognized his writing.* Who was the minister? *It was Stefán. He said, "Yes, it's him."*

As mentioned earlier, Stefán is one of the few remaining pastors in the national church who is also a spiritist. He once said to me, *How can you be a Christian and NOT be a spiritist.* He is the same spiritist pastor who did the wedding and confirmations for Jóhanna. Iceland is a small country. Such coincidences are not unusual.

Thorunn wanted to be doubly sure that this truly was the famous Einar, so she went to a medium for confirmation. The medium said, *Yes, it's him. He also came here just before you arrived. But,* Thorunn reminded me, **there's always this doubt, you know** [emphasis added]. It is a common dilemma in the spiritist belief system. She believes, but at the same time, she is not sure. It is a contingent belief.

In 1998 I asked Thorunn, are you a medium? I thought her answer was slightly equivocal. She said, *No, I wouldn't say that.* I took her answer to mean that she could be a medium if she chose, because she gets messages through automatic writing from spirits who are not part of her family. When I spoke to her of that she said, *It helps a lot with my family, but I don't want it known, because then I would have no peace.* In other words, with a son still to raise and, 2 years later, with the added burden of surgery and radiation, she is not able to work as a medium for the wider community. Not yet, at least, even though the medium in Norway told her how to carry on, and in that sense, prepared her to serve.

(5) Sigurpal

It was an extraordinary day for October. The sun was shining and the wind was quiet. I set out on my bike for the long ride to a 1 o'clock appointment at an address located in a cluster of modest apartment buildings on the edge of town, happy to get away from my office where I had been closeted all morning. Kristín, the graduate student who was assisting me, made the appointment for me a few days earlier based on a business card I picked up at the reception desk of the Icelandic Spirit Research Society. Sigurpal was advertising himself as a spiritist healer by passing out cards. The society allows almost anybody to leave brochures or other advertising for display on their reception counter.

I was of two minds about this meeting. According to my map, it was a long way to bike. At Kristín's urging, instead of going out the main road, heavy with traffic, I biked along the shore of the fjord, cutting back into traffic at City Hospital, where I had an interview appointment for the following week. It would be a trial run for that bike ride, since Sigurpal lived beyond the hospital. In addition, I was worried because Sigurpal didn't speak English, and I would not have Kristín to translate.

Somewhat uneasy about the whole endeavor, I knocked on his door and was met by a quiet, kindly man, about 60 years old, thin and tired looking from a lifetime of hard manual labor. Invited into his small, pleasant apartment, I was relieved to meet a student whom he had invited to translate for us. Sigurpal's wife immediately produced porcelain cups and saucers and poured coffee. I felt welcome and at ease. Still, interviews are never really satisfactory when it is necessary to depend on a translator, so I thought I would move fast and get back to the university. That would have been a mistake. It turned out to be a prize experience in participant observation.

Well into the interview, Sigurpal unexpectedly pointed to my right shoulder and told me it was hurting. How could you know that, I asked? He said he knew because he could feel my pain in his own shoulder. He was fairly well on target. Because of the long bike ride, I had a muscle spasm near the shoulder blade in the upper part of my back at the inner edge of the shoulder. He offered to treat it. I handed my video camera to the student and we positioned ourselves in two chairs facing each other.

With his right hand, which felt clammy, he grasped my right hand. That cold and damp hand, along with a subtle tenseness, suggested he was anxious about this encounter. Perhaps for that reason he got mixed up, since from then on his attention was directed to my left shoulder rather than the painful right side. He also placed his hands on my head, explaining that it controls the rest of the body in a way he didn't understand. We sat facing each other in silence for almost 30 minutes until he reported that the pain had left my shoulder and was now lodged in his. The session apparently ended with both of us having pain, because I felt no change at all. Finally, he asked if my right ankle and foot were cool or cold. I said no, they were not. He said he had picked up that feeling, and I might find that eventually I would have that feeling. Strike two.

Earlier he told me how he had reached this stage in his career as a healer. He spoke vaguely of encounters with spirits of the dead when he was a child, but I didn't take time to elicit details about those experiences. Instead, I encouraged him to tell me how he began to heal with the help of a team of deceased physicians, led by a dead Icelandic doctor named Jónas. He explained that in treating my shoulder and diagnosing my foot he was merely the means by which those physicians practiced medicine.

Mediumship was recent for him. His first encounter with a ghost doctor took place only 4 or 5 years before our meeting. At that time he was disabled by chronic low back pain. X-rays at the hospital confirmed that his condition was "very bad." They wanted to operate, he said, but he chose instead to seek out a medium. She told him he had the ability to heal with his hands, and he could heal himself with his own hands, which he did.

(How interesting I thought. Other mediums, including Ingólfur who is on staff at the Icelandic Spirit Research Society, have told me they can heal others, but not themselves. Because spiritism is only minimally institutionalized, it is quite common for mediums and advocates to espouse mutually contradictory claims about the spirit world.)

Since healing himself a few years ago, people have approached Sigurpal after work and on weekends for treatments, which he has provided willingly, always without expecting payment. *I have never received money,* he emphasized, *but in the future I want to leave construction work and do healing, so I will want to be paid.* To do that, he added, he needs authentication by the Icelandic Society for Spirit Research. They have told him, he said, that to be certified by the society he will need to demonstrate that spirits of the dead undeniably are working with him and that people are healed. To achieve that level of acceptance, he would no doubt profit from training or mentoring. But no medium has sponsored him thus far.

At that point, I realized why he was nervous in my presence. Kristín told him I had gotten his card at the society headquarters and that I was a professor at the university. No doubt he hoped I would testify in his favor, not realizing that I was not there for that purpose.

That misunderstanding does point out the importance of ethics in fieldwork. Anthropologists need to be sensitive to how their activities have consequences for the people they study—making sure they do not cause harm. I made a mistake in not realizing that he might think I was there to evaluate him for the society. Regrettably, in what mattered to Sigurpal, I did not and could not benefit him. To this day he still earns his living as a carpenter.

(6) Vigdis

When successful mediums talk about preparing for their careers, they predictably tell stories that emphasize early evidence of remarkable innate talents for accessing spirits of the dead. These stories are always well rehearsed, having been told and retold for years. When recited for clients, such stories become personal myths of transcendent power serving to justify faith in the teller's ability to intercede between the living and the dead. Inborn ability will qualify one for this line of work, but personal experience and guidance are also required.

Vigdis is a gracefully aging woman and possibly the best known medium in all of Iceland. During my semester in Reykjavík she was featured in a cover story of *Vikan,* the Icelandic equivalent of the American magazine *People,* and her life story has been written up in books and articles over the years. For a decade she lived just 20 minutes from my office at Mills College in California, but I didn't know her then. When we had our first conversation she talked about early evidence of her talent.

When I was very young—I was 5 or 6—my mother always had a helping hand in the house. The one I remember best was Laura. One day I saw a child standing next to her. I said to my mom, "Who is the girl standing next to Laura?" Her mother just told her to be quiet and gave no answer, but Vigdis never forgot what she saw.

The tension in that unanswered question was relieved only recently. *Three years ago Laura called me up because there was a book out about my work. She said, "Now I understand why you were so strange when you were a child. It was almost impossible to get you to listen. You didn't want to eat. You would always have your hand under your cheek, like your mind was not there and you couldn't understand. I was always trying to talk with you."* Vigdis then told Laura that 60 years earlier she had seen the spirit of a girl with her. Laura responded, saying, *That must have been my sister. She died that winter. See,* Vigdis said to me, *after all these years I found out who it was.*

One day when Vigdis was about 10 years old she was sitting at home talking with her mother. Suddenly she said, "Asa is going to die this week." That annoyed her mother, whose response was, "How dare you say something like that!" Asa did die of tuberculosis that week, but the story does not end there. *Half a year later,* Vigdis added, *I looked out the window, because we lived in an old house in Keflavík, and I said, "Asa is walking there." I waved at her and she waved back. My mother said, "I don't know what I'm going to do with you, girl. You're always making up stories." So I learned little by little, I'm not going to talk about it no more.*

When her children were grown, Vigdis moved to California to be near her oldest son. She attended a spiritist church and decided that she truly did have talent and ought to have some training. She began by taking a Reiki course. Reiki is a healing technique in which the practitioner directs energy into the body of the patient (Anderson, 2000: 85–86). It has nothing to do with spirits of the dead, but her teacher had the ability to see spirits and recognized that Vigdis achieved amazing results for a beginner because she had spirit helpers. Later, a medium saw the spirit doctor who was her main helper, and told her he was a German named Fritz. Later she drew a picture of him.

Edna Mitchell

Lake in an ancient lava flow

In California Vigdis also took courses in a spiritist church where she learned about the spirit world and how to practice as a medium. For years she also associated with mediums, including working as an assistant for one who told her she should practice mediumship herself.

During those years in the United States she developed self-confidence and gained experience. When she returned to Iceland she was given the opportunity to work as a medium at the headquarters of Icelandic Society for Spirit Research. At first she didn't want to do it. *To be a medium is a tremendous responsibility, a heavy burden,* she said. But she finally decided to work at the center once a week. Her schedule for the last 10 or 15 years has increased to 3 days a week, and she earns her living this way. *My task in this life is to serve as a connecting link between the two worlds, this one and the one inhabited by the dead. I bring messages from the spirit world that can be helpful to living people.*

Based on what I learned from these six people and from others whose lives are also powerfully shaped by spiritist thought and practice,

I will allow myself an anthropologist's prerogative and describe what I see as a pattern of recruitment and authentication.

THE UNDERLYING PATTERN

The culture of spiritism in Iceland is consistent with an anthropological description of cultures as "amorphous, unbounded bundles of ideas, knowledge, and beliefs that are continually being contested and renegotiated" (Cronk 1999: 117). The mediums I encountered differ from one another in many ways, just as Sigurpal differs from Ingólfur on the issue of whether a medium can cure himself. Even so, certain dimensions of practice appear to define the profession.

First, mediumship is not possible without an inborn qualification. At the very least, as Magnus clearly explained, a medium must display a huge innate talent for seeing or sensing the presence of spirits and for communicating with them. It is perhaps significant that not one of the five non-mediums talked about witnessing spirits of the dead as children, although I met other non-mediums who did. Every successful medium remembered spontaneous encounters of that sort.

Second, a successful medium typically relies on learned as well as intuitive skills. Success seems to require the encouragement and help of established mediums who serve as mentors and teachers. It is notable that of the five non-mediums, only Thorunn was instructed by a recognized medium, and then only briefly. However, it may be just a matter of time before she turns professional.

Third, to be a successful medium, the ability to communicate with spirits must not be limited solely to deceased members of one's own family, as was true of Klara and Jóhanna. Thorunn regularly communicates with nonfamily spirits, but only for her own purposes. Of the non-mediums, Sigurpal most closely approaches the status of successful medium. Like Thorunn, he interacts with non-family spirits and like her it may be only a matter of time before he achieves professional status.

Fourth, a successful medium serves the community, contacting spirits for the benefit of a network of clients. Non-mediums do not. Although I have characterized Sigurpal as a non-medium, for the last several years he has served the community marginally by intermittently attending to coworkers, neighbors, and acquaintances as a free service. About 2 months before I met him, he made a serious effort to upgrade into full professional status by distributing newly printed business cards. He also hoped to be authenticated and perhaps employed by the Spiritist Research Society of Iceland. Apparently nothing has come of these efforts.

Fifth and last, because social recognition is achieved by demonstrating success in communicating with spirits, which can include foretelling future events and curing disease, errors and failures can lead to the contestation and renegotiation of one's status as a medium. It is rare for a well-known medium to completely lose credibility, but aspirants are vulnerable. A status challenge was implicit in the case of Sigurpal when he missed a diagnosis and failed a cure in ministering to me. Thorunn questioned her own self-identity as future medium when she reminded me, *There's always this doubt, you know.*

THE HIERARCHY

Icelanders on the whole interact with one another as equals. Status titles are played down. The most powerful and the least powerful demonstrate mutual respect by addressing each other on a first-name basis, and yet, some enjoy extra benefits from high status while others do not. Spiritists do not give much public attention to ranking mediums, yet it is implicitly understood that they can be ranked according to a hierarchy of spiritual skills. The most honored and respected seems to be the physical medium, who, while in deep trance, is able to materialize physical objects or cause them to move without direct physical contact. Almost as high in the hierarchy is a transfiguration medium, whose body, when possessed, becomes physically transformed into the face, body, mannerisms, and voice of the spirit. At the third level down, a possession medium can be used by a spirit who speaks by means of the medium's voice, but does not change the face and body of the medium.

Most mediums rank below trance mediums in this hierarchy, and most of the mediums I came to know are in this fourth category. They are usually referred to simply as mediums, but also as clairvoyants in the usage of mediums I talked with. As part of meeting all of the basic defining criteria of mediumship, they possess a "sixth" sense that allows them to see and hear spirits and communicate with them directly, one mind to the other, without audible speech. Lowest in the hierarchy are individuals who exercise paranormal healing abilities, but are not defined by the pattern variables of mediumship. They are neither thought of nor referred to as mediums.

Deborah as a Healer

I never met a medium who explicitly said, "this is the complete classification scheme that we all accept." However, Deborah, the English transfiguration medium who regularly works in Iceland, recalls stages in her own career development as exemplary of these categories. In my first interview with her she talked about her first meeting with a medium. *I have always been able to hear and see the spirit world from being little,* she said, but when she met a medium for the first time, *He saw the healing ability within me. So I trained as a healer.*

Intrigued by that statement, I broke in to ask, How did he train you? *Just by watching me, telling me where to go with my hands, concentrating on a place where there was pain.* I interrupted for clarification, and she added, *He would heal with me at first, watching what I was doing. For many months he worked with me and watched me.* What kinds of things did he tell you? *He used to explain to me that I wasn't healing the physical body, I was healing the spiritual body. I was also told of the ethics. A lady healer with a gentleman, you always got to have somebody there. Especially when a gentleman healer is giving a lady healing, for your own safety.*

We talked at some length about the healing techniques she learned to use. *My teacher told me what to do, told me to just tune myself into the spirits. He said, all you are is a vessel for the energy to flow through. He said, it's not you doing the healing, it's the power of the spirit working through you. I learned to transmit the power through my hands into that person. Sometimes the patient would say there was an awful lot of heat, and sometimes it was ice cold. It just depended on which was needed. He said, just leave it up to the spirit world, because they know.*

Then Deborah told me that the schooling of paranormal healers in England has changed since she began. *Now, you see, they are trained differently. They've got about 3 year's work to do, a lot of paper work, exams, texts. They've got to know the inside-out of the body, the bones, everything.* Why would they need to know that? She ignored my question and continued, *They sit for a test. It takes about 3 years now before you can be called a healer.* Perhaps that answered my question.

Deborah as a Medium (Clairvoyant)

As she continued to tell me how she "developed" she said, *This other teacher came along, and she says to me, you stop the healing. Your mediumship is the stronger talent, right? Then I trained as a medium. I do, as a medium, see the spirit world.* By developing her clairvoyant abilities she soon became able to converse with spirits in the sense that she could detect their thoughts and gain impressions of their bodily and facial gestures, which she was then able to explain to her clients. As a clairvoyant, her purpose often was to serve as a means by which a sick person could be healed, so her ministry of healing was not abandoned, but it manifested differently and was no longer the only service she provided.

When I first was learning—developing—my daughter used to say I could walk into a room and my nose used to twitch, and she would say, "Mother, you're picking up something." I would say, "how do you know?" "Mother, we can see your nose twitching." And I knew soon as my nose started there was somebody in that room needed healing. I kept wondering why this was happening. Well, I got told after by a medium who could see what was going on. It was because I had a very big Zulu what worked with me. And he had a bone through his nose. My nose would start twitching. It was his way to let me know he was there. He would see somebody needed healing, so he would make my nose twitch."

As an anthropologist I know that septal piercing, although common in New Guinea, is never found in South Africa among the Zulu. I was there to listen and to learn so, of course, I let her statement pass without comment.

Deborah as a Trance (Possession) Medium

Over the years I would get messages that have to do with trance healing, and I thought, I don't do trance. How would I be doing trance healing? And yes, eventually I did develop trance. But now I'm a transfiguration medium. A trance or possession medium loses consciousness of her own body and mind, in that way allowing a spirit to use her voice in order to converse directly with a client.

I was intrigued by the language issue in possession. Whenever I heard Deborah speak while in a trance it was always in her own working class dialect of English. Yet, she would have ample opportunity to use other languages since in addition to her annual 2 weeks in Iceland, she also visits Denmark, Germany, and Hungary. So I asked her, how do you deal with foreign languages? *It just depends on what level they get me into. Last time I was here—very far north—in an old cinema—when I came around it was very, very quiet. I said, "What's wrong?" "We're in shock." "Why?" "It was the last lady what come through. We only put her in the coffin tonight at 6 o'clock, and half of them are going to her funeral tomorrow."* But, Deborah emphasized, she came through and spoke to them in Icelandic—had a conversation with them. *"We're just in total shock."* I was in shock and said, "Oh my God, she's not even cold and she's come back."

As further confirmation of how moving that experience was, Deborah added, *The next day a lady came for a private reading, and she said it seemed funny going to her funeral when she was talking to us last night on the platform.* So the spirits can speak Icelandic through you? *On occasions. It just depends. If they get me right deep they completely cut my mind out. Because I haven't got an Icelandic mind, okay? So they've got to get to that point.*

Then she offered another anecdote. *It's like, I did one in Liverpool, and a Japanese sailor came through. A lady who could speak Japanese knew this fellow. She spoke to him in Japanese and he spoke back to her in Japanese. It just depends on what level they can get me into, because I'm very nosy. I think to myself, I miss what's going on. It doesn't seem fair that I miss it all. My spirit guide, the Chinese gentleman, quite often will say, "She's being a very nosy lady. She is listening to what is being said." Then I just gradually go back down.* But in her sittings the Chinese gentleman never speaks Chinese, only English with an accent like Charlie Chan in an old Hollywood movie.

Deborah as a Transfiguration Medium

Very few possession mediums become adept at letting not only their voice become that of a spirit, but at yielding so completely that the face and body are remodeled with ectoplasm to take on the physical appearance of the possessing spirit. *I developed trance* [possession], Deborah explained, *and in one of these trance sittings this lady was there what had a slipped disk, and they called me out. I put my hand on her and when it was over she was all right.* You had no memory of it? *No. They told me after.* Did you know who the spirit was? *It was the Chinese gentleman. I didn't know while in trance, and when I come around, everybody was kind of staring at me, and I watched around. And they said, a Chinese gentleman came through, and you stood up and walked across the room and went to a lady, gave her healing, walked back and sat down.*

At this point I asked Deborah, How did they know it was a Chinese gentleman? Her answer explained how they knew and also why they stared at her with astonishment. *Because they could see him. My face changed.* So suddenly you were a transfiguration medium? *Yes.* And, I might add, in that first instance without sitting in a pitch-dark room illuminated only by a dull red light as is otherwise always required.

What did you know about being a transfiguration medium at that point in your career? *Before I ever had anything to do with mediumship I went to see a very famous lady called Queenie Nixon, a transfiguration medium. I didn't know what to expect, me and my friend, when we walked into the spiritist church. I was frightened to death,* she said, laughing. *And I can remember coming out of there, and I went, "Oh God,*

I would love to do that." And years later I got told I opened the door to it by expressing that wish.

I sat for 12 years, every Saturday night for 12 years, and I never missed, to develop transfiguration. Who taught you to do it? *No one. I just sat with the spirit, and the people who came and sat with me. I just had complete and utter faith in the spirit world. I just said, well, I'm being open to you. I've got every faith in you.*

I interrupted to ask, may I videotape your sitting tonight? Her answer was a firm, *No.* Is it okay to audiotape? *You can do sound.* I was not surprised by her refusal to permit videotaping, because in an earlier meeting I asked if anyone had ever taken pictures of her during a transfiguration, and she said never. When I asked what would happen if someone took pictures she said, *I don't know. Sometimes they tell us they don't want a strict supervision.*

So spirits don't want moving pictures? *No,* she emphasized, and that was that. The prohibition is consistent with doing transfigurations in pitch-black rooms lit only by a single dim red light that faces up from the floor. Under such circumstances an audience can only dimly see the medium's face. Skeptics might suspect a conscious effort to deceive. Even convinced spiritists sometimes become skeptical of these performances. When I told my friend Adalbjörg, whose son was treated by a ghost doctor, that I was going to be in the audience for Deborah's transformation she said, *I can't believe you will see somebody come. I think that's a fake.*

Deborah as a Physical Medium

It was years after the experience with Queenie Nixon before I actually went back into a spiritist church, but the spirit world are very crafty and devious, because I had no intention of sitting for it, but my teacher asked me, would I keep my eye on a young man who was developing physical mediumship. So this young man came to my home and I got three of the ladies to come and sit for him. And for 3 years we sat for this young man so he could develop his gift. What does a physical medium do? *Materialization.* He was materializing things in those sittings? *Well, he was developing.* I took that to mean he had not succeeded, but showed promise.

After 3 years he had some problems at home and he stopped sitting. And a lady, an old Manchester medium, said to me, "You go in the cabinet. You're the physical medium." And I said to her, "I'll go in the cabinet and keep the energy going until he comes back." He never came back. It was me who developed it. And it was me who developed the transfiguration. Now I'm sitting to develop materialization." You're still developing! *Yes!*

What does it mean, you sat in the cabinet? *I had in my home—and I have—a cabinet. It's all black,* (she gestured up the sides of herself and over her head and behind). *It has curtains* (gesturing in front of herself), *so it blocks out. The cabinet builds the energy inside. You pull the curtains back* (gesturing an opening movement), *and it's all pitch black in the room, and there's just a red light. And the energy and everything all build up. Actually, people say they actually see the spirit world moving in. They can see the shape of them all coming in.*

She told me about one sitting in which those sitting with her confirmed a partial materialization. *They said they seen the ectoplasm completely covering me, okay? Everything has to be just right for it to happen, okay? They actually saw the shape of a child what stood at the side of me.*

Two years later on a short visit to Iceland I just missed seeing Deborah by a week. Ragnheidr, whom she stays with on every visit, told me that the physical mediumship was progressing well. She had materialized a young girl who stood beside her. The child looked a bit gray, fuzzy, and incomplete, but most of the people in the room said they could see her, looking somewhat the way Princess Leia did when she materialized in front of Luke Skywalker and Obi-Wan Kenobi through the mediumship of R2-D2, the lovable droid in *Star Wars.*

Deborah as a Psychic

I got an early lesson on the importance of distinguishing psychics from mediums in a conversation with Vigdis, the magazine cover celebrity. She explained the difference between information taken from people in a paranormal way and information that the spirits provide. *When something comes through from the spirit world I'm not taking that from you, I'm taking it from the other side. Psychic work and spirit work are different.*

It was a distinction others also made, particularly when they discussed auras. *If I were just working with you psychically,* Vigdis said, *I would go into your aura and check on it. I do that sometimes. Sometimes I only listen to the spirits and sometimes they say to me, look around him, you need information from around him. I say, "Okay, I'll look around him," and then I might go into his aura. Then I'm taking it from your surroundings and from your mind, and that's different, see?*

When she told me that, I was reminded of what the president of the Icelandic Society for Spirit Research told me about mediums. *We have a medium who never connects with the spirit world. She just goes into your aura,* and he leaned forward as though wanting to outline an aura around my body. *That's dangerous, because you aren't connected to anything. We have people who see auras quite clearly and we have been investigating them. It turns out that some mediums work with auras all the time. Others do so only when tired, and still others, only when they wish to do certain things that can only be done that way.* I assume that Vigdis falls into that last category, supplementing what she learns from a spirit with what she can detect in an aura. According to what the society president told me, that should not be dangerous.

Several months after discussing psychics with Vigdis, I showed up at her apartment to see a picture of Fritz, the German spirit doctor who assists her in healing as a spirit medium. She has never seen Fritz herself, but another medium did and was able to draw a portrait with colored pencils. As we looked at that framed drawing, she recalled a time when her son was injured in an automobile accident. He was taken to the hospital, and she was with him when the doctor came in. Remembering that moment, she told me she knew the doctor was Norwegian, but not from his Scandinavian accent. *I said, "You're Norwegian." He said, "Yes. How did you know?" I said, "From your aura. I saw the Norwegian flag,"* and then, turning to me, *just like I told you that you have European parents.* Right, my parents were Danish. *I saw the Danish flag in your aura.* (Hmm, I thought, what about the red, white and blue? After all, I was born and raised in the United States.)

Continuing her discussion of auras, Deborah told me that when she was apprenticing as a paranormal healer, her teacher taught her that she could heal by means of an aura. *He used to say you don't need to touch the person. All you need to do is put your hand near him, into the auric field.* She explained that disease shows up in the aura before it enters the body, so it is possible to cure a person before clinical symptoms are detectable. Unfortunately, this painless form of preventive medicine is impossible to demonstrate to the satisfaction of medical scientists. From their point of view, you are claiming to have cured a disease that never existed in the first place.

CONCLUSION

In this exploration of the status and role characteristics of spiritism in Iceland it became evident that in spite of how much mediums differ from one another, they all reflect an underlying cultural pattern. Early in life they display a talent for being aware of spirits of the dead. That talent needs to be recognized by an acknowledged medium who provides basic instruction. Contact with the dead must extend beyond loved ones, because they are obliged to serve society at large. They must also demonstrate their ability by successfully putting people in touch with the dead, forecasting future events, and healing people who are ill.

Individuals who display some of these traits but not all are not mediums, although they may become mediums in the future. Finally, the ability of a psychic to see events at a distance or to see and use auras to diagnose and heal people defines a practitioner of the paranormal who is not a medium, although some individuals are qualified in both professions.

At this time in Iceland, it is rare to encounter a physical or a transformation medium and even possession mediums are uncommon. Most mediums communicate with spirits of the dead by translating what they see and are told through mind-to-mind communication. Vigdis practices in that way, and she enjoys an enviable national reputation. It is true that the current star of Icelandic spiritism is Deborah, the English medium who does transfiguration and who hopes soon to reach the pinnacle of achievement as a physical medium. Iceland is a very egalitarian society, however, and status rankings do not sit well with them, so the hierarchy is subdued and implicit. Vigdis describes her own career as a movement up from being a psychic healer to performing as a clairvoyant medium, and even for a time, demonstrating that she can do trance possession. But she characteristically plays down these status comparisons. *Each medium has a different way of working,* she told me. *We don't all work alike. Many work like me, but still, the energy is always a little different.*

DAILY LIFE IN
THE SPIRIT WORLD

DEATH FROM AN ANTHROPOLOGICAL PERSPECTIVE

Anthropologists have observed in societies around the world that people believe in the existence of a supernatural world and believe that people live on, somehow, after dying (Levinson 1996: 226). Because these ideas are virtually universal, they must serve very important basic human needs, but what are they? No doubt religion does many things for people, and different things in different places (Klass & Weisgrau 1999:2). Sociologist Robert Bellah says religion is fundamentally about the ultimate condition of existence (1964). Philosopher Martin Heidegger (1962) wrote about the terror of knowing that inevitably every one of us must die, and what happens then? Anthropologists Lewis Langness and Gelya Frank (1981) would add that people everywhere find ways to accommodate the inevitability of death. "One thing that every human life has in common with every other is this: certain death, and foreknowledge of that event" (p. 113). Similarly, classicist Walter Burkert (1996) targets such beliefs as the way individuals and societies cope: "The utmost seriousness of religion is linked to the great overriding fear of death" (p. 31).

Anxiety about the inevitability of morbid decay is assuaged throughout the world by conceptualizing the deceased as somehow surviving in one way or another (Levinson 1996: 3). It is certainly true that belief in life after death is widespread in Iceland. But it is widespread in a paradoxical way. It seemed very important to nearly everyone I talked with to know that they will still be alive after death. With a few important exceptions, however, almost no one gave any thought at all to what the afterlife actually is like on a daily basis. No one seems to ask or care how Vincent van Gogh passes the time of day when he is not sitting on the roof of his old house in Arles to answer questions about how he died. What was he doing there anyway?

Perhaps because I'm an anthropologist, with an anthropologist's insatiable curiosity about societies and cultures different from one's own, I wanted people to tell me what they knew about the daily realities of living in the afterworld, an ethnography of the spirit world, if you will. I was disappointed when it became clear that for most, how spirits comported themselves from day to day and from year to year was simply not on their mental TV screens. Fortunately, there are some exceptions. I met several mediums who had queried spirits on what life is like in the great beyond and early on I was also told about the teachings of Helgi Pjeturss.

Helgi Pjeturss (1872–1949)

Early in the 20th century, Helgi Pjeturss, an internationally respected Icelandic geologist, described the afterworld in detail. Many in Iceland took his teachings seriously, their authenticity enhanced by his reputation as a scientist. The year after his death his followers founded New Awareness (*Nýallsinna*), a society dedicated to practicing, propagating, and expanding his teachings. Around mid-century their meetings regularly attracted small loyal audiences. To this day, Helgi's books can be found in many homes. I have seen them myself when visiting friends. His best known work is *Nýall* (The New), which was first published in 1919, but he also wrote many other books and articles.

In earlier decades, the New Awareness membership included mediums who contacted spirits of the dead by means of trance possession, as I learned from Ingvar, a man in his sixties who is one of the founders of Asatrú, a modern revival of the old Nordic religion. *I used to go to séances at Nýallsinnar,* he told me. *I was not a member, but I found it very interesting. It was actually a very nice ritual. It was a ritual.* Did everyone sit in a circle? *No. It was like a lecture hall, or it could be smaller, and the medium sat at the front of the room.* Because I had attended some group séances in which the audience sang songs to set the mood while the medium went into a trance, I asked, did the meeting begin with singing? *Not that I can remember. People came in, said hello, and then sat in silence. The medium sat facing the group and, when all were assembled, entered a trance state. Since Helgi Pjeturss had passed on by then, usually a meeting started with Helgi himself coming through. He would say something. The response of the congregation was always the same. They would say "hello."* You have the feeling this had been honed for a long time, a real ceremony in a sense, the same group, the same place, the same *thing at regular intervals, done in a similar manner every time. First Helgi arrived from a planet somewhere. Then different personalities also came through from other planets.*

Ingvar continued, *Sometimes they came from ancient times. Many were from Asatrú, the religion of the Vikings. Their interpretation of the gods is that they are superior beings living on other planets, having simply gone much further than we. I think this was the interpretation of Helgi Pjeturss himself.*

What was the purpose of the spirit séance? Was it to ask about what life is like on other planets? Was it to give advice? *As far as I remember— it was many years back—the whole idea was that the dead who live on other planets are trying to give advice. They are in a more advanced plane of existence. They offer advice on how to behave. The main advice was how to achieve better contact between the two worlds, describing life in those other places. But a lot of it was personal messages, to family members who were not there and directly to those who were.*

The society is moribund now and Helgi's most innovative ideas are largely discounted. The few surviving members are old and inactive. A reunion in 1997 attracted about 20 loyalists who spent an evening sharing memories and thoughts. I was able to interview one of them, Thorsteinn Gudjonsson, a founding member. I also located a book Thorsteinn published in 1976 called *Astrobiology: The Science of the Universe.*

From Thorsteinn and his book, as well as by discussing Helgi's ideas with mainstream spiritists who know of him, I learned that New Awareness was never a big movement, even though Helgi's ideas were widely discussed for several decades.

Writing on what he referred to as "afterlife conditions," Helgi directly challenged the most fundamental belief of almost all Icelandic spiritists, which is that after death we live on without physical bodies. Geir, a medium I will introduce later on, once told me that spirits are able to move right through us because, as he put it, *their energy is a higher frequency, and we are a low frequency.* Gísli of the Spiritist Research Society of Iceland said much the same thing, telling me that his deceased wife was in the room with us *in a different frequency.* In sharp contrast, Helgi wrote, "life after death will be found to be a perfectly natural and biological affair" (Gudjonsson 1976: 115–116).

Helgi taught that after death the human spirit is transported to another planet. On that planet it is given a new body made of the stuff of that planet. Just as our bodies are formed from chemical compounds common to Earth, theirs are formed out of the chemistry of the world that they inhabit (Gudjonsson 1976: 116).

His most disputed claim was a theory of dreams, which grew out of the concept of telepathy. Minds can communicate instantaneously across the immense light-years of space according to this hypothesis. In dreams we do not evoke imagery from our unconscious as Freud was claiming in those days. Rather, dreams are actually the intrusive thoughts of people in outer space, thoughts that most people mistakenly take to be their own. The experiences of sleep are actually true pictures of life on other planets. Helgi recalled making that discovery in 1902. "Here I arrived at a conclusion that was at first glance staggering" (cited in Gudjonsson 1976: 41). He added that he was not referring to any of the planets in our own solar system. The planetary worlds of extraterrestrial humans and superhumans are located at much greater distances throughout the universe.

He emphasized that dreams communicate true activities of the dream-giver. Moreover, in such an encounter the sleeper is charged with energy, a process he termed *bioradiation*. It accounts for the restorative power of sleep. Additionally, one may wake up in the morning with new ideas or thoughts that in origin are also contributions from another mind (Gudjonsson 1976: 40).

Moving from one life to another, from one planet to another, souls grow in wisdom and goodness. This resembles the widespread belief in Iceland that people experience multiple reincarnations, and that the purpose of each is to learn new lessons as they progress toward perfection. The purpose of living is to learn about and aspire to what Gudjonsson refers to as "superhuman life." The cosmos as such has a purpose, which is to nurture the evolution of life to higher and higher levels of attainment (Gudjonsson 1976: 116).

However, contact with the dead is not confined to highly evolved beings. A person's own departed loved ones may return as dream-givers from their new home planet. Gudjonsson published an account of the dream-visit of a man's father who saved him from death by drowning when he advised him to have the local blacksmith forge a backup tiller for his fishing boat, even though to do so was not ordinarily done. He did as he was told, and it was a good thing, too, because next time he sailed a powerful storm blew up the that broke the tiller as he struggled against wind and water. If he had not followed the advice of his deceased father, he would surely have lost his life (Gudjonsson 1976: 108–109).

Today, those who remember the writings and teachings of Helgi Pjeturss generally forget or reject the two concepts that are the most difficult to reconcile with what most spiritists in Iceland postulate or believe: That spirits in the afterworld obtain physical bodies, and that dreams are the intrusive experiences of space aliens. The cultural menu is permissive in this way. Given the absence of dogma about the spirit world, it should not come as a surprise to learn that one can respect the theories of Helgi and still conceptualize the dead as having ephemeral bodies and conceptualize dreams as being encounters rather than takeovers.

His theorizing can also be used to provide explanations for other mysterious events. Thorsteinn told me, for example, that *there cannot be the slightest doubt that UFOs come from other inhabited planets* to visit Earth. I want to mention this, because I spent a lot of time with Magnus, who categorically dismisses Helgi's theory of dreams and of the dead obtaining physical bodies, but, like many others, is very open to the possibility that people live future lives on distant planets.

MAGNUS SKARPHEDINSSON

The founder and director of the Spirit Research School (*Salarrannsóknaskólinn*), a nonprofit voluntary association, thinks of himself as a historian, but he seems more like an ethnographer of the afterlife to me. He does his "fieldwork" in group séances that convene 15 to 25 people on a regular basis to speak with spirits through Sesselja, a possession medium. Addressing spirits as they use Sesselja's body and voice, Magnus quizzes each one about its activities and surroundings. Where are you? Tell us about your daily activities. What is the landscape like? Describe the sounds you hear. Are there animals? What do you eat? Do you have sex? What sort of democracy do you have? Do you meet people from other nations? *They answer all of these questions,* he assured me. Then, with unabashed hubris he added, *We have been doing this for 25 years. Only we know what their lives are like. As far as I know, we are the only ones in Europe to do this kind of recording and taping. My dream is to put our records on the computer, to be able to hand a CD disc to all of the students in our school, indexed. I would love to put it on the Internet and let the world see it.*

Everything said in spirit school séances is recorded on audiotapes, and just as Ingvar characterized New Awareness séances as following a predictable pattern, those of the spirit school are also highly ritualized. The medium is a monolingual woman in her seventies who obviously enjoys the meetings and the regulars who attend. They always end with socializing over coffee and waffles. *She gets no money from us,* Magnus once told me, an important reminder that not all mediums expect to be paid. *Twenty or thirty years ago, none of them got paid,* he added, but I don't think he is right about that.

When a spirit is about to take over Sesselja's body, she begins to assume the visitor's postures and gestures, stretching or seeming to look

Robert Anderson

A medium as she is possessed by a spirit from the Gray Place

around with closed eyes, perhaps yawning, shivering from the cold, or taking a deep breath. At that point, Magnus will say *good evening*. He will say it again if he gets no immediate response, and eventually the spirit will answer. After that Magnus initiates a conversation, asking the spirit's name and circumstances of death and inquiring about home and community, daily work, social relations, values, attitudes, church life, religious beliefs, pastimes, amusements, and so on.

One afternoon in another part of town while I was chatting with Gudmundur, who was president of the Spiritist Research Society of Iceland at that time, I mentioned that Magnus always wants to know what daily life in the spirit world is like. *I know,* Gudmundur answered. *I have been to many meetings with Magnus. I have lectured at his school. He asks spirits to describe, and from that you get a picture.* Laughing, he added, *The life they describe is not so different from our lives here!*

I was intrigued with Magnus's ethnography in part because he thinks it likely—although, he cautiously adds, *not proven*—that after death we go to other planets, which is what Helgi Pjeturss taught. *I fancy that idea,* he once told me. *I'm not sure about it, but what I have learned in working with other mediums is that some conditions of the afterlife are generally accepted. They tend to agree that spirits live on hard land surfaces that include landscapes of trees and rivers and they experience changes in the weather. They are places with suns and moons.*

Continuing, he said, *Different mediums come up with the same descriptions. The only difference from Helgi is, they say that in the spirit world we live in another dimension. Or, simply, they say we live in a world that has no special place. It's just another world in another dimension, nowhere and elsewhere. But the more I work with mediums who do not have backgrounds with Helgi Pjeturss, the more I gain confidence in his theories.*

In other ways Magnus diverges from New Awareness beliefs and practices. He categorically rejects Helgi's theory of dreams. He also rejects Helgi's notion that after death we acquire new physical bodies. Magnus teaches that in the afterlife we possess only an ephemeral presence. *A spirit can sometimes become visible, but to do so requires very high energy. Occasionally a spirit can become visible and physical as well, acquiring what is called an ectoplasmic body. But that is very difficult for the spirit and is rare. I have only seen it once.*

Magnus actually struggles against the intrusion of Helgi's ideas into spirit school seances, which formerly happened a lot. Sesselja was originally a member of New Awareness. Her spirits tended to act the way Helgi described them. When I asked Gudmundur how that could be, he told me that what spirits say can be heavily influenced by the experience and personality of the medium, so Helgi's ideas might come through when Sesselja is in a trance. That is also what Magnus told me. *The background of this medium is Nýallsinna. That's why many of Helgi's ideas come through. Fortunately or unfortunately, mediums seem to reflect very strong echoes of their backgrounds. Those who have ideas of reincarnation are totally stuck in that,* which Helgi rejected and which Magnus believes is unproven. *Those who were with Helgi Pjeturss are totally stuck in Nýall,* Magnus concluded.

Continuing in that vein, he added this assertion. *But we have managed to train her so well that she is much more open than she was when we first met her 20 years ago.* Some months later when we returned to this issue, he said, *We have systematically trained her not to voice the Nýall background, to be as open, as wide, as possible; to have all the ideas possible, so they can get it through to us.* How did you train her? *We taught her that Helgi Pjeturss did not possess the only version of truth.*

Puzzled, I found an opportunity one day to ask Gudmundur to explain how Magnus could train Sesselja so that the spirits would describe their lives differently from when she was in New Awareness. He paused before answering, and then made this statement. *I don't know how Magnus does this, but [smiling] he is a man who wants to be in control, so maybe he can influence the medium. If he does, I don't know. It may be that the medium is responsive to Magnus's wishes.* At this I was reminded of a comment by Thorunn, the active spiritist who does spirit writing, **there's always this doubt, you know** [emphasis added]. It certainly reinforced doubts in my mind about the extent to which spirits and the spirit world truly exist apart from being mere figments of the imagination.

The Gray Place   According to Magnus, *Good people go to good places. Bad people go to bad places.* An ethnography of the spirit world according to Sesselja's spirits includes a place they refer to as the Gray Place. It is inhabited by those who, when alive, committed suicide, were drug addicts or drunks, committed murder, were overwhelmed by severe guilt, overpowered by hatred, or in other ways led troubled lives.

Everything you did when alive waits for you after death, Magnus told me. *When you die, you have to deal with it. If you murdered someone, the first person you meet is the person you killed, and the issue between you has to be resolved. If you tortured someone, you have to get his forgiveness. You will probably experience his feelings if you don't understand them. The punishment in the spirit world is not that you will be tortured, but that you have to learn to understand what you did. You are put in their situation and it's played again, and again, until you have gone through everything. You are completely stuck in the Gray Place until this is taken care of. It's not a matter of God, or Jesus, or a judge. It is a physical thing. If you do this, then this and this happens.*

The Gray Place is not the Hades of eternal fire and unquenchable thirst that Lazarus looked at from the bosom of Abraham (Luke 16:23–24). To some extent it reminds one of the pre-Christian, pre-Jewish afterworld described by the ancient Sumerians nearly 5,000 years ago, a neutral place that is neither a heaven nor a hell. In Mesopotamia at the dawn of history the dead existed in complete isolation from the living, surviving "in a pallid half-life without either reward or punishment," according to my friend and colleague, Alan Bernstein (1993: 3, 5). *They seem to be stuck in some sort of personal hell,* Magnus said, echoing thoughts from literature like *No Exit,* or *Waiting for Godot.*

In any event, the first spirit that Magnus wants the medium to attract is always someone from that world, and it always happens. The purpose of making contact this way is to help the spirit move on to a higher plane as well as to elicit biographical and cultural information. *We usually talk with one person at each meeting who is stuck in this situation. We help them get out by telling them to change their thinking. We tell them that rescue teams in the spirit world are trying to help them. They can't help themselves because they are so totally lost. Some don't know they are dead. They know they are stuck somewhere and haven't a clue where they are.*

One spirit encountered in the Gray Place when I was present was a man who only recently died and didn't know it. He told us, *I don't believe in life after death.* He was located in a desert where he was sleeping in a small house under a cliff, but he told us he didn't know where he was. A second man came through that evening who was also on the desert. He said he had been a ghost for 6 years before he finally got away from that. The following week a man came through who also didn't know he was dead, complaining about the cold and talking a lot about horses.

Another visit from the Gray Place took place one evening when we encountered a lady who had died of lung cancer 8 years earlier. She could remember her death, but nothing after that except for waking up and falling asleep in a hospital at the edge of the Gray Place. Somehow, 10 people were hospitalized there, 5 women and 5 men, each in a single-occupancy room. The rooms opened onto a corridor, the men's rooms on one side and the women's on the other, with a door at each end of the corridor. They all thought they were dying, but there were no doctors or nurses. They just lay there, sleeping almost the whole time, mostly in darkness, but at times with light. They had been transported there from the central gray area where it is completely dark, but they didn't know how. They desperately needed Earth energy to break out of this hospital-like prison. Sesselja's guide asked us to talk with them and send light and energy. Under Magnus' leadership, we managed to awaken eight of them and get them out of their rooms, out of the hospital, and into a park nearby that had a beautiful, bright view. Two remained behind, to be worked on at a future séance.

Summerland   On death one's spirit may languish for years in the Gray Place or it may go directly to Summerland, which, according to Magnus, *is another planet, or maybe it's a dimension.* Summerland is distinguished by two suns, one like ours and the other a little bigger and blue. It has five moons. When Magnus told me about the suns and moons I pointed out that Helgi Pjeturss had written about that. *Yes,* Magnus agreed, *and it is consistent with the findings of modern astronomy, which has discovered a solar system that has two suns.*

In one séance a ghost physician named Kjartan showed up. He had practiced in a town in southern Iceland before his death. Magnus asked him how many planets are included in Summerland. It turned out to be four, all in a solar system that belongs to our galaxy but is located much nearer to the galactic center. Kjartan said that our Summerland, that of Europeans, is the third of four in terms of distance from the two suns. Magnus asked, *What do you call the four planets? We call them Europe, Africa, Asia, and America. People from each of those continents go to their own planet.*

Summerland is a place much like Earth, and spirits live on it much the way we live in Europe and North America, just as Gudmundur and others told me, including Stefán, the elderly Lutheran priest who is a spiritist. *Life in spirit is much the same as for us,* the priest told me, without trying to reconcile that with theological dogma relating to the concept of heaven. Do they have bodies? *Oh, yes,* he added, *but not as we have. They have spiritual bodies.* Magnus reflects that opinion, except that he emphasizes how Summerland is a utopia. *They exercise 100 percent control over the weather and don't know darkness, although at midnight it is a little darker, like nights in Iceland in the summer. They have gravity. There is no disease there, and no pain, no grief, no war, no problems.*

It is not uncommon to think of the spirit world as utopian. I once asked Jóhanna, the homemaker whose deceased grandparents visit her daily, what she thinks it is like to be a spirit. She said, *I think it is very like here on Earth—except, no weather problems or anything like this,* nodding in the direction of the rain and wind that were glowing against her window pane. *They have everything they need.* Do they have bodies? *No. Well, I don't know. I think they are souls. When they visit they put on their bodies.* That's when she told me that they chose how old they want to look, calculating whether they will be better recognized looking as they did when young, middle-aged, or old. Do they enjoy eating? *No. They don't need food.* I felt it would be inappropriate to ask Jóhanna about sex in the afterlife, but I had no hesitation in addressing that question to Magnus.

They have sex, Magnus stated, categorically. So I asked, How about gay sex? *In the spirit world they can choose their sexual orientation. They can be gay, hetero-, trans-, or bi-.* What would influence choice? Would it be their experience in the earthly world? *Probably. At least for a start. They have told us they are very hooked on sex, especially young people. They also say, "we totally understand your horny feelings. That was necessary for the species to survive, but it's a disadvantage here." When you die you have sex, but you don't have as much physical reaction as on Earth. It grows into love without sex that you enjoy much more. In the end people stop having sexual intercourse.*

Do spirits have children? *Usually not. Those who have a deep need of children can get pregnant and have babies. But so many babies float up from Earth that nobody suffers from a lack of babies to care for.* Do the babies grow older in Summerland? *Yes. Kids from abortions grow up.* Is it a bad thing for a woman to have an abortion? *Yes, terrible. It's the murder of a baby. One of the first things all ladies meet when they go up, they meet the babies.* Is the aborted child angry with the mother? *No. Her act makes them sad. Abortion denied both the evolution of the baby and of the mother.*

We then talked about mothers who miscarry or whose children die, and specifically about Jóhanna who lost several children. *The spirits of those babies come to her and she watches them grow.* I suppose it will be a beautiful reunion when the mother passes over! *You just can't imagine. That's what women who have miscarried tell me. It is the high point of their lives when they die and meet those grown up children.*

I wish now I had asked him how spirits without physical bodies were influenced by weather, gravity, and light, enjoyed sexual intercourse, and in some cases even got pregnant and gave birth. I suspect an inconsistency here. I also neglected to challenge him with the contention of others, equally sure of themselves, who say that children in the afterworld never grow up or, as still another cosmic scenario, are reborn on Earth in a new incarnation. There is a rich cultural menu here from which people can chose.

So people live trouble-free lives in an otherworldly utopia, I acknowledged as an inquisitive probe. *The only problems they have are those that float up from Earth.* They worry about people on Earth? *Oh, yes. Nearly half of their time is spent helping us with doctors and protectors, guides who protect us every second of our lives. There are several of these guardians for each of us, working in shifts, day and night. When you drive, walk, pilot, shoot, fall, play, they are on shift.*

Why do the guardians do so much for us? *We asked them. It's part of every person's obligation. [It is necessary in order] to evolve. In the spirit world you have to spend certain years being a guide to somebody who usually is totally unconnected to you. Occasionally it's a relative.* Do they protect loved ones that way? Yes and no, he told me. Deceased loved ones continue to relate to those they have left behind, but the protectors are nonrelatives.

We all have bad things happen to us. Why don't our protectors save us from that? *Couldn't manage. It could have been an accident he didn't foresee. But they say, if you lived in the world without us you would have many times more accidents, and so on. What I am telling you is not totally scientific.*

One evening we encountered a deceased pediatrician in Summerland named Kristjonn who talked with Magnus about his daily life. It was 10 PM his time, 7 PM our time, when we interrupted him. He was in a clinic. He planned to go home soon and was looking forward to reading a book that evening about the history of Ghana, because he had once volunteered in that country with a team of doctors and he wanted to know more about the people.

Magnus asked him what he had done earlier in the day. He said he began his day by making several house calls on Earth to provide care for sick people. After that he went to the children's department of the university hospital in Reykjavík to assist the doctors there in the treatment of a very sick child. That left him quite tired, so he took a nap, and then rejuvenated himself by swimming in the pool next to his house. The water is different from that of a swimming pool on earth, he said. It is filled with a special kind of water that is very refreshing because it contains minerals and carbonation.

When asked about other recreation he said he especially likes to take walks in the forest among the trees. At the end Magnus asked about his family on Earth.

Do you stay in touch with living members of your family?

Yes, definitely.

Do you see them every day?

Well, not unless there is something wrong.

Do you visit them just to know what they are doing?

Yes, sometimes. I listen to their conversations.

Finally, I asked Magnus if spirits of the dead are still Christians, or Jews, or whatever. *Yes, they are,* he told me, *But their view enlarges so they understand all the other religions. But still, they say we are Christians because that is our background.* If Iceland had stayed with the old Viking religion, would that have been a good thing? *It would have been terrible because of the violence. The dead Vikings who went to Valhalla, the heaven of warriors, killed and wounded each other every day, after which they were instantly restored so they could spend their nights banqueting. It was a very positive thing for Iceland that we converted to Christianity.* Interesting, I thought, he doesn't deny the reality of Valhalla, only the desirability of it.

People on higher planets are more evolved, but I didn't learn much about them. One such planet is Sunland. Another is called Heaven Place. Magnus told me that the previous year he asked to have a conversation with Indridi, Iceland's famous medium of a hundred years ago. *Now, right now, we want to talk with Indridi Indridasson,* he told Sesselja's spirit guide. Everyone was thrilled when Indridi responded. Magnus asked where he was at the moment. *I'm in the Heaven Place. That's where I live,* he said. *I just now sat down, but I have been walking through a big, beautiful forest.* Magnus asked how he had gotten our request to appear. *Well,* he answered, *it came through a series of connections and then a "dong"* [pointing to his ear] *that you wanted to chat with me.* He went on to explain, *I am working here with some Norwegians on their spiritual evolution, helping some people in Norway with mediums. I can only talk for a minute or so.* He spoke with Magnus while the Norwegians were walking in the forest, but when they stopped he had to leave. *I have to say "bye" now and catch up with them.* That didn't provide much information about the Heaven Place, but to the extent that it did, it seems similar to Summerland and to Earth itself.

SIGGI IN AKUREYRI

Conversing over coffee one evening in the home of friends in Akureyri, Siggi, a highly respected medium began to get somewhat ethnographic. I noticed it first when he said something about alcoholics in the afterlife. I recalled immediately that George Rich had asked me to inquire about that before I left for Iceland. George is an American anthropologist and a friend who carried out ethnographic research in Akureyri in the early 1970s. At that time he was told that an alcoholic's craving for liquor can be caused by the spirit of a dead alcoholic who drinks vicariously by getting a vulnerable living person to drink for him, but he wasn't sure if the idea was widespread.

My chance came because Siggi was talking about the pain of alcoholics. He told us that they take their pain with them into the spirit world, a statement that resonated with what Magnus says about the Gray Place. It seemed like a good time to insert George's factoid into the conversation and ask if the spirit of an alcoholic can satisfy a craving for alcohol by borrowing the body of a living person. Siggi said yes, that can happen. *When you drink it opens light upwards, and spirit drunks seek that light.* Well, I wasn't sure what that meant, but I took it to imply that even though they do not have liquor in the spirit world they nonetheless continue to struggle with the addiction.

Emboldened, I next asked if spirits enjoy sex, having in mind what Magnus told me about younger spirits being horny. *No,* Siggi said categorically, *There is no sex on the other side.* He then added, *I was called to meet with a woman who said her dead boyfriend was raping her. I told her it was impossible, and shortly after she was admitted to a psychiatric hospital.* How can experts who contact the spirit world report back in such mutually contradictory ways? Whom can one believe? Should one believe any of them?

Having gotten some fairly unsatisfactory information on alcohol and sex, I thought it wise to ask a more mundane question. Can spirits eat food? *Not the way we eat,* Siggi said, without explaining. So, referring to Iceland's most well-known living medium, I said, Vigdis told me that they get their nutrition by smelling flowers. She said that's all they need. *Yes,* he said, *They can do that.* Then, following his own logic rather than the trend of my questioning, he added, *When I visualize the other world, sometimes it is very beautiful, and sometimes not.* Basically, Siggi just did-n't have much ethnographic curiosity, which seems to be true of many mediums, maybe most, so we talked about other things for the next 2 hours. Then I asked again about life in the afterworld.

Do spirits go to heaven? *It depends on what you mean by heaven. I am prepared to say it could be heaven.* Reflecting on what I had been told by Magnus and had learned about Helgi Pjeturss, I said I had been told that there are different levels in the spirit world. Siggi agreed that there were. What are the higher levels like? Unfortunately, Siggi didn't direct-ly respond to that question. He simply said, *Often they say there are 13 levels. Yogis say there are more.* Yogis! The cultural menu of spiritism reaches from Nordic Gods in Valhalla to Hindu religious practices. It is definitely global in reach, both historically and geographically, in some ways extending far beyond Icelandic contacts with Denmark and the United Kingdom, as is quite explicit in New Age spirituality.

Shifting from places to people, he then told us that spirits live in dif-ferent stages of maturity with different tasks to complete at each stage. He then presented his version of a common theme in spiritism, which is that *the purpose of living is to grow in understanding and love.* In this view, the cosmos is like a school. Magnus spoke of this. So did Deborah, the English medium in Iceland who said, *Everything is meant to be a les-son.* The theme also popped up in a conversation I had with Águst, a young construction worker with bookish interests in the occult. *We are only on this planet to learn,* he told me. *Most of our lives are in the spir-it world. We come down here to get experience, to learn different things. Then we go upstairs again, that is, we go home to evaluate what we learned and plan the next lifetime.* Siggi put it this way, *Every soul must learn its lessons and move higher and higher in the knowledge hierarchy. Important lessons are learned on earth, but others must be learned in the spirit world.*

The metaphor of the cosmos as being like a school is associated with conflicting canons of life progression. The learning discussed by Helgi Pjeturss and Magnus Skarphedinsson takes place by progressing from one planet or dimension to another that is more advanced. The concept of reincarnation offers a competing scenario. Every soul must return to Earth to learn new lessons each time. Some mediums specialize in acquainting clients with their past lives. Again, the lessons taught in séances are often mutually incompatible.

Siggi, however, did not talk about either moving through different spirit worlds or being reborn on Earth. Instead, he simply spoke of being given specific learning tasks to accomplish. As we talked over coffee and cakes he was distracted when he suddenly realized that the deceased mother of the host of our coffee klatch was in the room with us. He told us that her task as a spirit is to help her family. A different mother spirit, he explained, may be given the task of receiving babies who died. Usually she will take the child to some place the child can relate to. Still another will contact the spirit of a miscarriage. The aborted fetus will develop and grow until the mother herself dies. He told us that one woman encountered a dead brother at a séance, even though she had no brother that she knew of. Later she learned that the brother was actually her mother's miscarriage who had grown up. So, as often was the case, in this conversation, we seemed to be ricocheting from one thought to another, a conversation directed by simple word association that was not very helpful.

Some spirits are more advanced than others, so they will teach newer spirits who arrive in the spirit world. Well, I asked, somewhat exasperated by this otherwise knowledgeable and delightful man who simply wasn't accustomed to think about ethnographic things, do advanced spirits live in the same world as the less advanced? *I don't know exactly,* he answered, implying that figuring that out was a very low priority for him. *Apparently there are different regions. Families of souls live in different places.* This conversation was going in circles and I was abusing his patience. Sometime after midnight he finally said, *There's a medium in Reykjavík who has studied this. You really should talk with him.* And that's how I ended up on the phone nearly a year later to arrange a meeting with Geir, who is respected by other mediums for his knowledge of what I call an ethnography of the spirit world.

GEIR IN REYKJAVÍK

Our conversation on life in the spirit world began with a statement that was totally at odds with Helgi's contention that spirits of the dead obtain new physical bodies on other planets. According to Geir, in the afterlife people live as energy frequencies. *Because spirits do not have physical bodies,* he said, *they cannot experience sickness or shed tears.* That was consistent with what many spiritists told me, but then he spoke of something that probably many would dispute. Spirits cannot feel love, sadness, or courage. *You can be happy in the spirit world. You can enjoy singing. You can have creative thoughts. But you have to come to Earth and get a body to do it in a physical form, to feel it, to be in it, to be with it. That's why they reincarnate on Earth, to be able to understand the emotions of being a husband or wife, of being a parent, of loving or hating.*

Robert Anderson

A medium describing life in the spirit world.

The key to understanding the human body according to Geir is the concept of a chakra, a widely encountered Hindu contribution to New Age thought. Others occasionally spoke of body chakras, but only Geir made it central to his thinking. He explained chakras by contrasting love and hate as being like the polarities of a battery with plus and minus poles that create an electric flow. *If there is no flow in a battery, it is dead. Chakras have positive and negative poles. Each chakra spins. All of the chakras in a body are connected. The universe itself is a chakra, made up of chakras. Earth is a chakra. Galaxies are chakras. Each galaxy has a different "earth" with different life forms. Some earths have two suns. Some have no moon. Others have one or two moons.*

Talking about different earths, each with different life forms, and mentioning plural suns and moons sounded very much like the planetary scheme of Helgi Pjeturss, so I asked if his ideas came from him. He denied that influence, insisting that he was reporting his own findings. His exact words were, *I don't know much about his theory. From the way I have seen the galaxy, Earth is a unique place where* **souls can learn to share and to love** [emphasis added].

He then offered an explanatory scheme that sounded like the four planets of Summerland I learned about at the Spirit Research School. You will recall that Magnus was told by a spirit that Summerland is an interplanetary system of four different planets called Europe, Africa, Asia, and America. Geir told us the same thing, the dead of Europe, Africa, Asia, and Native America each go to their own Summerland planet.

Yet, Geir's version of spirit astronomy and of the universe as a cosmic university differs from the others in significant ways. Noting that the inhabitants of Earth include *all kinds of color, all races,* he said that souls come here *to share and learn to love.* He then showed me a drawing of our galaxy, with other galaxies around it, like chakras, each of a different color. One galaxy is African, another is Asian, another, Amerindian. He didn't mention a European one, and I failed to ask about it, but logically it should exist in his intergalactic system. At any rate, spirits come to Earth from those galaxies, *to learn how to live in peace.* The reader will want to ponder that purpose. Is Earth a good teaching model for loving race relations and peaceful nations? Apparently it makes sense if we listen further to his explanation.

As a related aspect of interplanetary spirit life Geir shifted from planets and races to individual souls. Speaking of people as individuals he said, *We are all changing. In one of your lifetimes you are black. In another you are Asian. You mature as you experience being of different race because you learn that all those people are looking for the same thing: love, sharing, appreciation of what God has given them. To learn that lesson might take a thousand years, two thousand. But eventually each will go home and tell the people of their galaxy, there are no differences among the galaxies, in spite of differences in skin color. We are all going the same way. We are here to get the experience and to bring knowledge back.*

As I reviewed those statements with him, he added a further explanation. *It's up to each person how many lives it will take. It could be one or it could be thousands, but eventually you will take the knowledge back and share it with those who didn't have the opportunity to come here. In the fulfillment of yourself, you will build up to God's image of creation, the God Force.*

Helgi denied reincarnation. Magnus is skeptical of it, although he considers it a hypothesis worth pursuing. Geir is committed to it. I asked if a person lived in spirit between births, and he said yes. How much time passes between births? *It can be a few hours or a few hundred years,* was his answer. He then unexpectedly added his version of the Calvinistic doctrine of predestination, *All your life is written in the Book of God.*

I wondered aloud if we get reincarnated as animals, fish, or insects. He said no. *We are reborn from one life to the next with similar bodies. You will not always be born as a man, but always as a human. When Buddha said you may come back as a dog, he means you will behave like a dog, but you will be human.* I asked if karma determines what your next life will be like. He answered with a bit of numerology, saying that everything that God creates will be in 10 parts. If you do something evil, you will pay 10 times over.

With so many scrambled ideas spilling out, I nearly forgot that I had come to find out about daily life, so I tried again to bring up the subject. He told me that spirits exist as pure energy. They travel as light in the form of an infinitely long tube. After arrival they chose how to present themselves. They can transform into the person they once were, as young or old as they wish. So far this resembled what some others had said, but then he went off into his own space again, talking about what a living Earthling can do.

We can live on the Earth plane in different times. That statement intrigued me, so I asked what happens when you go into the *Twilight Zone,* referring to a television series, or go back to different times in history? He responded by saying, *The past and the future are taking place here. Where are you? Are you willing to go back in time? Or, into the future? That's what Edgar Cayce did in trance states. Nostradamus did it without trance. I have done it to see for myself how they built the pyramids in ancient Egypt.*

Finally, he told me how he sometimes prays with people, and in particular, how he explains to dying people what kind of world they are going into. Without trying to reconcile what he tells them with what he told me about reincarnating in African, Asian, and Amerindian bodies, he explained, *In the spirit world our thoughts create houses, living rooms, and books. But we can come down to Earth and look at books too.*

And then, suddenly, we were back to talking about ourselves living on Earth. *You don't need to read a book page by page. Often I buy a book and put it by my bed. The next day, I realize I know everything in it without reading it. The next day I take another book and do the same. It's like your subconscious mind is working differently from the conscious mind.*

Wanting to get back to daily life in the spirit world I said, If a spirit can create a house just by thinking it, how do they spend their days in those houses? *Very much like we do,* he said. *Reading. Communicating with friends. They do not drink coffee from a cup. In the spirit world they like the smell. For that reason, a spirit will come back to visit a living wife or daughter, because he likes the smell of her perfume. He will also come to the Earth plane to give her a hug. That's one of the reasons they come here. They go into the kitchen to smell the foods they liked. They fill their needs through smell because they don't have to eat. They go into nature to smell it.* Do they also see it? *Yes, they also see it.*

Geir's comments resonated with what Águst told me about life in the spirit world. *I'm not saying this from experience,* Águst said. *It's described in a good book, Journey of Souls, by Michael Newton. Newton says spirit is like balls of energy, same as I say. I see spirits as balls of energy. But they can project an image of themselves, from past lives.* How do they spend their time? *Mostly learning. Not like in a classroom. They have buildings made of energy that look like this house, because for some souls, it is more comfortable than just hanging around loose.* It sounds like life on Earth in some ways. *Yes.* With buildings and streets? *Yes.* And gardens? *Yes.* And they live with other people in the same way, talking with one another? *No, that part is very different,* Águst countered. **Everybody has unconditional love** [emphasis added]. *No arguments. Just love.*

I asked Geir how a spirit can hug a living loved one? *The spirit can feel it, but he doesn't have a body to feel it with. He feels it with emotions, by means of the energy flow between them.* Then, suddenly, he got into dream theory. *As living people, we have a spirit form as well as a physical form,* he said. *You dream you were with a person. Your spirit and the spirit of that person were communicating and touching one another without physically touching. That's how the spirit works. Through dreams we learn how life is in spirit.*

Geir's theory of dreams resembled that of Helgi Pjeturss, but in fact was quite different. *Through dreams we learn how life is in spirit. All the thoughts you create when dreaming, good, bad, and evil, all are creations of your mind, your thoughts, and how your thoughts can be real. You are more or less living in the world of spirit.* That is very different from Helgi's belief that our dreams are actual visitations by real people from other planets.

In this way, Geir said, people learn during their lifetimes how life is here on Earth and in spirit. *I rise up in bed and say it was just a dream. In the spirit world, they wake up and realize that life on Earth was just a dream, and they say, "I had the strangest dream." Some of the people in that dream will go into the future in space ships.*

So how should I sum up Geir's ethnographic insights? I would characterize them as eclectic. He acknowledges that he was influenced by books in his father's library. He has obviously been influenced as well by books he has acquired, those of Edgar Cayce, for example, and by movies and television, by New Age ideas that are ubiquitous, by the Bible and Christian teachings, and by other spiritists. From these variable sources, he has created his own unique mix of ethnographica, which is why Siggi deferred to him when he felt pushed to the wall by my quizzing. But Geir has not had any wider influence that I could detect. I met no one, not even Siggi, who repeated his cosmology when I asked about daily life in the other world.

CONCLUSION

Anthropologists agree that belief in a supernatural world is ubiquitous. It is also good anthropology to point out that how the supernatural world is described and addressed varies from one culture to another. In Iceland, I found it useful to identify two cultural patterns that characterize spiritist concepts relating to that world. One is the highly elaborated and thoroughly narrated cultural pattern of mediumship described in Chapter 4. That pattern is defined by five characteristics that set limits on individual variation, in spite of being open to some divergence. The other, explored in this chapter, is a sketchy, weakly articulated ethnography of the afterlife that describes what life is like in the spirit world. It reveals a cultural pattern delimited by six characteristics, each of which is acknowledged by some and contested by others.

First, one characteristic of the world of the dead is that spirits have ephemeral bodies. Helgi disagrees. However, spirits in many ways behave as though their bodies are like ours, which tends to minimize the implications of Helgi's contrary assertion and points up how uninterested people are in clarifying internal contradictions.

Second, spirits live in another dimension. However, whether they occupy Earth space on a different frequency, live in some undefined space, or occupy distant planets is not so much disputed as it is simply not known. After more than a century of communicating through mediums, almost no one seems disturbed about not knowing quite where the spirit world is located.

Third, daily activities in the spirit world are nearly the same as in our world, with some differences. One difference widely agreed on is that people smell for nourishment rather than eat. They enjoy forests and fields. They live in houses. But little detail is provided. Social, family, and marital life are only rarely discussed or thought about, and sex is never voluntarily mentioned, except by Magnus.

Fourth, for most, the spirit world is a utopia, with no disease or distress, although Magnus commits delinquents to the Gray Place, from which ultimately they can and will escape, somewhat as one eventually will be released from that Catholic afterworld known as purgatory. The burning pits of hell are not part of the cosmos. People are healthy and happy, but a statement like that suffices and is not rounded out with stories or descriptions. Apparently it is a world without interpersonal anger or conflicts, police or armies, politicians or lawyers, churches or chapels, hotels or restaurants, but such realities and their implications are rarely discussed.

Fifth, the purpose of life is to grow in spiritual maturity as measured by increasing one's knowledge of the purpose of the universe. Living in different dimensions is like working up through the school system to culminate in graduate work at the university level. It seems to be mostly about love, but beyond that the course goals are rarely spelled out, and then only abstractly.

Sixth, spirits evolve to higher levels by doing good things for people on Earth. Only this characteristic is well narrated and filled with detail. Spirits continue to care about loved ones, to follow their lives, and to help when they can. Every spiritist can give examples. Spirits of the dead help strangers as well. All agree that deceased physicians continue to provide care for the sick. As part of what life is like in the afterworld, altruism is well documented and consistently emphasized.

Five of the six characteristics are notable for being largely nonspecific. Details are missing. Mediums do not pass on very much information about what it is like to live as a spirit in another dimension, and clients don't ask. For that reason, the culture of the spirit world that I was able to elicit by means of persistent questioning is very unsatisfactory. I believe the reason the culture of the afterworld is so poorly conceptualized is because the interest was mine, not theirs.

When Icelanders communicate with spirits of the dead, the most important information they want at first is simply to know that humans live on after death. Beyond that, they want to be assured that deceased loved ones are happy in the spirit world. They frequently ask for help from ghost doctors. And very important, they want spirits to warn or advise them about events in the future. To inquire into ethnographic matters ranks as at best a remote interest for almost everyone except for that unusual man, Magnus.

To the extent that people like Magnus and Geir do want to know what spirit life is like, they are not trained anthropologists. They lack the skill it takes to elicit the information they need from spirit informants in order to describe a culture. They do not challenge or explore inconsistencies and incompleteness.

Not the least, those who are at least slightly curious fail because they are trapped in a dualistic theory of body and mind. They seem unaware that the sense of self of a disembodied spirit has got to be radically different from that of a living human being who has a body as well as a mind, a body-mind monism. If they smell instead of eat, it is a body-dependent act. If they hug for the emotion of hugging, it is still a brain function. It cannot logically be so. If spirits have no bodies, their sense of self, of the meaning of being somehow alive, of finding pleasure in existence has got to be virtually beyond comprehension in human terms.

Gudmundur was right when he observed that daily life in the spirit world as described by Magnus seems just like daily life as people know it in the West. It is equally true of everyone else I talked with. Daily life is embroidered with magical adjustments, as when Geir teaches that spirits create houses with their thoughts. Gudmundur, highly intelligent and with years of experience in spiritism, comes as close as one can to providing a brief description of the Icelandic cultural pattern for life in the spirit world. Mediums teach that life in the spirit world is just like life as we know it on Earth, and Gudmundur is understandably rather skeptical about how that can be true.

CHAPTER 6

GHOSTS AND CHILDREN

COMING OF AGE IN ICELAND

Since the 1920s, anthropologists have done intensive research in societies of all kinds on the lives of babies, small children, and adolescents, with a heavy emphasis on how they end up as culturally committed adults. Margaret Mead (1928), for example, wrote about the way adolescent girls in the South Pacific grow up. Her investigations there and in other societies documented differing ways in which culturally shaped parenting and community practices impacted adult personalities, and they remain a continuing source of stimulation, discussion, and controversy for anthropologists (Haviland 2002: 129–132; Roscoe 2003).

As concerns children and religion, anthropologists want to know how religious ideology and practice are transmitted—how child rearing eventually may result in a personal commitment to religious beliefs and practices. Hutterite children in the American Midwest and in neighboring parts of Canada, for example, are taught in religious schools by teachers who reinforce parental values of simplicity, hands-on work, neighborliness, and pacifism. These values and beliefs are reinforced by a remarkable community uniformity that manifests outwardly in plain clothing, houses without radio and television sets, and the activities of farming occupations (Hostetler 1974; Park 2003: 7–11).

In Iceland most families have little direct involvement with the national Lutheran church. Peter Stromberg's (1986) assessment of formal religion in Sweden applies equally to Iceland when he writes that "the state church is legendarily moribund (which is not to say that there are not vital churches and active Christians within it)" (p. 28). Richard Tomasson (2003: 61) agrees, noting that the national churches in all of the five Nordic countries are characterized by extremely low attendance rates and high levels of unbelief, even though nearly everyone is listed on official membership roles. The main opportunity Lutheran ministers have to teach children the basics of Christian belief and practice occurs when nearly every adolescent attends classes in preparation for the sacrament of confirmation, but little seems to come of it. In contrast to the religious indoctrination of Hutterite children, Icelandic children grow up to be overwhelmingly secular. Just as Stromberg (1986: 11) found in Sweden, Icelandic children grow up to be quite diverse and uncommitted as concerns official dogma and the meaning of Christian symbols.

I would suggest that spiritism, in a sense, is a secular religion that is unrestrained by theological dogmatism, and in that way is quite suited to the Icelandic mentality. I did not systematically look into how parents or agents of the national church attempt to teach Christian practices and virtues, but I did inquire into early experiences with ghosts and spirits. What I found is diverse, as is to be expected for a minimally institution-alized and rather eclectic range of beliefs, but I did identify some consistencies. Descriptions of the experiences of children with ghosts sort out into one or another of just a limited number of scenarios.

GHOSTS AND LITTLE KIDS

Occasionally I was told of a child who described encounters with ghosts. Such a child, I suppose, could be considered to have one of the qualifications that seems to be required to become a medium, but that possibility was never suggested to me. One such childhood experience was recounted by Marta, a middle school administrator who earlier told me about two different times when she herself had encountered ghosts. In the following conversation she described the ghost companion of one of her daughters. I asked if her girls, like she, could see spirits of the dead. *No*, she answered, *not as such. The older one did have an imaginary friend when she was 2 years old. She's a very calm, relaxed child, clever, but very easy to raise. However, she would become frantic if we closed the door and "Lapannany" wasn't in the room with her yet. So we started asking, "Is Lapannany in? Can we close the door?"* I reacted to Marta, saying, that sounds like a common experience for small children, to have an imaginary playmate. *Perhaps, but Lapannany was an adult and was her constant companion in her second and third years. Then it ended. We left Lapannany in England.* Was it a man or a woman? *We never found out. I think it was a spirit, and not just an imaginary friend.*

Gudrun Bergman, famous in Iceland as a novelist and spiritual guru, recalled that as a 3-year-old child she and her brother lived with their mother in a small apartment with just a kitchen and one room. *Everything took place in that room. When we went to sleep at night my mother would usually be sitting in the center of the room sewing or such. She would say to me, "Go to sleep." And I would say, "What about the man in the corner? Isn't he going to go to sleep too?" This man was always in that corner of the room.*

I asked her to talk more about that invisible man whom she alone could see. Did he ever speak to you? *No. It was just that I could see him in the corner, dressed as though he were going out or something. So I always asked, "Why is he here? Why doesn't he do something?"* Where do you think he came from? *It was an old apartment building. It's possible he had lived in that apartment [before he died].*

How did you feel about him being there? Did it frighten you? Did it comfort you? *I was very indifferent. I thought it was very strange that he dressed as though ready to go out when we were ready to turn in for the night.*

Sometimes people completely forget that they were involved with invisible beings as small children. My physician friend and fellow explorer Jósep Blöndal gave the example of his daughter Ida. *We were at her grandparents house in a small north Icelandic community where I was cramming for a course I was taking at the medical school in Glasgow. She stayed with me for 6 weeks or so. The weather was beautiful and we had lovely old people tending to our daily needs. All the while, she was seeing a woman multiple times every single day. She described the woman in detail to her grandparents, who spent hours trying to figure out who it must be. I think they finally narrowed it down to two or three old women who had died, but I particularly remember that she was so frank and honest about it that it never crossed my mind that she was making it up.*

Ida herself told me that she had no recollection at all when her father talked about it after she was an adult. She added, *Children don't talk about these things. If they feel there is something wrong about it they become especially shy. My niece is now 4 or 5, and she has at least two or three playmates. She can stay alone in her room for hours playing and talking with these children we can't see. Last Christmas her mother told us about it. When I asked my niece, however, she said, "I don't want to talk about it" and clammed up.*

As the subject was about to change, Jósep offered a last word on that topic. Referring to Ida's stepsister, he said, *Gudrun had an imaginary playmate for quite a while. She had a name.* But before we could learn more about Gudrun's ghost, the conversation took a turn in another direction.

However, I did hear other such stories. Margrét, a university student, said she did not remember that when she was 3 or 4 years old she had an invisible friend. She learned of it years later from her mother, who told her she was always playing with someone as a child. Her parents could hear the noise of playing, but they were never able to see the playmate.

Konrád, 31 years old, unemployed, and on psychiatric medication when I met him, came to talk with me because his girlfriend thought we would probably hit it off well together, and we did. When the conversation turned to spirits of the dead I asked when he had his first experience of this kind. *I was just over 5 years old,* he said. *My mother and I lived in the home of my grandparents. For many years my mother's little sister, who was my age, played with a girl none of us could see.* What did you think about her having an invisible playmate? *I gave no thought to it. It was just part of my life.*

Did you have a friend like that yourself? *No, but when I was 5 I saw someone and later learned she was dead. I didn't realize that it was a spirit. I just saw a person.* Where your eyes open? *I think so. I remember seeing her. Later when I looked at old family photographs I realized it was my great-grandmother on my mother's side.* Did you talk with her? *No, I just saw her.* What did that do for you? Did it make your life better in any way? *As I look back on it now I think it helped me settle down. We had moved from my grandparent's house, and seeing her gave me strength.* Would you say she gave you comfort? *Yes, even though I had never known her.* Did she come again later in your life? *No, only that one time.*

Konrád then told me about a similar experience when he was 6 or 7 years old. *I was leaving the house with my mother, going down the stairs, when I saw two people on the staircase. One was my mother's friend, and the other was a woman I didn't know. I asked about it, and my mother said only her friend was on the stairs and no one else. So we looked at photos to see who the second person was and found she was related to a friend of my mother.* Did she say anything? *No, she didn't say a word.* Well, you know I want to ask if it was in any way harmful or beneficial for you. *It did nothing for me. It was just an experience. In fact, that's why I feel it was a true happening, because I had nothing to gain from it.* Why do you think she appeared there at that time? *I have no idea.*

The anthropology student Haukur told me about the experience of his girlfriend's little girl. It was a bit unusual, because Haukur and the child's mother were frightened, even though the little girl was not. *We live in student housing,* he informed me, *and when she was about 2½ years old she used to see a person while watching TV. She would suddenly turn and talk to somebody who was standing by the door. We sat there and couldn't understand what was happening. It was kind of scary.*

That was frightening to you? *Yes, very.* Do you know who she was talking to? *No. She said a clown was standing there, a funny looking guy.* Was she afraid? *No. It didn't frighten her. It surprised her. But we were spooked out by it.*

I had the impression that seeing ghosts as a small child was never frightening and often pleasant for the child. However, after half a year of interviews I learned about two children, related as cousins, who were quite upset at the experience.

Nónni is a young woman in her late twenties whose sister-in-law was a student of mine. Her 5-year-old son Olaf started talking about an invisible man when he was about 2½. *It always happened when he was sick with a fever,* Nónni told me. *When he came into my bedroom he would see a man next to my bed. He would point to him and whisper, because he was afraid to have the man hear him, "Mom, Mom, look, look." "At what?" I said. "At the man, the man standing there." I would then ask what the man was doing, but he was too young to explain.*

Later, when he was 3 or 3½ and still seeing the man he would say, "The man is making a face," and Nónni mimed a grimace to illustrate. *He told me the man is ugly and he didn't like him. Eventually he was quite scared by him.*

She continued, *About a year ago when he was almost 4 he woke up every night for a few weeks, terrified and screaming. But then he talked about a woman. He was so scared. I went in the dark to pick him up. He didn't realize it was me and thought it was the woman. That continued night after night for weeks. He was so scared. He thought this woman was bad and would do something to him. But he couldn't describe what was going on.*

A few weeks after that started I had a dream in which a woman was in the living room of our apartment. She was naked, with long black hair, lying in a corner of the room in a kind of fetal position. She looked up at me and I could see her face. She looked as though she had been on drugs for years and was selling her body. When I awoke, something told me this was the woman Olaf was seeing. I had never asked what she looked like, so I said, "Olaf, what does she look like? What is her hair like?" "Mom, she has long black hair and is ugly." He described her exactly as in my dream. Did you ask if she was naked? She answered, *No, I didn't,* but then added, *she was trying to get something from him.* What would she be trying to get? *I don't know. I thought she was a person who accidentally came into our apartment.* Do you think she was dead and that it was her spirit that had come? *Yeah.*

Whatever happened? *Well, I started praying. Every night I make the sign of the cross over his bed and mine, over him and me.* What do you say in your prayer? *I say, if there is anybody in there, leave him alone.* Do you say that out loud? *Yeah, and it stopped, about 4 or 5 months ago.* Do you feel that your prayers kept her away? *Yes, and other people also prayed for him.* Oh, who were they? In response she explained that it was church people, but not from the church she belongs to, which is the national Lutheran church. It was members of a Pentecostal church that one of her friends attends.

Ah, but you still seem to be concerned. *Yes. He still talks about the man being present. The man was present while the woman was there. He was always there, but Olaf wasn't so scared of him. I make the sign of the cross every night, but he comes anyway. Olaf talked about it just this morning. He told me that the man said I was a shithead, and she laughed.* He's at that age. *Also, now I don't know whether I should believe him or not.* He's at that age. *He's always saying something. But sometimes I think he really does see the man. He always asks me to turn on the lights, saying, "otherwise I'll be scared." "Scared of what," I ask. "Of the man." I say, "Forget it." Sometimes he says, "All right," but at other times he says, "I know he's here."*

Have you considered having a minister come in to bless the house? *Yeah, I've thought about it, but I haven't done it.* Do you think the Icelandic Society for Spirit Research might help? *No,* she said, without explaining why. With that our discussion shifted to her brother's son who is 2 years younger than Olaf. *My 3-year-old nephew sees several people during the day as well as at night. It started 4 or 5 months ago and got to be really bad, so my mother telephoned a medium.* Both of these cases of children worried about the presence of a ghost were still ongoing and unresolved the last time I inquired.

What surprised me about the experience of Kristján, Nónni's nephew, is that two of the ghosts turned out to be a loved one who intended no wrong, but who were strangers to the little boy. It reminded me of decades ago when I returned from a summer in China where I had grown a beard. Meeting at the airport, my daughter Robin, 5 years old at the time, was frightened and hid behind her mother's skirt when I tried to pick her up, because she had never seen me with a beard before.

Speaking over the phone, the medium said that two of the men the child saw were his grandfather and a great-grandfather, both of whom had drowned at sea while still quite young. They told the medium they only wanted to touch the boy's face with gentle caresses and to be loving with him. Realizing that their presence frightened the boy, they said they would return no more.

However, the boy was also disturbed by a small man with black hair and two women wearing green dresses and white shoes. *He would tell* his mother, Anna, *"He is walking there,"* and, *"They are going there."* Anna made an appointment to see a medium, but she also called a [Lutheran] pastor who said he would pray for him. He did, and Anna reported that for the next few days he was free of the apparitions, but then, 2 or 3 days before our conversation, they started again, although not as bad as they were.

I asked Nónni if Anna intended follow up on her appointment with a medium and was told that she did not. *She's not going to this medium,* Nónni told me, *because—I don't know—sometimes when you go to a medium they accidentally put someone through you. They want to help, but to do so they have to open your—you know what I mean—ugh, so accidentally somebody might get in.* In other words, Anna felt that her son might be exposed to even worse visitations than those he has now if she took him to a medium. Nónni told me that maybe her own son was exposed to the ghosts because she went to so many mediums when he was a baby. *I've heard that spirits try to get something from people who are weak, who are not strong enough to resist, like children who have something wrong, like my son. It was always when he was sick that the man and woman appeared. You get so open when you are sick.* I hadn't heard that before, but evidently it is an idea that is around as part of the cultural menu. A ghost can be scary, but in no way as horrifying as the saga ghosts of the past.

GHOSTS AND ADOLESCENTS

Konrád, who recalled seeing ghosts as a youngster, went on to relate a spirit encounter from when he was 15 years old. *I was at a friend's house,* he recalled. *He had lost his father in Denmark where he was living. It was a shock for everybody, because his father was only 44 years old and my friend was heartbroken at his sudden death. There was a reception with food and drink after the funeral service. I was standing at the top of the stairs when I noticed a man go from one room to another. I called to my friend and said, "Who is that?" He hadn't seen him, so we went downstairs to find him, but we found no one, and the only way out was in front of us. Later I found a picture of the man I had seen. It was his grandfather who had been dead for some time.* Have you had any other such encounters since you were 15? *I'm not sure,* he said. *I'm very skeptical. I don't believe my own feelings.*

The novelist Gudrun, who used to see the spirit of an old man when she was a 3-year-old, had a somewhat different experience as an adolescent. *Later at the age of about 10 when I went to bed there was this woman talking to me, this voice. I remember going to bed and thinking, "Is she going to come tonight or not?" I had this special world all to myself. She said very soothing things to me. She spoke in a very special tone of voice that I have never heard from anyone else. She spoke very slowly and it was almost hypnotic. However, it made me uncomfortable when I reached the age of 12 and I didn't want it anymore, so I put out a request for her not to come, and that was the end of it.* She then added, *It's interesting that many years later when I opened up again for this kind of understanding or intuition I heard her voice again, but only once.* It must have given you great pleasure to have her come back, I said. *Yes, it did.* Did she say anything meaningful to you when she came back? *No.*

Where do you think she came from? *I have no idea. It was just in my head.* Do you think she had formerly lived in that building like the old man possibly had? *No, because at that time we lived in a house we had built from scratch.* She then added a bit of interesting analysis. *Experiences differ. For example, I saw this man very clearly as a 3-year-old child. When I was between 10 and 12 the woman's voice was a completely different experience. What I see and sense today is yet another kind of experience, because I don't see people who have passed away very much. I seem more able to sense or see the hidden people* [elves] *or garden spirits* [fairies]. *Some people seem to have an ability to see old people who have passed away. Others describe seeing people as if they were watching part of a movie. People seem to become aware of very different worlds.* (I will return to Gudrun's experience with elves and fairies in Chapter 9.)

I did not find any correlation of contact with spirits of the dead and socioeconomic status or level of education. Konrád, for example, exists on the fringes of the economy while Andrés is a well-paid mid-level executive in his forties. Andrés told me one afternoon over coffee that he encountered a ghost when he was a teenager. *In my opinion ghosts do exist,* he asserted. *What they are, I don't know. But the thing is, I have seen one. One morning when I was 13 years old, I was delivering newspapers near my home in a suburb of Reykjavík. At a house down the street from my own house I walked around to the back and up the stairs to deliver a paper at the kitchen door. The ground was covered with newly fallen snow. It was early in the morning, maybe 6 or 7 o'clock. A man was standing on the porch when I reached the top. His appearance was quite unexceptional. A nondescript parka obscured his face, but there was nothing the least bit sinister about him. He seemed quite ordinary.*

I attempted to hand him the paper, but he signaled "no," and pointed to the door. So I turned my back on him, stepped over to the door and put the paper on the threshold. When I turned around he was gone. I was mystified. How could he have disappeared like that? The only footsteps on the new snow were my own. He couldn't have walked away, and I

Robert Anderson

Frozen Lake Tjörn in Reykjavík

would have heard if he had jumped off the porch. There was enough early morning light for me to see clearly. I just couldn't find a logical explanation, except that he was a ghost.

Andrés also offered a variant of how an adolescent may have a spirit companion, since he had one without knowing of it for a long time. *I've been told that my father, who died when I was 12 years old, was with me in spirit until at least 10 years ago.* What do you mean by saying you were told of his presence? *I was told by a medium. She didn't know me, but she told me that a man was with me. When she described him I realized it was my father the way he was when he died.* How do you know it wasn't just any man? *Because she gave a very clear description of him. He had a beard trimmed in a particular way. He had glasses that change in the sun, which was unusual at that time. He had gotten them abroad.*

What did he do for you in his spirit form? I asked. *Well, he just was* **my guardian spirit.** Do you think he helped you in life? After a pause, Andrés said, **Yes. I've always felt that I am well looked after** [emphasis added]. *And I still feel that way.* You said he was with you until about 10 years ago. Do you think he is still there? *Yes. Probably.* You were only 12 years old when he died, but he was able to stay with you as your grew. *Yeah. Well, I didn't know about it.*

Is your mother alive? *Yes.* Has she ever had a visit from your father? *I don't know. I haven't asked her.* So you don't talk about this very much?

No. You talk about it when things come up, but, you know, Icelanders live a double life. We are a rational society. Very modern. But we live a second life with our ancestral spirits, the hidden people, elves, and his voice trailed off. I responded by saying that it is not necessarily irrational to believe that your father lives on as a spirit. It could be a perfectly natural occurrence that we simply do not yet understand in objective, scientific terms. *Yeah. To many Icelanders, this is normal.*

For the last decade Ingólfur has worked as a professional healer and medium. He recalls that early in childhood he had the gift of seeing spirits of the dead. I asked how old he was the first time that happened. He answered, *I started seeing people I knew were gone away when I was about 10 years old. I could see them just as I see you. Now I don't see them exactly that way anymore.* As an adult he senses their presence but he no longer sees them in a vivid way.

Berglót told me a child's ghost story that had been a more frightening experience than most. Berglót is a nontraditional university student in her early fifties who seemed psychologically stressed to me. *When I was 11 or 12 a man who rented a room in our cellar died. He had no relations and was dead for 3 days before his body was discovered. After his possessions were removed, my sister and I moved into his room.*

One evening while my mother was sitting with us I was trying to close the door, but again and again it opened. Finally mother said, "leave it alone. The poor man is standing in the doorway." After that, he was in our room all of the time.

I was so scared of death. My mother sees spirits of the dead. I am the only one of my sisters who sees things. It was very scary, always seeing dead people around you. They don't speak. Nobody else sees them. Gradually I overcame the fear. When you were 11 years old, did it bother you that he was there when you were undressing? *No. He was an old man.*

Now I feel at peace near these people. I always believed in God, and that he will help me. I asked him to help me to help these people if I could. My grandmother always said, "Perhaps they are not so very happy. Perhaps they want to leave some message. Just be kind. Don't be afraid of them."

Baldur is a massage therapist who told me, *When I was maybe 6 or 7 years old I could see dead people.* Did it frighten you, I asked. *Yes. It was a very tough time for me, the worst experience of my life. By the time I was 14 or 15 I fought them off really hard.* You fought them off? How? *I found out that if I moved all the time, kept busy, then when I came home I was so tired I would fall asleep like that,* snapping his fingers. *If I slept I didn't see the spirits.*

He told me, though, that he was troubled with nightmares. *I fought these feelings for many years and was so distraught that I stopped believ-*

ing in God. Hard work made me feel better, but in the end I started to drink. By the time I was 19 I found that if I had just a bit of alcohol I would be free from the spirits for 4 days and could sleep. Then I got into sports and stopped drinking, but the spirits returned.

By then I was old enough to leave home, so I went to Sweden where I became a vegetarian, met other people, and got interested in Sai Baba and other Indian masters. I began to think that maybe I should open up to God again. After that ghosts continued to appear to him, but they were very different from before. *Although I don't give thought to who they are,* he explained, *I know that some are Icelandic and Chinese doctors who back me up when I work with patients.*

I wondered if any loved ones come through to him, so I asked. *If I go to a medium,* he said, *they come, my grandmother and grandfather. Now my father also comes.* Do you talk with them when they appear? *Yes, I do, it's really true. They talk about things I am thinking about.* Oh, can you tell me more about that? *Sure. I just started with a medium one of my friends recommended. He said maybe she can help me to sort things out. She is just starting out as a medium and was obviously quite nervous, but a spirit did come and speak through her. It seemed like it was a man I knew really well, but it was difficult for her to get it out. In the end it turned out to be my father, who died 6 years ago. It's not the first time he has come.*

What did your father tell you? *We talked about my work. I'm trying to find a new place for my practice. He said, the place for you is in Kópavogur [a suburb of Reykjavík], not far from where you live, and the time is right. He also told me other things. It was really good for me. I was never close to my dad. He was a sea captain, and all five of my brothers went to sea, but I didn't. He was never happy with that, but I didn't realize why until near the end when he was crippled from a stroke. One day he went to the man I was working for at the time, a house painter, and complained that he [the painter] had employed me. He said that I was the only son he expected to become a captain like himself. He said that he had a gift for feeling things, for locating fish, and he knew that I alone also was really sensitive. But he was a very distant man. He never talked about feelings. He never spoke about that sort of thing to me or to anyone that I know of until that day. On that one occasion he had been drinking and was half-drunk and he brought his feelings out into the open.*

When I met him through a medium, Baldur added, *I asked him what he was doing in the spirit world. He said, "Now I am dancing,"* and Baldur beamed at me through teary eyes. Yet, as a middle-aged man, Baldur is still haunted by private ghosts. *You can go crazy,* he concluded, *if you go to a medium with bad things on your mind. You must be in balance.* He seemed to be referring to lessons he had learned from

Indian mystics, because nobody else spoke of needing to be in balance and free of harmful thoughts. He is a troubled man who seems still to confront fears that first materialized as spirits of the dead when he was just a small boy and a growing adolescent.

ADOLESCENTS AND OUIJA PANIC

The Ouija board is well known in Europe and the United States. In Iceland it is called *andaglas* or "spirit glass." It is a game in which a flat board the size of a square café table for two is marked with numbers, letters, and words such as "yes" and "no." The way it is played in Iceland, it is usually done in the evening with flickering candlelight, and although it is played a lot, the participants are usually teenage girls. Two to six players pass the glass from person to person, each one performing a little ritual to attract the spirit. That involves making a sign of the cross with the glass, blowing in it, and outlining a circle above one's head, although not all do it the same way.

In semidarkness and ready to receive the spirit of a dead visitor, the glass is turned upside down on the board and each player puts an index finger on it. One girl may say, "Is the spirit in the glass?" If there is no answer, the question is posed again. They wait patiently, fingers bundled in place until, slowly at first, the glass mysteriously moves to make one-word statements or spell out words or count numbers. "Who are you?" is usually the first question. After that, any question is fair game, although a younger girl will usually ask if a certain boy likes her, when she will marry, how many children she will have, and so on.

I wanted to observe and videotape a game and several university students thought they might arrange for a younger sister or friend to organize one, especially since it was then winter and Ouija is sort of a winter sport for kids. But that winter, nobody was willing to play and I soon found out why. They had all been traumatized by a Sunday TV horror movie involving the playing of Ouija.

The TV story, titled *Andaglas,* began with two young women, maybe 18 years old, who were walking through heavy rain and darkness to an apartment. The scene was set inside the apartment to elicit fear as they turned off the lights and lit candles while it stormed outside. As the plot unfolded they moved from preliminary questions to ask one that made them nervous. Each queried, "How will I die?" They were tempting fate. The first was told she would die in a car accident. The second, known to have a heart condition, was told she would die of a heart attack.

Suspense built up to an important scene in which the one with a weak heart tried to be funny by falling to the floor and faking a heart

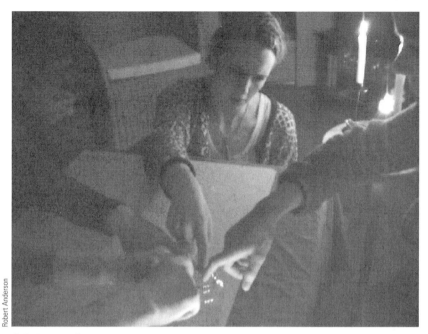

Robert Anderson

Quizzing the Ouija board

attack. She seemed to be dead. When her friend leaned over her in alarm and despair the jokester started laughing. Angry beyond words at the hoax, the other grabbed her coat and dashed out of the building. From inside the apartment viewers could hear the sound of screeching brakes and a crash. Looking out of the window, the young woman saw her friend lying dead on the street, whereupon she truly did collapse with a heart attack. Both of them died as a consequence of playing at the Ouija board. In a final fadeout, to the sound of eerie music, a mysterious wind blowing through the room snuffed out the candles, one by one.

I thought I would never witness young people at a Ouija board until in mid-winter, nearly at the end of my stay that year, five students invited me to videotape them at play. It seemed like it would be fun for them as well as for me, and the evening started off with laughing and joking. But I was concerned about the organizer of the evening, Björg, who told me some months earlier that she had been warned as a girl never to open herself to the spirit world until she was at least 30 years old because she was vulnerable to evil spirits.

Björg wanted so much to do this for me that she organized the meeting in spite of misgivings. While I watched, her smiling, cheerful face transformed at times to a fearful face clearly visible in the dim candlelight.

A cause for fear revealed itself when the spirit said she was still alive. How could her spirit enter the glass if she was alive? Perhaps she was sleeping, someone said, speculatively. But the real cause for alarm came when the spirit said that Björg's friend was going to have a serious accident. Her friend laughed it off, saying she didn't believe in spirits, but she looked worried. Björg, a very caring person, was devastated. They decided to stop the game and the evening ended when fresh baked cake and coffee were served.

Although I only watched a Ouija game once, I was told of Ouija experiences by many students at the university, most of whom recalled moments of terror. Gudny, for example, told me of one game she played. *We were all afraid. It ended in hysteria, five 16-year-olds screaming out in the yard, burning the board and breaking the glass.* Kolbrún recalled that she played Ouija only once, with her friend Salvör when they were 17 years old. *I got terribly scared,* she said, laughing. *The glass moved, of course. We did it a couple of times, and the last time it kept telling us to stop. Ohh, that was frightening, so we stopped right then and never did it again.*

Others included Huld, the bank clerk who encountered a ghost at work. *I never did it. It was a common practice when I grew up but I was afraid and didn't dare. I was convinced there was something to it.* The seaman Eyjólfur recalled that he was not frightened, but his friends were. *They asked, who does the spirit want to come to? The glass started to spell out the name of one of the girls, but before it could finish she stood up, screamed, and the glass exploded.* Another student, Karólina, told me she did it when she was 10 or 12 years old. *It was a terrible experience. All of a sudden I heard somebody say my name. I thought it was one of the girls at the table, but they swore it was not. The glass then started to say something about me by moving to the word "is," so I left. I was so scared and I never did it again.* Sigrún recalled from when she was maybe 11 or 12 years old that she and her friends played it from time to time, always with a good outcome. *Once, however, it was a bad spirit. We got frightened and broke the glass against a stone. That was the last time I played Ouija.* Agnes, a student who played it a lot between ages 12 and 16, recalled that it was very exciting and strange. *I was always scared something bad would happen. That the glass would explode. I felt I was working with energies beyond my control.*

As a last example, I give you another university student, Birna, who said she had a very bad experience. *I did it twice,* she recounted, *and I will never do it again. The first time was just a joke. One of us consciously moved the glass. But the second time, about 4 years ago, three of us tried it, two girls and a boy. We tried to really let a spirit come through.*

Nothing moved. The boy didn't feel anything, but my girlfriend and I were shaking with fear, so we stopped.

But the glass didn't move, you said. *No, it didn't.* Well, then, why did you feel so shaken? *I don't know. We did it in an old house that has a lot of history. I wouldn't be frightened of doing it in a new house. Also, all of the kids were doing it. We weren't the only ones getting scared.*

Birna then told me about a couple of her friends who had a bad experience 3 years earlier. *It was a year after one of our girlfriends was killed in an automobile accident, and she came in the glass, no doubt about it. She said things like, "I had a lot of unfinished business when I died," and she spoke of ill feelings she had about people who had treated her badly. She was only 17 when she died and had been my roommate. It was upsetting to have her say those things. The rumor is that her mother has a kind of altar for her with pictures and stuff on it, and that her mother goes to the graveyard and feels her presence there. Even kids who never knew her sometimes say things like, "I heard her laugh yesterday."*

Also factoring into Birna's fear of Ouija was the fact that Magnus Skarphedinsson of the Spirit Research School had come to counsel them about Ouija. *It was a small school,* she said, *with about 80 students between 16 and 18 or 19 years of age. The building was old and someone committed suicide there once. Some of the kids were upset. A couple couldn't sleep at night, so the principal, who is a friend of Magnus, asked him to talk to us.*

Tell me what Magnus had to say. *He said we shouldn't play it because when a spirit comes into the glass, whether it is a good or a bad spirit, you can't control it because you don't know what you are doing. You can't just say, "Oops, I'm scared. I'll just quit." That's not possible. He also played a couple of audiotapes of séances and handed out a lot of printed material about how many are fake, how many are real, and so on.* When you listened to the tapes, did you feel that spirits really were coming through? *Yeah, sometimes. Some of my friends freaked out.*

Not long after talking with Birna I had a chance to ask Magnus about that episode. *I have often been asked about those things and have visited schools a number of times,* he affirmed. *I remember that visit, in an old school building where many supernormal things had happened. The main part of the building was destroyed by fire in 1963 and was rebuilt in cement, with the second and third floors about a meter higher than the old floors. When mediums saw spirits there, they only saw the top halves of their bodies on the third floor and the bottom halves on the second floor because the spirits were standing on an old floor of the original building.*

Birna told me that you warned them not to play *andaglas* and that you had them listen to séance tapes. Do you remember? *Yes.* How did they respond to the tapes? *The response was positive. They asked lots of questions. I told them there were benefits in doing Ouija. You get in contact with dead people. You can sense a lot of things. The glass moves. Exciting things happen. Those are the benefits. But there are also disadvantages and dangers. You can't control it and lots of incidents occur around that.*

In one school, he continued, *the glass flew from the board against a wall and smashed into smithereens. That frightened the kids so badly that they ran out of the room, all but one boy and a girl. They didn't get away because they were overtaken by some force. When that happened, everything in the room began to shake. Things were thrown around. They dove under a blanket on the floor and lay there shivering, absolutely scared to death. By then it was the middle of the night and they managed to reach a phone and call me for help.*

I told them to put their thoughts on Jesus or God and pray, but they were too irreligious to do that. So then I said, reach up and take something that will come floating down from your grandfather and grandmother who are dead. **Your grandparents are protecting you** [emphasis added], *I said, and will push away the bad. In the end they managed to escape.* Generalizing on his extensive experience he concluded, *Kids ask, "Is it a reality?" I answer, yes, it is. You can get in contact with dead people, but it's dangerous. You can get into trouble.*

For a moment our conversation flagged, which gave me an opportunity to ask about something I found puzzling. I said, at the Ouija game I videotaped last Friday a woman came through the glass who is alive. She said she was sleeping. Can a living person come through that way? *It seems so,* Magnus acknowledged. *I have heard of it a number of times, but I can offer no explanation. If you ask the person who was asleep, "Did you dream?" they usually report that they had a very strange dream at that moment, perhaps a nightmare. Others remember no dream at all.* Struggling for a logical explanation, Magnus speculated that it might be the person's soul, part of the soul, or perhaps some energy.

Changing the subject again, I mentioned that Birna had told me you said that doing Ouija in an old building where someone had committed suicide was dangerous, but it's safe to do in a new building. *Yes, that's correct,* he agreed. *In an old building with a history you can get stuck in some old drama that may have occurred there. I don't know why, but if you want to do Ouija, do it in a new house where there will be no tragedy, no trauma, nothing that you might get sucked into. But an old place can be dangerous. I know of a girl in the north who became totally, totally insane after playing Ouija in an old building.*

A POLTERGEIST

I nearly finished my exploration into the ghosts of Iceland without encountering a poltergeist, the kind of ghost who haunts a house in a disruptive way, as happened to Indridi a century ago. Poltergeists usually make their presence known only when a young person is in the house, and that was true of the one story of a poltergeist that I jotted down. It happened to Björg, the student whom I worried about when I videotaped that game of Ouija. *When I was 14,* Björg told me, *I lost a classmate who had been one of my four closest friends. He died of meningitis. I was grieving. My hormones were working. Two months after he died I started to get the feeling that someone was in my room. I didn't pay much attention at first, but I saw those shadows. My mother is a nurse in a psychiatric facility, so I knew a few things about mental disorders. I thought, okay, I probably am schizophrenic because I am seeing some stuff I probably shouldn't be seeing, so I tried to ignore it, but it continued. One afternoon I was playing the piano when the shadows came, but I just played on. Then the stereo went on and off, on and off and the volume turned higher and lower. At first I just stared at the stereo, fixated. I was terrified. At last, I ran out of the house.*

I didn't know what to do, so I went to my school and tried to read. When I knew it was late enough for my mother to have returned home I went to her. I always talk with my mom. She said, "It's probably your grandmother." That was great, because she didn't say, "Oh, you're schizophrenic. I didn't want to be schizophrenic."

But when I was alone in the house I continued to hear noises. It just went on and on. Books fell off shelves. The stereo went on and off. The door to my room opened and closed. A glass of water on my piano shattered. It was like a poltergeist, always in my room, not in the whole house, just in my room.

Then one day I heard a voice, and that was it. I heard it say "Björg." It came nearer and said "Björg" again. I thought, Is it in my head? What's happening? Then right next to my ear he said, "Stop!" "Stop it," he shouted. I ran to my school. I thought, okay, I'll commit suicide and get it over with. I can't do anything. I can't do anything. I was terrified. Actually, I wasn't able to talk about this with anyone, except for my mother. My friends tried to understand, but they couldn't.

I had one friend who wasn't in my group. She lived in another part of town and had been a friend and classmate when I was 6 years old. We were good friends then. Well, we met again at this time, when we were both 14 and she moved to my school. She told me she could see things others couldn't see and that all winter she had been upset by a spirit. It was so disturbing to her that she just stayed on a couch. She couldn't get up or eat. Our teacher said she was probably depressed, but her mother had seen it, and so had some healers and, all together, five mediums. The spirits cured her, getting rid of the spirit that was disturbing her. Being aware of my interest in deceased doctors she added, *some of them were spirit doctors as I recall.*

After hearing all about how upset she had been I told her about my experience. We talked about this for hours and hours. She told me the poltergeist was the spirit of my friend or of his helpers. They were telling me to stop grieving, to let go. The problem was, I couldn't stop grieving.

The following day her mother called me and our teacher. She told me we two must never meet again. I asked why, and she said, "Your souls are not compatible." My teacher, however, told me I had to go to a medium who could help me. I was glad to know that the medium could help, so I went. It was 1 o'clock when I sat in the chair across from her. Suddenly I woke up and it was 5 PM. Yet I was awake the whole time, but I couldn't remember a thing. She didn't do anything except talk. I didn't fall asleep, I know that, but it was like being asleep.

After that, the poltergeist never appeared again. She told me I shouldn't do anything in the spirit world because I draw in energy. I use it in a negative way without knowing it. I can't control it. "You can never have this experience again," she told me. "You mustn't go to a spirit class or to a spirit circle where they try to connect. Absolutely not. And not to a medium again until you are 30. Until then, you are not mature enough. And I was not supposed to meet with my friend again, who was transferred from my school to another. She gave me no hope of ever having a positive relationship with spirits. She told me I would have a difficult life until I was 30, and then I would be mature. I am 24 now, and it has been a difficult life. I have been successful as a musician, in a job as an administrator, and as a student at the university, but my private life with men I have cared about has always been mixed up.

CONCLUSION

I was often told that children are quite gifted in spirit awareness, but tend to lose that gift when adults convince them that they are deluded. Yet an awareness that people can be in contact with spirits of the dead is so pervasive in Iceland that children on the whole seem to know of the possibility. While most children apparently do not encounter ghosts, some do. Contact would seem to prepare them for spirit experiences later in life, and perhaps even to become mediums if they develop their gifts.

For the most part, childhood and adolescent encounters with spirits are recalled as benign, but they can be upsetting. The recollections of people who had played Ouija as adolescents seemed always to describe games that ended in shocking fright. Similarly, in the past, the ghosts of Iceland tended to be evil and murderous. They may also be frightening in the present day, although much less so than in saga times. However, many only want to do good things for living people, as exemplified in the ghosts of deceased physicians. Others seem merely to want companionship. In a society with recent roots in isolated farmsteads in which sociality consisted of spending long evenings in dim candlelight telling stories from the sagas or reciting poetry, where wealth and power were no cause for snobbery, and where intellectual gifts were prized, perhaps anthropologists should not be surprised to find that ghosts mainly just want to be included in quiet activities.

Most of the ghosts who frighten people seem to do so without intent, and those who are frightened often speak of how they learned not to be upset. The remaining bad ghosts seem more mischievous than evil. Poltergeists, who in other societies make such a nuisance of themselves that they frighten people into abandoning homes and apartments, are so rare in Iceland that I only encountered one example. Ouija ghosts scare pubescent girls who actually want to be scared, the way teenagers do when they attend horror movies.

Jósep once commented that he was happy to return to Iceland after living and working as a surgeon in Sweden, *because I wouldn't want to live in a country without ghosts.* That comment makes sense for Jósep. The ghost stories he knows are mostly about friendly ghosts and do-gooders. The worst of them seem merely to be pranksters and practical jokers. The sadistic evil ghosts of Jósep's ancestors have entirely faded away, as have the marauding Vikings themselves.

PRIESTS VERSUS MEDIUMS

CULTURE AS A REPERTOIRE OF OPTIONS

It is not my intent to describe how the national church is structured except to offer a reminder of what is obvious. The church is a rational-legal organization—a bureaucracy—with a clerical hierarchy of pastors who are salaried by the state. Clerics, who may be women as well as men, constitute a highly educated, socially privileged elite with personal and professional values that are inculcated during formative years when they study theology as university and seminary students. Responsibilities and job descriptions are formalized by laws and regulations.

Relations between the priesthood and the laity are most obviously and regularly formalized in ritual settings. In ceremonial activities, social distance is symbolized by seating arrangements whereby those who attend worship services and partake of the sacraments sit apart from officiants and assistants, including musicians and choir singers. Churchgoers and ritual leaders sit or stand in separated spaces facing each other across an architectural no-man's-land, a symbolic chasm.

I hasten to add that in spite of the distancing behavior imposed by these institutional constraints, warm and intimate relations can mature beyond the pleasantries of shaking hands with the pastor on exiting the church. I certainly do not mean to suggest that pastors are not caring individuals, and I know that on the whole they are dedicated to the well-being of their parishioners. I merely want to suggest that formal structures are not inherently set up to facilitate informal relationships, and the national church is a highly formalized structure.

Often it seems that culture is a trap. Individuals in some societies can be said to go to school, marry, work, and worship in ways so heavily pre-

scribed by their cultures that individuality and deviance are scarcely tol-
erated at all. In that sense, culture is a trap. As Ioan Lewis (1986: 315)
points out, institutionally based, well-entrenched, authoritative religious
leadership will expectably be very controlling of people in a community
who challenge church orthodoxy. Yet, in other societies people seem to
enjoy a wide range of choices about how to live their lives. Taking a cue
from the philosopher Michael Polanyi (1968) and my own application of
his ideas to anthropology (Anderson 1996: 32–42), I have found it helpful to examine cultural practices in terms of whether they impose constraints or support freedoms (see also Powell & DiMaggio 1991: 11). As
an analytical tool, this binary opposition helps to make sense out of the
confrontation between the Icelandic state church and the practice of a
New Age kind of spiritism.

CONSTRAINTS AND OPPORTUNITIES

Every Icelander surely has some knowledge about the church and
Christianity on the one hand and on the other hand has some awareness
that people talk about individuals who have survived as spirits or ghosts
after death. As a result, every reflective individual has the opportunity to
think about personal beliefs in these terms, that is, about accepting or
rejecting the beliefs of Christianity and/or about the spirit world.

It is the "and/or" of belief that is problematic. Can one be a spiritist
and also be a Christian? For half a year, I raised that question with many
people in Iceland, and found that the answer depended on whether spiritist and Christian beliefs are conceptualized as competitive or as complementary. That is, it depends on the extent to which acceptance imposes
constraints or allows choices. If the constraints of Christian commitment
forbid contact with the dead or deny its possibility, then it is an "or" situation. You must choose one or the other, because you cannot have both.
However, if biblical authority condones spiritist practices, then it is an
"and" situation, offering the opportunity to subscribe to both sets of
beliefs (Anderson 2003b).

Most of the clergy come down on the "or" side of this debate, justi-
fied by ordinances in the Bible. Leviticus 19:31 reads "Do not turn yourselves to the spirit mediums and do not consult professional foretellers of
events, so as to become unclean by them. I am Jehovah your God." (See
also Deuteronomy 18:9–14.) This injunction survived into the New
Testament where, in Revelation 22:15 Jesus compared spiritists to dogs,
branded them as liars, and excluded them from his realm. "Outside are
the dogs and those who practice spiritism and the fornicators and the

murderers and the idolaters and everyone liking and carrying on a lie." (See also Galatians 5:19–20.)

Currently, high-ranking prelates in Reykjavík as well as clergy in neighborhood churches characteristically offer a contemporary, much more tolerant, but nonetheless categorical, condemnation of all attempts to communicate with the spirits of dead people. Hafsteinn, pastor of the national cathedral, told me, *I am against this. You see, it doesn't do anyone any good. It does great harm. I think it can lead people astray, lead them away from the true Christian faith.*

But, I countered, it can be a great comfort to know that one's loved ones are still a part of one's life. I then told him about Halldór, who said he is never alone, because his long dead grandfather is always with him when he is in danger. What harm is there in that? Hafsteinn's response was, *I would say that this man believes in his grandfather. He should believe in God. And the protection of God. And God will send his angels to watch over him.* Further in our conversation he added, *How can he be sure it was really his grandfather and not some evil spirit who was leading him astray?*

I rejoined that in countless difficult circumstances over 15 or 20 years, the spirit of his grandfather had always been benevolent, saving his life when he seemed doomed. Is that evil? *No,* he countered, *but there are all kinds of spirits, and they can be good and evil. The devil can pass himself off as a good spirit.* In short, cavorting with spirits is forbidden to Christians because it is dangerous.

Although a number of statements in the Bible forbid intercourse with mediums and spirits, they do not deny their existence. As documented in the Bible, a medium can contact the dead to get them to speak, and even to foretell the future. The prime example is in I Samuel 28:3–17, which recounts how Saul was distressed because Jehovah had not answered questions about his future as king. Disguising himself, he visited the medium of Endor and asked her to bring Samuel from the place of the dead, which she did. Samuel then spoke to Saul, but only to reprimand him. "Why have you disturbed me by having me brought up?" He then told Saul what would happen to him in the future: "Jehovah will rip the kingdom away from your hand and give it to your fellow man David."

Now, on the one hand, this experience with the medium of Endor and the spirit of Samuel is consistent with injunctions against meeting with the dead. Overriding the taboo put Saul in the bad graces of Samuel and his future looked bleak. On the other hand, it also demonstrates that as far as the Bible is concerned, the dead do live on, and that, indeed, mediums can call on them, and that future events can be predicted. But are spirits of the dead evil? Samuel was not an evil man! And are they inevitably harmful?

On the unorthodox side of this disagreement, I spoke with two Lutheran pastors who survive from earlier decades when a substantial number of clergy preached that involvement in both Christianity and spiritism was not only permitted, it was good. For these two, the biblical constraints are negotiable.

One of them was Stefán. When asked if one could be a spiritist and also be a Christian, he responded with evident fervor. Gesturing forcefully by opening out his arms he answered my question with a question of his own. *How can one be a Christian and NOT be a spiritist?*

He then explained that in part he based this theology of opportunity on the biblical narrative describing the most famous ghost in all of human history, that of Jesus after he was crucified. He spoke of Luke 24:13–31, where it is said that a couple of days after Jesus died on the cross and had arisen to be alive again he joined two of the apostles who were walking and talking together. As long as the three of them were on the road the apostles did not realize that the man who joined them was the revenant Jesus. When they stopped to have dinner together, however, they did. "And their eyes were opened and they recognized him; and he vanished out of their sight."

That unexpected appearance and sudden disappearance was possible because Jesus was in a spirit body for that encounter, Stefán told me. He then added that the resurrected Jesus apparently had a physical body in a later episode when he appeared to some men in Jerusalem and asked, "Have you anything here to eat?" According to Luke 24: 41–43, "They gave him a piece of broiled fish, and he took it and ate before them." It's hard to imagine how he could have eaten if he did not have a solid anatomy and intact visceral organs.

Hjörtur, the other clergyman hospitable to spiritist beliefs, offered the same theological argument. *The resurrection of Christ is the main point in everything,* he told me. *Christ proved for us that your soul lives forever. . . . I believe that when you leave this Earth you come into a new world and you don't need this body anymore. You get a new one. When the departed comes as a vision, he shows himself as he was when he was perhaps at his best. He shows himself to the people as they knew him.*

Until Stefán retired and Hjörtur gave up his pastorate at the national cathedral, the two were exceedingly popular for conducting funerals. For a decade they officiated at approximately 50 percent of all funerals in the capital city, leaving the other 50 percent to the remaining 15 or 20 clergy. Why? *It was our theology, our preaching. We tell people they will live after death, that they will find their loved ones.*

Hjörtur told me several stories of encounters with spirits, but the ones that touch most directly on the syncretism of Christianity and spirit beliefs and practices are from his experiences as an officiant for funerals.

One of the farmers was a trance medium in my first parish in the western fjords. Another was a clairvoyant. Both could see the dead. When I was officiating at my first funeral, they were in attendance, although they were not sitting together. After the service, speaking separately with each one, I asked, "Did you see anything?" They independently reported the same vision. They each saw the dead man standing on the floor of the church beside his coffin. He was holding a little girl on his arm. That was the only person he had lost from his family. It was his daughter.

Hjörtur also told me that the spirit of his deceased grandfather frequently assists him when he is in the pulpit. *Many clairvoyants have said to me, "there is another priest standing behind you. He is very tall and stout. He is sending light from himself to you." I am sure it is my grandfather. He was a very big man, and he was a clergyman. Perhaps I can thank him for some of my popularity.*

The Menu of Christian Culture

Identifying constraints versus freedoms can serve as a useful analytical tool when your goal is to understand how a culture can integrate conflicting ideologies and practices. A different pair of oppositions, the comparison of how a culture or a trait is like or unlike another, is so basic to anthropology that anthropologists hardly think of it as an analytical concept, but comparative analysis on that basis proved to be very useful when I wanted to explore more broadly the extent to which recourse to mediums and the practice of communicating with spirits of the dead can be reconciled with Christian theology.

I interviewed representatives of four small, proselytizing Christian churches that are part of the Icelandic cultural scene (Pentecostal, Salvation Army, Catholic, and Mormon). What guided my inquiry was to look at how these churches are alike and different on the issue of spiritism. I must emphasize that this was not an investigation into formal academic theology. What I am interested in is folk theology, what ordinary people believe. For the most part, what I learned about spiritist beliefs in Iceland is just that. In the questioning I did of Christian congregations, however, I found myself gathering data at a kind of in-between level. Most of what I learned was from neither ordinary folk nor theologians, but from members of the clergy. Of course they explained theology to me as they know it, but on the level of an intellectual conversation. For these small mar-

A nearly empty state church on a Sunday morning in Reykjavík

ginal denominations I got my information primarily from a Pentecostal minister, a Salvation Army captain, a Catholic priest, and, since the Mormon church does not ordain ministers, four lay leaders of the Church of Jesus Christ of Latter Day Saints in Reykjavík. Robert Redfield (1955) suggested an analytical framework for comparative research that contrasted what he called the great tradition (based on written literature and professional experts in a complex society) with the little tradition (which derived from the oral traditions of small, often face-to-face communities). In those terms, mine is a study of the little tradition of Iceland.

SMALL DENOMINATIONS ON THE FRINGES

The national church today is a strong, stable institution financed by a universal church tax. Essentially unopposed by politicians and the electorate, it is housed in beautiful, well-maintained church buildings that stand high as reminders of a national allegiance to Christian values that have shaped Icelandic culture for a thousand years. These structures also serve as much used resources for weddings, funerals, and other rites of passage. Yet the official church is sidelined as an organizational basis for religious enthusiasm, godly devotion, personal growth, or spiritual evolution. Although the architecture is generally stunning, the pews are rarely occupied.

One senses that loss of vitality by the marked contrast encountered in crowding into the sanctuary of one of the few Pentecostal churches. There, young born-again Christians with accordions, guitars, and electronic keyboards sing devotional songs to a rock beat and the crooning of gorgeous young women who hold microphones close to their lips as they sway sensuously to a dance beat and passionately intone, "I yield myself to thee, oh Lord." The pastor preaches revivalist sermons that climax in altar calls where sins can be forgiven, salvation achieved, and health restored. What a contrast to the stiff formality of official church services!

Less charismatic but none-the-less captivating are the meetings of two other small but active Protestant sects, the Salvation Army and the Mormons. Even the Catholic church, with its mainly foreign supplicants, is active and well attended by the small number of Catholics who live in the capital city, perhaps because most of them are young working people who have come to Iceland for jobs.

These religious denominations seduce very few dissenters from the national church. Their overall small membership numbers clearly indicate that competition for affiliation is no big deal for most people. Even so, given what I learned about the repudiation of spiritism as a policy of the national church, I hoped to gain insight into Iceland's "'tool kit' of symbols, stories, rituals, and world-views," its cultural menu, by talking with Christians who were active and committed in contested, oppositional denominations.

THE PENTECOSTAL RESPONSE TO SPIRITISM

The pastor of the downtown Pentecostal church in Reykjavík told me that the Bible is quite explicit in saying that mediums are not permissible for God's people. *Those who have been saved have been set free from the evils of spiritism,* is the way he stated his position. When I countered with my example of Halldór and the importance his dead grandfather has for him, the pastor was dismissive. *We know better when people say they have communed with the spirit of a grandfather or grandmother. It is not the spirit of a person who has passed away, it is an evil spirit. The Bible says the devil can appear like an angel.*

He then told a story that was meant to prove beyond question that spirit contact is unredeemable bunk. *We know of a few people who have gone to mediums to get news about fishermen in danger of drowning at sea. In one example, relatives who were worried at the news of a terrible storm at sea were told by a medium that their menfolk had perished when the*

Robert Anderson

The Sunday morning crowd at a Pentecostal church in Reykjavík

ship sank. They were told that the deceased had arrived in the spirit world. They wanted those on Earth to know that they were fine, the medium said, and that they send greetings. Their story was published in a newspaper.

The pastor continued, *Grieving friends and loved ones took solace in knowing that the lost seamen were still alive in spirit. Their mood changed a few days later when word reached them that the ship had not sunk and that every one on board was alive and well.* Then he added, *And there are more examples like this. We know the devil can lie. Those who were in spiritism but have found salvation in Jesus all tell us that it was exciting and tempting to go to mediums, but also that they were fearful. We know that it was not spirits of the dead they communed with, but evil spirits.* The Pentecostal pastor, in short, is far more outspoken against spiritism than even the most opposed of mainstream Lutheran pastors.

THE SALVATION ARMY RESPONSE TO SPIRITISM

Captain Júlíusdóttir of the Salvation Army is equally intolerant of communing with spirits. *According to the Bible you're supposed to leave the dead alone—very clearly. People call themselves Christian. Iceland is a*

Christian country with a state church, baptism, confirmation, and so on. So call yourself Christian. But there's a difference in being a born-again believer. The born-again believer realizes that spiritism is not the same as Christianity. Sometimes they discover they were bound in spiritism and needed to be delivered.

As an example of being "bound," she told me of a somewhat vaguely situated incident. *In a place where these spiritist things were happening the participants felt they had lost control and they became frightened, so they asked a Christian to come and pray. I believe that when you start doing things like that, you call in spirits, but it is not the spirit of God. It's evil spirits. Things like that happen. That's why it is so important to be saved and be covered with the blood of Jesus.*

When people come to the Lord, she added, *they find that they get delivered from spiritism. That's part of their past, and they are freed from that. Some people just see that it isn't true; others have to be informed. But for all of them, something happens when they decide to take Jesus as their savior.*

As we talked more about being "bound" in spiritism she confessed, *I don't know how it happens. It's like all the different things you go into. It affects you, like anything that has to do with occultism. You get into areas you are not in control of. It says in the Bible, Ephesians 6, that we have a battle not with humans but with the power and authority of darkness. So we have to be dressed in the full armor of God and truth.*

Later when I checked her reference I found that in Ephesians 6:11–14, Paul wrote, "Put on the whole armor of God, that you may be able to stand against the wiles of the devil. For we are not contending against flesh and blood, but against the principalities, against the powers, against the world rulers of this present darkness, against the spiritual hosts of wickedness in the heavenly places. . . . Stand, therefore, having girded your loins with truth. . . ."

As I had done in other interviews, I told her about Halldór and his deceased grandfather, after which I asked, Is that bad? She responded by explaining that to look for help from deceased parents and grandparents is a deception, an infantile regression to the dependencies of childhood, adding, *I don't think the dead are roaming around someplace. I think they are with the Lord.*

Then she added a provocative and appealing way of thinking about dead loved ones. *But I believe you have their memory—a special feeling. Memories are good. They stand for real truths. You remember what they stood for.* That comment about the persistence of remembrance must be a deep-rooted Icelandic concept because I encountered it earlier when conversing with a middle-aged accountant who was knowledgeable about the old Nordic religion. He emphatically denied that we survive death as living individuals, but he spoke in a beautiful way how important his grandmother had been to him as a child. He went on to say that she still lives almost daily in his thoughts, and he encouraged me to look up verse 77 of the Eddic poem, *Hávámal,*

> Cattle die, kinsmen die.
> You yourself shall die.
> I know one thing which never dies,
> The reputation of each dead man.

Captain Julíusdóttir contrasted what death means to a born-again Christian as against the certainty of spending eternity in a lake of fire and brimstone. *I believe we go straight to be with the Lord. He conquered death. That means we don't have to face death.* So you go to heaven? *Yes. My brother died of cancer. He went to heaven and is with the Lord.* Living on in heaven, he and the others who were saved are not free to communicate with loved ones back on Earth. For those who don't make it into heaven, she added, there is no hope. *It's too late to pray for a person after death.* Pentecostal Christians would agree. Catholics and Mormons would not.

The conversation lagged for a moment, so I asked, Is it risky to go to a medium? *Yes,* she shot back. *I recommend that you avoid that completely. It's like going to a devil thing. First thing you know you are hooked. It's the same with alcohol and drugs.* She also told me that it is based on a completely misinformed notion of what happens to people when they die.

Changing the subject I asked, Where do the evil spirits come from? *I don't know. I know there is Lucifer, the angel that disobeyed, but I don't know where the evil spirits came from.* I respected her forthrightness in acknowledging what she didn't know and moved on, asking her to tell me more about angels. *There are all kinds of angels and I believe they watch us. I believe there is an army of angels. They have different names. Some are just like human beings.* Do we each have a guardian angel? *Yes, I think so. I believe I have one. The Lord sends out angels—I don't know— as good spirits or whatever. I've been in situations where I should have been killed. The Lord protects with powers we don't see. Angels are watching over me.* There doesn't seem to be much difference between an angel and a deceased loved one watching over you, I said. *Well, I don't think the spirit of a loved one will be watching. I believe it will be an angel. They are not humans. They are a separate creation.*

THE CATHOLIC RESPONSE TO SPIRITISM

One Sunday after mass at the imposing Catholic church high on a hill above Reykjavík I approached the officiating priest, hoping to arrange a meeting when we might talk about spirits of the dead. Unfortunately he was Irish, and I felt it important to meet with an Icelander. Turning to a second priest who was approaching as we spoke, I discovered he was Belgian. Are there no Icelandic priests in this place? *Ah yes*, they said, as much in unison as English permits when spoken simultaneously with a Gaelic brogue and a French lilt. *Father Agúst would be just the man*, and so he was when I met him a few days later in the attached church school.

I think it made a difference that he is an Icelander who did not convert to Catholicism until he was 24 years old. I detected a penchant for avoiding conflict and a capacity for tolerance that I had grown to expect in Icelanders, although it is not noticeable in everyone, and was certainly not evident in the Pentecostal or Salvation Army clergy I spoke with, a reminder that cultures do not predict individual personalities, except as a sometime thing.

According to the Bible you should not attempt to have contact with the dead, he told me, as soon as he understood why I was there. But then his open-mindedness came crashing through. *On the other hand, the Catholic church has always been of the opinion that you could ask for the prayers of dead people—for intercession of the saints who are dead and who are in heaven, according to our belief. You can ask them to pray for you.* And can you also ask loved ones? *In your prayers you can also ask parents or loved ones to pray for you. They can always pray, including for us.* Well, that was a surprise. It seems that you can talk with loved ones who have passed over; it's just that they can't speak to you in return.

Also, the Catholic church has a history of belief about "poor souls" in purgatory. In old times we would say that a dead person spent some time in purgatory to cleanse the soul in order to be ready to meet God. Father Agúst explained that purgatory used to be thought of as a place. In the Middle Ages they painted pictures of a pit of fire. Now, however, it is more common to conceptualize it as a state of mind. That fit with what I was reading in Jacques Le Goff, *The Birth of Purgatory* (1984).

Father Agúst continued, *There are stories of people who have had contact with poor souls who came to them and asked for prayers.* Since he didn't tell any of those stories I found some on my own. Le Goff (1984: 42) tells a few. Taking Gregory the Great as his source he writes of a man, a spirit as it turned out, who helped a priest regularly with his bath, scrubbing his back and handing him the soap, I suppose. He was assigned to do it as a way to expiate his sins, but he used those bathtub encounters to persuade the priest to pray for his release and it worked. He got out of purgatory and moved on to paradise.

In an old book written by a Jesuit priest I read about the ghost of a Benedictine monk who appeared at the abbey daily around noon for a whole month in the fall of 1859. When a novitiate finally asked why he was showing up that way he explained that he was suffering his 77th year of purgatorial punishment because he sinned by failing to celebrate seven masses of obligation when he was alive. The souls in purgatory suffer frightfully, he said, but with help from the living they can gain deliverance (Schouppe 1986 [1893]: 104).

My favorite story from Le Goff (1984: 178) is of a 12th-century dead woman who showed up as an apparition in a basilica where she was observed by worshippers. She made her ghostly way there after being liberated from purgatory in order to personally give thanks to the Mother of God who had interceded on her behalf. *So,* Father Agúst acknowledged, *even if the Church is opposed to the use of mediums to try to contact the dead, it doesn't say that it is not possible. There are people who have had this experience within the Catholic church.*

Is it false, harmful, or evil to approach the dead through a medium? Again, the Catholic priest was not as categorically judgmental as the evangelicals, speaking in the subjunctive rather than the accusative. *There is the danger of misuse. And also of being misled.* The good father then explained in more detail. *If you read about the development of the soul in the descriptions of church mystics, all describe the same thing. So do Zen Buddhists. At a certain stage in your development you start to have visions. Now, it is very harmful to dwell on this stage, because it can be a delusion or some evil power trying to lead you down the wrong path. For that reason the church says it is very dangerous and may be evil. Saint Paul tells us that the devil can appear like an angel. For that reason, as it says in the Bible, you shouldn't try to have contact with the dead because to do so can lead to all kinds of dangers.*

Have you had parishioners tell you that they communicate with spirits of the dead? *No.* Would they ever say that to you? *Probably not. But I know many who are interested in supernaturalism. There is nothing wrong with that. Many supernatural things are natural. It's just that we don't have an explanation for them.* Can you give an example? *Sure, take people who use divining rods to find water, or a pendulum. There is nothing harmful in that.*

What he said next thoroughly surprised me because it indicated an unexpectedly positive attitude toward contact with the dead. *What I find strange with spiritists,* he said, *is they explain contact with dead people as supernatural. It may be something that is natural that will be explained later.* Wow, I thought, that likelihood or possibility is exactly what inclined the national church to be receptive to Indridi, the first modern medium at the beginning of the 20th century. I guess it's an idea that continues to have some currency in Icelandic thought.

My colleagues from abroad may not agree with me on superstition. But I know people in my own family who have had experience with spirits of the dead. My aunt, for example, my mother's sister. She used to tell of things she saw. She claimed she saw dead people. I don't think she was lying. It is something I cannot understand. She was not a medium or something. She was a completely normal person and she saw these things.

How do people reconcile being a Christian with spiritist practices? *It seems not to be a big problem for people. Not even for those who claim to see elves. I have never personally seen anything like that, yet I have had strange experiences even as a priest. I was a priest for 10 years in Hafnafjödur....* As soon as he said that I realized he was talking about that small town where elves and spirits are said to abound. *About 3 years ago a man phoned to make an appointment to see me. He had been confirmed as a Catholic when he was a child, but he had not practiced. He said, "Something strange is going on where I work and I wonder if you would come and bless the place."*

He was an ironworker in the shipyard. The company moved into an old building in which the men, who worked hard and were not highly educated, were having all kinds of strange experiences. For example, somebody seemed to stand behind them and breathe down their necks. They thought there must be some ghosts there. So I came and blessed the workplace with holy water and prayed in every room. I also said a prayer for the dead. A week later he said everything had disappeared. Turning to catch my eye Father Agúst added, *I didn't sense anything, you know. But it doesn't do any harm to pray for the dead or to ask God's blessing for a place.*

You have an interesting point of view; it doesn't do any harm to pray. *No, on the contrary, it's a good thing to do. But I cannot believe that these men—there were 24 working there—it was no joke, you know. It was completely honest. How do you explain it? I don't know.*

THE MORMON RESPONSE TO SPIRITISM

Knowing very little about the Church of Jesus Christ of Latter Day Saints, often referred to simply as Mormons, except that they live healthier lives than most of us (in part because they don't carouse, smoke tobacco, or drink alcoholic and caffeinated beverages), I naïvely assumed that

Robert Anderson

Hallgrimur Church in Reykjavík

their strict adherence to the Bible and the Book of Mormon would make them as intolerant of spiritism as were the Pentecostal and Salvation Army people I spoke with. Not so. They were even more open-minded than Father Agúst.

The first time I attended a Sunday service I was amused by the Mormon's in-your-face presence in Reykjavík. They are few in number, with a congregation that fits tightly but adequately in a rather small sanctuary located on the second floor of an ordinary-looking apartment building. However, that unimposing building with its prominent sign identifying it as a Church of the Latter Day Saints is positioned at the edge of the imposing square that frames a high-standing statue of the Icelander who discovered America, Leifur Eiríksson, and is confrontational to the opposite side of the square that fronts on the entrance of Hallgrimur Church, which, with its tall pyramid-shaped tower, is the most dramatic church in all of Iceland. The two churches, face to face across the plaza, are an architectural David and Goliath, emblematic of a battle over Christian allegiance that continues (although no longer architecturally, because the Mormons have since moved to larger quarters elsewhere).

Since the church does not have ordained ministers I was able to meet with Loftur, a businessman who is president of the local congregation, and Elínborg, the executive secretary. The first thing I did when we got together was to describe my interest in spirit mediums and contact with dead loved ones and then to ask, how do you make sense out of that? To my surprise Loftur said, *We accept that there is a spirit world and that spirits can communicate with people. Whether good or bad, I don't know.*

That's the question, I said. Are they good or bad spirits? Elínborg picked up on that. *We believe that the spirit world is really at work all around us, and some can see it more than others. But we believe that it is dangerous to open our bodies to spirits, because there are bad spirits. That's why we counsel strongly against that.*

As we talked I began to understand that they made a clear distinction between encountering spirits of the dead, which was not inherently dangerous, and possession by a spirit, which was extremely so. *As I said,* Elínborg continued, *we just don't open up our bodies for it. You can feel them. You can even see them. But opening up your body for them, that's what makes it dangerous.* Loftur extended her thought, *We know that evil spirits like to have the experience of bodies like ours. They want to feel our joy, our peace, and that we can eat, enjoy meals, and experience good things in marriage.* In response I mentioned that I had been told that the spirit of a former drunk might succeed in drinking vicariously by means of possession. Elínborg responded by saying, *I've heard that, although I have not encountered it directly.*

Loftur went on to say, *When Jesus was casting out 5,000 demons from the man they had possessed, the demons transferred themselves to pigs, who then killed themselves by jumping off a cliff. Evil spirits like to have the experience of bodies, even those of pigs.* Elínborg added, *In the Bible it says that one-third of the host of heaven were thrown out. They were deprived of the experience of having heavenly bodies. That's our teaching. So they aim to get hold of our bodies.* Those are the evil spirits? *Yes.*

I told them about Halldór's grandfather, which introduced a confusing digression and suggests that I wasn't paying close attention, since Halldór was not possessed by his grandfather, but anyway, when I asked, is he an evil spirit? Elínborg answered, *We don't know. It could be. The spirit world is all around us. You have to be very careful. That's what we teach, to be very careful.*

Loftur picked up on that thought. *Evil spirits can deceive, but, of course, good spirits can also communicate with us.* Now, to say that good spirits can communicate with us is to diverge sharply from what other fundamentalist and conservative Christians told me! I snapped back to sharp attention.

Have you had that happen, Loftur? *Well, I have had the Holy Spirit communicate with me. But that's God. Yes, that's God. I think God sometimes sends good spirits to convey some message to us in dreams.*

Elínborg chimed in, *Yes, dreams,* while Loftur continued, *I don't think a spirit from God will go into our body, but it will communicate with my spirit.* How can you know if that is happening? *Well, can you tell me why salt tastes like it does?* (Pause) *You can hear a voice, but not through your ears. It's a spiritual communication. And you see, but only with spiritual eyes. To hear and see a spirit, you don't need your bodily ears and eyes.*

I turned then to Elínborg. You said you have had that experience? *Just once. I felt something touch me, very strongly. It happened in one of our temples, so,* she said with a knowing smile, *I don't think it was an evil spirit.* Who was it? *I don't know for sure. I was doing baptismal work for a deceased lady and there was a nice-looking lady sitting next to me who was also doing the work. I had my eyes closed and all of a sudden I felt this soft touch on my shoulder. I thought it was the lady next to me. I was sure of it because it was such a strong pressure, and then I felt a kiss on my cheek. When I felt the kiss I opened my eyes and could see that the lady next to me had not moved. The caress and the kiss were from the lady I was working for.*

After acknowledging what a remarkable example that was of loving contact with a departed soul I asked, what happens to people after they die? Loftur answered, *They go to the spirit world, the same place Christ went after his death on the cross.* I immediately flashed back to that moment during the crucifixion when Jesus said to the thief who was also on a cross, "Today you will be with me in Paradise" (Luke 23:43). So I said to Loftur, You mean he went to paradise? *Yes, to paradise—the spirit world—which has two parts, both of which are subdivided. Christ went for 3 days when his spirit was away from his body in order to organize the preaching of the gospel to the spirits so they also might be redeemed.*

That belief was not part of my upbringing in Baptist and Pentecostal churches, but according to Alice Turner (1993: 66), it is a widespread part of the Christian tradition that Jesus descended into the netherworld between Good Friday and Easter Sunday in order to straighten out the thinking of Old Testament patriarchs so they would know how to qualify for heaven.

At this point we got into additional Mormon theology as Loftur told me, *We believe every human who does the best according to his own conscience will go to the same place—the resting place of peace and happiness—while waiting.* Will I go there if I live an upright life? *Yes. We Latter Day Saints are not the only ones who will be happy.* Silently taking note that Mormons were far more generous on that score than Baptists or Pentecostals, I then heard myself ask, Well, then, what is the benefit of being a Latter Day Saint? *The benefit is that you get more knowledge from our Heavenly Father—more spiritual communication and heavenly vision—a picture of the purpose of the universe. Also, of course, you will have the necessary ordinations for being admitted to live with our Heavenly Father: baptism, priesthood, and a special ordinance performed in the temple that we don't talk about.* While muttering, I see, I began to realize they were talking about a spiritual equivalent of graduating from an Ivy League school and that the Mormon heaven is caste-ranked on that basis. Wondering about my own prospects as an apostate Baptist I asked, will I still be growing in the afterlife so that eventually I can achieve those ordinances? *Yes, in time,* but as he continued I began to understand that I would never succeed fully as well as a saint. No surprise there.

At some point in this quite long conversation we discussed the Mormon practice of baptizing deceased members of one's family, a practice considered anathema where I grew up. Loftur told me the unequivocal biblical authority consisted only of one solitary verse in the New Testament, 1 Corinthians 15:29, which reads, "Otherwise, what do people mean by being baptized on behalf of the dead? If the dead are not raised at all, why are people baptized on their behalf?" You will have to get the details from the Book of Mormon. Quite beyond my depth in trying to make sense of that one and only biblical reference to a rite that is so important to Latter Day Saints, I initiated a shift from theological niceties to down-on-the-earth pragmatics by asking, how would it benefit my long dead grandfather, who was a member of the Danish national church (Lutheran), if I were to baptize him posthumously? How would it change his existence? How would he be better off? *He would be more able to learn and communicate with God. He would progress. He would have the Holy Spirit with him all the time to teach him. Of course, he would have to act according to the gift of the Holy Spirit.*

Still confused, I encouraged him to continue. *There is a prison and a paradise in the spirit world.* So, is he in prison? *No, only if he was very bad.* What is the prison like? Laughing, Loftur said, *I haven't been there.* Elínborg carried on, *It says in the Bible, Jesus went to prison.* Ah, yes, where the rich man was when Lazarus looked down from Abraham's bosom and saw him suffering in the pit of fire? *Yes, well, fire is just a symbol—maybe it represents pain. People have to face their lives and repent; to make something good out of their lives.* Still a bit worried about my grandfather I asked, can people work their way out of prison? After all, hell in the church I grew up in was eternal. *Yes, they can be released.*

At this point we got heavily into an ethnography of the afterlife that I won't go into here, other than to share their explanation about angels and elves. As concerns angels, Loftur explained, *We believe angels can be just spirits or they can be resurrected spirits, like Jesus. We don't believe angels have wings. Angel really means, from Hebrew, messenger. An angel is just a messenger from God, from heaven to Earth with some specific message, and then they just go away.* Are you saying that an angel can be a person who lived on Earth? *Yes, like Gabriel. He was Noah. No one will be a messenger to this Earth except he belongs to this Earth.* Hmm. Let's move on, I thought.

I mentioned that I had been talking with people who have encountered elves or hidden people who live in rocks and hills. Loftur said it is just mythology. Do they exist? *I don't think so. They might be spirits or something. We believe that Satan is really working hard and can deceive people about everything. I'm not saying that the people who are deceived are good or bad—they could be either—but he deceives everyone.* Their tolerant attitude was refreshing. Elínborg affirmed her own tolerance. *We used to believe in the elves and the secret people. It doesn't seem to do harm in any way. It even seemed to help people in the old days.* Does that belief do any harm in terms of spiritual growth? Loftur picked up on that question. *It can set a limit on how much you can develop. If you keep your mind on what is not true, the devil will make sure you will not progress.*

Our conference ended with the emotional story of Elínborg's encounter with her deceased parents. *Well, it was after my father died. It was in a dream. I was in Sweden attending a genealogy seminar and was going to fly to Copenhagen in the morning. That night I was staying overnight with a friend, a lady of the church. I woke up in the morning when I heard her baby cry, and then I fell asleep again. My experience is that usually you dream something like that when you are sleeping lightly.*

What she then described was an out-of-body experience. *Well, in my dream I felt I was leaving my body. It was such a strong feeling. I still remember exactly how it was—a very strange feeling—not a bad feeling—far from it. I was thinking, "Well, I must be dying. I'm leaving my body." Then, all of a sudden I was standing in front of a huge door—a double door that opened up like that,"* and she gestured opening wide with both of her arms.

First it seemed rather dark inside and it took some time for me to adjust to it. But then I saw a very long table with people sitting on both sides. It was so long that I couldn't see the end of it. But close to me I saw my father. I ran up to him and was so happy and I embraced him. Then I saw my mother sitting and of course I embraced her as well. It was a little less than a year since she died, but about 3 years after my father died. I was crying, I was so happy.

Then I looked around and I could see my mother's sister and her husband and my mother's brother on the other side of the table. So I ran to them and greeted them also. I loved them too. But I felt it was dark in there and I didn't feel good. I said to my father, "Dad, I don't feel good here somehow." He answered, "Well, it doesn't need to be that way." I sat down and started talking with him. There was so much to talk about. But I kept feeling worse and worse. At last I said, "I don't belong here. I'm not supposed to be here. I don't feel right about it." Then we stood up and I said, "I have to go." My father stood up and said, "I know." He put his hand on my shoulder, looked at me very seriously and said, "But please remember, it doesn't have to be this way."

After I went out through the door I felt I was going back into my body again. I woke up, still within the dream, in bed. My youngest son was sleeping beside me, crying. I reached out and took his hand and said, "I'm not dead. You don't need to cry." And then I woke up.

Elínborg concluded, *I returned to Reykjavík, but kept thinking a lot about my dream. One evening after I was in bed and thinking about my dream I wondered, why weren't my other ancestors there. Why not my grandmothers and grandfathers? And then, all of a sudden, I remembered. I had done all the work for my parents, uncles, and aunts, but not for the others. Then I understood the dream completely. So, the last time I went to the temple I did the work for them. I believe I was shown into the spirit world there, and I think there are many, many, many people waiting.* What a joy for you to be able to do that for your loved ones. *Yes, I always go to the temple whenever I can.*

The very next day I was invited to dinner in the home of Elder Gustafsson and his wife. A retired American couple from Utah, they were attached to the church in Reykjavík for a year or two as missionaries. Missionaries are addressed in very formal terms, so I never learned their first names. Nonetheless, we had an informal and cordial conversation that evening that included a discussion of my interest in spirits of the dead.

Elder Gustafsson told me, *We don't believe in ghosts or in talking to ancestors. We do believe they are sometimes with us, our mothers or relatives, but not as apparitions. I was telling my wife, since coming to Iceland I've been thinking a lot about my mother who died in 1969, even though I hadn't thought of her much in the past.*

What caused you to start thinking about your mother? *Being here. They're very active in genealogical work here and have family reunions. They keep excellent ancestral records.* Would you say you've felt her presence? *No, I wouldn't say that. It's just that I think about her.* Do you dream about her? *No.*

We digressed to other topics, including how much I was enjoying a home-cooked American meal, and then Elder Gustafsson returned to the subject of spirits. *Although I haven't known any personally, I believe that some people, not necessarily in our religion, have special kinds of ability for that. Some can do it better than others. It's a special gift.* How do you feel about Icelanders who go to mediums? Mrs. Gustafsson broke in to make their reply. *We're told that they are maybe coming from the wrong source—the power of the devil, or whatever you call him, the adversary—I mean the opposite of God the Father and Jesus Christ. It can be the brother of Jesus, who was Satan.*

A version of predestination was mentioned next. *We believe in a preexistence before we came here. Jeremiah, for instance, when he was called as a prophet, was told by God, "I knew you before you were in the womb. You were foreordained to be a prophet." We believe very strongly that we were with God in a spirit condition. That everything is created spiritually before it is created physically. Jesus existed in a premortal condition,* and then she talked more about Jesus and his brother Satan. Remembering Plato's allegory of the cave and his concept of ideals as the true reality I silently wondered how ancient Greek philosophy found its way into the thinking of Joseph Smith and his fellow pioneers on the American frontier, but I said nothing. I waited for the conversation to return to our discussion of spirits of the dead, which happened over dessert.

We had an 18-year-old grandson die recently, Mrs. Gustafsson told me. *Our daughter believes very strongly that in some way she has had strong impressions from him. We haven't experienced them ourselves, but she believes very strongly that he has been near.* How is that? I wondered out loud, which led her to describe two kinds of encounters. *He loved to cook. She has felt his presence in the kitchen very strongly. Also, she'll be out riding in the car and all of a sudden a song will come on [the radio] with words that have a particular meaning. When that happens she thinks Billie may be communicating with her through that song, and it gives her comfort.*

Elder Gustafsson added, *I think our daughter had those feelings for quite a while after he died, but they have become less and less frequent. She kind of got closure on it. She got a signal from him that he's okay and let it go.* Mrs. Gustafsson then interjected, *He has things he has to do. He's got to move on, and so these things are happening less and less.* In antiphonal response, Elder Gustafsson concluded, *But right after his death and for many months she was having these experiences. I think that some people are much more in tune with that than others. Some are much more sensitive. Our daughter is one of those.*

CONCLUSION

The Christian presence in Iceland, the cultural menu as concerns competing denominations, is largely limited to Lutheran, Pentecostal, Salvation Army, Catholic, and Mormon, with almost all Icelanders self-identified as Lutheran. I have the impression that the overwhelming majority of Icelanders are simply not troubled by any need to reconcile being a Christian with also being a spiritist. Since that issue is not problematized, the cultural tool kit is not unpacked in a search for options. However, insofar as some might, they will find as I did that Pentecostal and Salvation Army Christian leaders vehemently oppose efforts to converse with the dead, Lutheran and Catholic priests officially oppose such practices but are much more tolerant and to some extent permissive, while Mormons are comparatively accepting and unconcerned. I hasten to add that my exploration on this issue was quite limited. A proper quantitative study would be most welcome.

SOCIALIZING TO ACCESS SPIRITS

INSTITUTIONAL THEORY

It has long been the practice in anthropology and sociology to describe and theorize social institutions such as the family, the church, the school, a business enterprise, a social club, and so on. More recently these disciplines have given attention to how an institution can shape the way people think about themselves to form a revised concept of self, how it can structure the way members organize themselves to take action, and how members may give meaning to their lives based on institutional values (Powell & DiMaggio 1991: 3, 12). Social scientists especially want to understand how institutionalized belief and ritual shape people's lives. In the preceding chapter I examined churches as institutions. In this chapter I will investigate the formal and informal associations that organize and regularize spiritist thought and behavior.

It has been customary for social science researchers to dichotomize customs as either sacred or profane. Churches and scriptures belong to the sacred part of a culture; that is, they are holy in the sense of inspiring reverence, veneration, or respect. In contrast, schools or research facilities would be defined as profane or secular because they are worldly and nonreligious. Emile Durkheim (1915) popularized the sacred-profane distinction more than 90 years ago, but it has never been easily applied or consistently used.

In my work in Iceland I had to drop it altogether, because mediums do not contact the dead in clear-cut sacred places even though a sense of the sacred may intrude. They may work out of their homes or rented rooms, and to the extent that their activities are institutionalized, the institutions are described in profane ways as schools or research centers.

Ritual is another old concept in the social sciences that originally was closely associated with sacred activities, such as Sunday morning church services, but that has changed. Ritual can be secular, as is explicit in the definition of Roy Rappaport (1999), for whom ritual is "the performance of more or less invariant sequences of formal acts and utterances not entirely encoded by the performers" (pp. 24, 32). In other words, ritual participants follow established procedures that they have not invented themselves.

Just as the ceremonial life of Christian practice is highly ritualized, so too are the acts and utterances of séances. Words that sound a lot alike can cause problems. The word *spiritism,* for example, refers broadly to a Western tradition of rituals and beliefs that facilitate communication between the living and the dead. Spirituality, on the other hand, is quite another thing. Although I could not escape my skepticism about the reality of spirits I encountered in séances or that I was told about in conversations, I always felt that appearances were misleading, and that what is truly important about contact with spirits of the dead is that it has to do with how important people are to one another while they are alive. At the risk of sounding maudlin, it has to do with love, in other words, with caring for and needing one another. I call that spirituality.

Fundamental to this way of thinking is a distinction anthropologists and sociologists make between manifest functions, which are conscious and can be explained by those involved as the reasons for a ritual or other activity, and latent functions that are neither expressly thought of nor clearly articulated by participants (Merton 1957). In identifying the latent functions of séances and meditation groups I was impressed with how they create a social space in which mutual caring and sharing can take place.

It helps to better understand the manifest/latent distinction to think of rituals as a three-stage process in which one separates from ordinary daily life, spends time in a space that is outside of normal life and activities, neither here nor there one might say, and concludes with reentry into the prosaic activities of daily life. Arnold Van Gennep (1960) described this approach to analysis in a very influential book called *The Rites of Passage,* first published in 1909, but it was a mid-century anthropologist, Victor Turner (1967; 1969), who elaborated anthropological thinking about that transitional period as a space of liminality in which people cease to interact in terms of the accustomed constraints of status and role. Liminality implies a breakdown of social controls and inhibitions that Turner called *communitas.* In group séances and spiritist circles *communitas* was experienced as the freedom to feel and share love.

As noted earlier, the official church of Iceland is rigidly institutionalized in a familiar way, with church buildings, parsonages, a bishop, and ordained pastors. Just as Protestant Christianity is widespread in Western Europe, so too is contemporary spiritism. However, spiritism is much more loosely institutionalized. In England and America some local groups own structures they refer to as churches, but not so in Iceland, where meeting places are conceptualized differently. According to the semantics of Icelandic spiritism, their church-building equivalents are described as research societies, schools, or retreats for personal growth. In addition, the institutionalization of spiritists includes small meditation gatherings that are quite unencumbered by charters, officials, and real property. Yet, these societies, schools, retreats, and private gatherings function as modest, often invisible chapels from which a flowering spirituality sends out tentacles to brighten an otherwise spiritually arid secular society. Many Icelanders only seem to be uninterested in religious values, because their beliefs and feelings are packaged differently from what is encountered elsewhere in the Christian world. They are, in fact, a deeply spiritual people.

THE ICELANDIC SOCIETY FOR SPIRIT RESEARCH

As described in Chapter 3, when modern spiritualism first attracted public attention in Iceland in 1898, those who spoke and wrote about it thought they were investigating a natural phenomenon that was susceptible to testing and documentation in scientific ways. That approach was quite at odds with the way one converts to religion based on faith. A belief in spirits tends to build up gradually. It is a process, and a key to that process is to become convinced that the belief is about something that is real or true (Rambo 1993: 1, 35).

Chapter 3 also showed that institutionalized spiritism in Iceland began in 1905 with the appearance of the first modern medium, Indridi Indridasson. From the beginning, leading scientists investigated Indridi's claims. According to Swatos and Gíssurarson (1997), "this very 'scientific' verification would provide the groundwork for the spiritualistic [spiritist] claim in Icelandic theology to be a more 'modern,' and hence more authentic, understanding of Christianity" (p. 122).

Almost without exception, every spiritist at the beginning of the commitment process puts the believability of mediums to a test. Taking a "show me" approach, each insists on having proof that the spirits are real, that what the spirits reveal is not merely a series of lucky guesses or astute intuitions by mediums or, as some suspect, a telepathic trick whereby the medium was not conversing with a spirit but was "merely" reading the mind of the client. As explained by Gísli, a building contractor who once was president of the spiritist research society, *I have a system. Anything I know can be retrieved from my mind. So for proof, I want to hear something I don't know and can check out later.* But once satisfied with the proof they have identified, many seek further contact with spirits of the dead. The result has been the growth of institutional equivalents to churches where people share an involvement in acts of spirit communication, and in my view, more importantly, where they also share experiences of personal spirituality.

The new spiritism began with a newspaper editor named Einar Kvaran, who set out personally to explore claims that mediums could establish contact with spirits of the dead. He collaborated with friends and relatives as early as 1904 to see if they could entice a spirit into their midst, but without success. They were especially discouraged when one participant received news by way of automatic writing that a relative had died, only to find out later that the man was still very much alive, an early version of the Pentecostal pastor's story of seamen still alive who were said by a medium to have perished in a storm.

After a year of disappointing experiments Kvaran and the others were ready to stop trying when young Indridi happened to attend one of their meetings. To the delight of all, he demonstrated clairvoyant abilities in their very first encounter. It was clear he had potential as a medium, and the informal research group rapidly geared up to center their investigations on him.

What began as casual gatherings became institutionalized as the Experimental Society. Kvaran was elected president and enough money was collected to pay Indridi a modest salary. Instead of a day job, he worked evenings as a professional medium. Séances were held in private homes at first, but eventually the society was able to build a small structure that served not as a church, but as a laboratory for investigative work (Swatos & Gíssurarson 1997: 82–85, 96).

In 1918, the Experimental Society was reformatted as the Icelandic Society for Spirit Research or *Sálarrannsóknarfélag Islands*, SRFI. *Sála* is related to the English word *soul*, but because that term is loaded with Christian implications I have translated it as *spirit; rannsoknar* means *research* and *félag* is usually translated as *society*. To this day, SRFI remains the most prominent organization for spiritualism in Iceland.

The old experimental building has long since disappeared. It was replaced at mid-century by a second-story walk-up apartment on the edge of downtown Reykjavík which serves to this date as a headquarters and meeting place for the society. Closed during the summer months, its dominant winter activity now is to organize the activities of mediums who make themselves available on regular schedules. It is no longer a research society. It has become a kind of spiritual counseling center.

I was told, but did not verify, that some 800 dues-paying members support the center by paying 2,200 kronar per year, about $25 in 2001. In return they are entitled to certain benefits. If there is a waiting list to see a medium, which is usually true of Vigdis, they are given a priority as VIPs. They also pay less for the sitting and are entitled to priorities and discounts for the monthly open meetings when mediums offer public demonstrations. Approximately 10 or 15 attended when Kristjan did his last demonstration, but Vigdis attracted a full house of 35.

According to Gudmundur, the immediate past president of SRFI, 3,000 to 5,000 clients a year come to the headquarters for appointments with one or another of the 10 or so mediums and healers who work as paid professionals. Three or four of the professionals have been on staff for years. Other mediums and healers come and go in unpredictable ways. Some visit from the United Kingdom once a year to work for a week or two at a time, contributing in that way to an international commonality of beliefs and practices. Between October 1999 and May 2000, five English mediums—three men and two women—worked in Reykjavík, which is about the average from one year to another. In addition, Siggi regularly comes south from Akureyri once a month.

The usual charge for a sitting is 4,500 KR (about $50). Clients come for a variety of reasons, but most often to visit with deceased loved ones, to inquire about past lives, to seek healing, to get advice about personal problems, or to ask the spirits for predictions of what the future holds.

Some come mainly out of curiosity or just for the fun of it, as Gudmundur explained. *I often participate in testing mediums who want to practice at the center. When I meet with a candidate, I don't especially want to connect with the spirit world or to meet with loved ones. I want to talk about the energy available to me. When a relative dies, yes, it can be a great comfort, especially since you usually have to wait a while for the first encounter, but I don't need to repeat that visit very often.*

Except for occasional pick-up conversations in the waiting room, like patients waiting to see a doctor, these appointments are solitary affairs between the client and the medium. Individuals come and go without socializing or forming a collectivity.

The steep entry stairway leads to a reception and business office on the right where Ragnheidr, the salaried administrator, greets everyone, answers phone calls, handles correspondence, does bookkeeping, arranges schedules for mediums and healers, sets up appointments for clients, processes money or credit cards, and issues receipts. Moving from Ragnheidr's domain to the left of the stairway, clients are invited to sit and meditate while they wait to be seen.

In contrast to the well-lit, efficient, no-frills office, the waiting room offers a soothing, quieting opportunity to ease out of the city and into another dimension. The window curtain is always closed, admitting only a soft glow through its blue-patterned folds. Lighted candles abound, illuminating the Salvador Dali picture of Christ Ascendant and old photographs of Kvaran and other founders of Icelandic spiritism as well as a tall white porcelain figurine of a winged Madonna holding baby Jesus, softly illuminated by a candle. Sinking into a comfortable chair, a sense of the sacred in this supposedly secular establishment is further enhanced by soft, soothing meditational music, the harmonies of outer space.

When the appointed hour arrives your medium ushers you into a room that has its own closed curtains, candles, pictures, and porcelain figurines. The medium will seat herself in a comfortable, well-upholstered armchair, directly under a statuette of Jesus, and you will sit facing her. If you brought a friend or relative, he or she will be invited to sit nearby on a couch and will probably be alerted to the possibility, even the likelihood, that a spirit may come to see him or her rather than you as the primary client. When my co-investigator Kristín was with me to videotape one of my sittings with Vigdis, a spirit ended up offering medical advice to Kristín, leaving me to handle the camera. It is unusual to videotape a séance but I was welcome to do so because it is quite usual to do an audiotape that the client can review later and share with others.

The waiting room can be rearranged for small meetings by placing chairs in a semicircle facing the visiting speaker or medium. Remember, the headquarters was originally constructed as a small apartment, so as an assembly hall it will only seat a maximum of about 35 people. When Deborah, the English transfiguration medium, did her demonstration for members of the board of trustees, chairs were set out for 22 people, and for the demonstration by Catherine, the new medium from England, only 13 chairs were occupied. This room, with a mere hint of the sacred, resembles a small college classroom more than the sanctuary of a church.

Audiotaping meetings with spirits of the departed is so much the custom that the waiting and séance rooms are wired for easy plug-ins. The original goal of documenting spirit contacts was greatly eased after World War II when electronic recording equipment made it possible to preserve what might transpire for later review and analysis, but inexplicably, no archive was created. The society cuts a tape of nearly every séance, but they are for clients to take away. When Gísli was president some years ago, he accumulated an estimated 700 tapes as a personal archive, but no one has systematically transcribed them, and they gather dust in his attic without ever having been described and evaluated. As mentioned earlier, research is no longer an active part of the society's program.

When I discussed this matter with Gudmundur, shortly after he stepped down as president in 2000, he explained that he had never believed in the value of doing scientific research. *We have no research agenda,* he told me. *It is more important that each individual research the correctness of what spirits tell them, and that they learn how to achieve spiritual development and growth.*

Beyond Reykjavík, the society maintains a loose affiliation with a network of more than a score of affiliated societies in other Icelandic communities. The only one I visited was in Akureyri, a city in the north of Iceland. It was essentially a smaller and quite independent replica of the mother society, centered on providing facilities and organizational support for a few local mediums. The Akureyri center has its own unique logo, which Siggi told me was given them by the spirit of an American Indian. It consists of a pair of praying hands, a cross, and a triangle. The hands symbolize belief, the cross, to Siggi at least, is like a candle, a symbol of light, and the three corners of the triangle represent faith, hope, and love. Printed prayers, both Christian and generic, are given to clients to take home for later devotional use, a reminder that most people see no need to choose between secular spiritism and sacred Christianity.

The society in Reykjavík organizes meditation and spiritual development circles in which, for a quite modest fee, clients meet weekly in the winter for spiritual exercises. I never attended a circle meeting sponsored by the society, but most mediums in Iceland do not work out of the society and most spiritist circles are informally organized, often without including a medium.

I spoke with several individuals who are active in spiritist circles, two of which were sponsored by the society and two of which organized themselves informally. I could detect no difference based on whether or not they were SRFI sponsored and was told that they all function in much the same way for spirituality and socializing. These are the hidden chapels I referred to, but before describing them, let me continue to discuss the formal institutions that have evolved.

THE ICELANDIC SCHOOL FOR SPIRIT RESEARCH

In 1994 Magnus Skarphedinsson rented space in an office building and branched off from the Icelandic Spirit Research Society, proclaiming there was a need to return to the original scientific agenda of the old Experimental Society and to establish a school where spiritist thinking could be studied and taught. Without a doubt he also branched off because he is personally ambitious and works best when unencumbered by committees and board members. His so-called spirit school, sometimes referred to as the elf school, because he offers a short summer course on that subject for tourists, was not so much a heretical breakaway as an independent, unaffiliated extension of the SRFI program.

He spoke of his vision for the school as becoming *a bridge between the religious experiment and the experiment of life on Earth. To learn to cope with the big disadvantages of Western civilization, its frustrations, violence, abuse, alcoholism.* He paused, and then added, *I don't know any other way to raise ethics and morality than to tell people about the benefits of spiritism, which changes people totally, because that is when you get plugged into reality. You see all the answers, the logic in it. You see what God might be. You see your life in perspective. Peoples' lives in the afterworld are many times fuller than ours.*

When I examined my videos and notes to write about the daily life of spirits, I was not able to confirm that claim to greater fullness. From the descriptions I got, and especially from those I got from Magnus, I concluded that daily life in the spirit world is described as being very much what it is on Earth for most people: humdrum, predictable, and uneventful.

Magnus continued, struggling to help me understand. *Society needs to know that there is life after death and that everything you do waits for you. When you die, you have to go over it. If you murdered someone, the victim is the first person you meet, and you have to resolve your differences. If you tortured someone, you have to get him to forgive you. You will be totally stuck in the Gray Place until these relationships are worked out. It is not a matter of God, of a judge. It is not Jesus. It is totally a matter-of-fact thing. If you do this, and then this, then this happens.* (I don't see that, for example, as living a life that is fuller than ours, but evidently Magnus does.)

Fast-forwarding a bit, Magnus affirmed another seemingly religious concept, but why not? For him as for most spiritists, religion and science are not merely compatible. They are mutually supportive, defying social science analysts who would differentiate the one kind of institution from the other in their search for neat binary oppositions. *Prayer does work. You can get rid of grief and get good health, but it's just physical-technical things. You must think about life. You can call it Jesus, whatever you want, you know.* He folded his hands as he proceeded his wrap-up on how to live a moral life. *It's very good to go directly to the energy, the powers that float round you, and you feel much better. It has nothing to do with religion.*

Given that he had just said we were not talking about religion I did a double take when he added, *God does exist. You can talk with him anytime.* But then I remembered that God for Magnus is not a bearded patriarch on a throne. *God is whatever you call him: super-mind, super-character, super-force, care, whatever. God is on duty all of the time.* With that he gestured a prayerful attitude with his hands and made a statement that reminded me of what I had learned when Halldór talked with me about the protective presence of his long-dead grandfather. **My students don't feel alone** [emphasis added]. *They manage much better in life. The crux of this education is to teach them the benefits of spiritism—not religion—but what comes out of scientific research.* To paraphrase André Droogers, a Dutch anthropologist, one might say it is true that Magnus does not have a religion, but it is also true that he is very religious (Greenfield & Droogers 2001: 156).

The school is listed in the telephone book as *Sálarrannsóknarskólinn Islands*, SRSI (the "s" stands for *skólinn,* which means *school*). As a voluntary association it was complementary rather than competitive with SRFI until 1999. The ability of these two institutions to coexist for 5 years when, in fact, their leaders were not true admirers of one another, is testimony to the tolerance of Icelanders for deviance and independence.

It helped, too, that until 1999 the two institutions met different needs. The spirit school did not organize one-on-one sittings with mediums, which are the bread and butter of the older society. Instead, its main activities, not duplicated in the old society, were to convene weekly group séances, which were tape-recorded for research purposes, and to teach evening courses about the history and nature of spiritism. As a minor fund-raising activity, it also operated the summer elf school for foreigners. The old society does not organize regular group séances, maintain a research archive, or schedule classroom programs.

As the program director, business manager, and sole full-time professor of the school, Magnus offers lectures and demonstrations in the winter courses. His teaching is supplemented by visiting lecturers, usually mediums who discuss their work, and occasionally by others. Gudmundur, while president of SRFI, taught there a couple of times before their complete estrangement. So did I.

Three 12-week courses are taught, ranked as introductory, intermediate, and advanced, although I did not have the impression that the curriculum is all that rigorously organized. Each course meets once a week for 3 hours plus time after for coffee, waffles smothered in berries and whipped cream, and conversation. The last meeting convenes solely for a class party, when the most important task is to pose for a group picture. One wall of the school is covered with these class pictures. In all, Magnus

A full classroom at the Spirit Research School

estimates that they enroll about 100 students each winter. The fee is 2,800 KR (approximately $30) per student, which students tell me is a bargain.

GROUP SÉANCES AS A RESEARCH PROGRAM

A second major activity of the school has been and is to schedule group séances. Participants pay 1,300 KR (about $15) each time they attend. They come because it is interesting, fulfilling, or convivial, but research is the primary official agenda. Magnus reports that as of November 2000 he had 307 tape recordings of séances. He wants spirits in this way to teach people about the afterlife, to document an ethnography of the spirit world, so he always asks about what they are doing, what they like, their beliefs and rituals, almost as though he kept a copy of the old *Notes and Queries* handbook for anthropologists on his lap. At present these tapes constitute a resource primarily for the courses he teaches, since he sometimes plays excerpts to illustrate a lecture. His hope is to have them transcribed someday and posted on a website for the use of scholars all over the world. He also hopes to publish scholarly reports in five

European languages sometime in the future when he expects to establish a journal.

Unlike the classroom which is brightly lit, filled with chairs, and oriented to a blackboard, the séance room is small, dimly lit, and suffused with gentle background music. About 20 chairs are arranged in a large circle. Located farthest from the door, the medium sits in the circle with everyone else. The moderator, who is always Magnus, is positioned at a small table facing the medium, keeping as busy as the pilot of a small plane. Using a handheld remote control he modulates the volume of meditational music from a CD player perched on a shelf above and behind the circle. At the same time he constantly adjusts the tape recorder that picks up from microphones dangling over the medium's chair and his own command table. He also makes written notations on a form that will be filed away as a permanent summary of what transpires in each meeting.

Obviously skilled at multitasking, Magnus manages simultaneously and without apparent difficulty to do nearly all of the talking as well, the main exception being that spirits also speak as they respond to his questions and converse with him through the possessed medium. Others in the circle may also question a spirit, but only occasionally and briefly. In every séance I attended other than these at the spirit school, the conversation was always between a client and either the medium speaking for the spirit or the possessing spirit as such. No third party was involved as moderator.

Magnus breaks with tradition in other ways as well. While everyone is settling in he likes to tell jokes, which he reads from joke books. They have nothing to do with spiritism, and not everyone finds them amusing, especially since they are invariably quite corny. He invites participants to tell their jokes as well, but the response is usually desultory. I guess he is demonstrating that in contrast to church gatherings with their staid formalities, his soirées are secular. Spirits are as natural as living humans, even though they are usually invisible. (It takes enormous energy for a spirit to become visible, Magnus once told me, so it is rare for them to materialize.) Being neither sacred nor supernatural, good-humored laughter is not inappropriate.

The sitting takes a serious turn when one of the regulars is given a few pages to read out loud. Usually the reading is from the folklore of elves and hidden folk, another practice that breaks with spiritist custom. One evening, for example, the reading was about events that supposedly happened on a 19th-century farm partly owned by elves, whose property included one of the hayfields. When a new owner took possession, he decided that leaving a field unharvested for the hidden folk was just nonsense, so he started to cut the grass. That night, an elf approached a hired woman in a dream and told her to warn the farmer not to cut their grass. The farmer disregarded that warning and was punished when his best horse died later in the winter. The next year he brought in the elf harvest again, and that time half of his sheep died. With that he finally realized he had to take the elves seriously, so he stopped stealing their hay, and from then on prospered.

The séance room, which also serves as a library, is filled with plaster of Paris dwarfs, looking exactly like Santa's helpers in an American department store window, and with soft plastic trolls with bushy hair and shiny eyes that were popular items a decade ago in carnivals and toy stores all over Europe and North America. Most of the figurines are thoughtful-looking men with beards and pipes who wear bright colored stocking caps and knickers or lederhosen. Some look a lot like Disney's seven dwarfs. Magnus assured me that clairvoyants who can see dwarfs and trolls have confirmed that they really look like that. Disney, Neiman Marcus, and Toys R Us somehow got it right.

Also, invisible elves regularly possess the medium and answer questions. This is rare outside the school. I only heard of it for one other medium. Even more surprising, many of the elves are not dead at all, although they may be a couple of hundred years old. It should be noted, however, that while elves or hidden people appear in every Magnus organized séance, the medium mostly is possessed by the spirits of dead human beings.

Magnus warned us that what we learn from the spirits of deceased humans is confidential because we will be talking with spirits about their former lives and present circumstances. We must respect their privacy and the feelings of surviving friends and relatives, including those who may be mentioned by name as the spirit talks with us. Of course, it is also those private revelations that make it possible to "prove" that they really did once live in Iceland, where death certificates and funeral notices can be checked to confirm the truth of what they say about themselves.

After reminding us of our ethical responsibilities, Magnus led us in a "meditation," which I would characterize as an hypnotic induction. *Think about what is going on in your body,* he said. *Imagine yourself suffused with power. The flow of energy is excellent today. Feel it moving through your body from top to bottom. The stresses of the day are beginning to fall away. You are relaxed, and now we are going on a journey.*

From a manuscript provided by Magnus, one participant then read out loud in the same vein. *We are going on a journey to the east of the country,* the reader intoned. *Settle comfortably into your seats. We are leaving this room. Now we are on the roof of the building* [which is 6 stories high]. *Imagine that we are floating over the city, sitting in this circle as if in the gondola of a balloon. We can see the streets of Reykjavík below us. All is quiet and calm. We see the whole city as we look around. Most of the people are peacefully in their homes. We move eastwards towards the mountains. A different energy blows in from the mountains and we feel it flow into ourselves, coming through our feet and upwards. High over the mountains we sense energy that is also blowing in from the sea. We stop for a while, enjoying the breezes and feeling refreshed. The energy from the sea is very different from the energy of the mountains and we feel how they blend. Now it is time to turn homewards again. We gradually move from wintry cold over the mountains to being warm and comfortable in the city. We find ourselves in the building again and back in this room, filled with the energy we have absorbed on our flight. We give thanks for this.*

After that virtual flight to a mountaintop, we hold hands to close the circle. One person says his name, which is followed by silence. The next person silently counts to 10 before saying her name. Magnus tells us that by waiting before speaking your name, you shift the energy from the last person to yourself, after which you think about the next person and shift the energy to him. In that way, a wave of energy slowly unites the circle.

Still holding hands, Magnus prepares us for the first spirit who will arrive. *Let's think about those who are in the Gray Place, those who are cold. And as we think about them they are getting warmer. Let us continue to think about them.* As he speaks the medium is stirring. Her body gestures and facial expressions are changing. She is deep in trance and becoming possessed. Magnus senses that the spirit has now occupied her body and taken over her consciousness, so he utters a welcome. *Good day.* (Pause) *Good day.* (Pause) *Are you awake?* The spirit answers sleepily and with hesitation, *Yeah. Yeah.* With that Magnus begins to draw him out. In this instance it is the spirit of a man who died the year before.

At the end of the conversation between Magnus and the spirit Magnus says, *Thank you very much. Goodbye.* We hold hands again and Magnus informs us that we would like to talk to another spirit, on this evening, a second spirit from the Gray Place. It, too, ends with *thank you very much and goodbye.* Magnus is ready now to continue his ethnographic documentation of the culture of hidden people. He quietly murmurs, *Let's try to feel how the energy feels from above. Let's all hold hands and we'll do an experiment. Feel that energy flowing down. Let's think about the Supreme Being as we take off on a small journey. Floating high in the sky we are approaching a place in the far north near Akureyri where we see a valley in which the hidden people live. It is covered with snow. In the distance we see the lights of Akureyri, but below us in the*

Robert Anderson

Coffee and conversation in the spirit school kitchen

valley we see two hidden people, a man and a woman. We wonder what their relationship may be with nearby rock people. The world of the hidden people [elves] and the world of the rock people [trolls] are in conflict. We continue to direct our thoughts to the Supreme Being.

As this monologue droned on, the medium began to fidget in her chair and to stretch her neck and turn her head. A hidden lady who is still alive began to speak with us using Sesselja's voice, continuing until it was time again to say goodbye. Then Magnus said, *Let's hold hands and prepare for what's ahead. Let's think about the Supreme Being.* We fell into a prolonged silence. The mood music, present but unnoticed, increased in volume. *Let us concentrate on how the energy is flowing through us. First we're going to float upwards 2 meters high, then 5 meters. Now we are 10 and 20 meters high. We feel warm as we float above the fjord. Down below we glimpse the lights of a small town. Now we have turned from moving northwards to a southwards return and are gliding back into Reykjavík. We see city streets and cars moving. Our building comes into sight. Now we are descending through the roof and are back here in this room.*

Let's think now about the medical clinic. Quiet takes over for a minute or two. *Let us concentrate on the energy that flows through us as we sit comfortably in our seats.* The medium shows signs of possession. *Good day.* This time it is the spirit of a deceased physician, a man who was personally known to her and to Magnus before he died. After a brief greeting, we take turns, each asking him to make a house call on someone we care about who is not well. After making those appointments, Magnus questions the doctor about his activities that day as a part of his ethno-graphic research, but then the answers seem to indicate that it is time to part and Magnus says, *Well, goodbye. Goodbye,* the doctor answers.

Magnus continues, *Now we are holding hands. We are going to fly over the highway,* and so on. We meet a deceased farmer who tells us about his life in a rather pleasant part of the spirit world known as the Summerland. Finally, Sesselja's guide possesses her and asks, *Yeah, yeah. Do you want to stay longer?* Sesselja herself responds to the spirit saying, *No, they are getting back pain, and that's not a good feeling.* Magnus joc-ularly interjects, *No, it's not their backs, it's their stomachs. They're think-ing of waffles and coffee.* The medium or the guide, I'm not sure which, responded in equal good humor, *I think that is enough for today. I hope you felt good and that it did you some good. Thank you for the time we spent together, and goodbye.*

For a last time, Magnus has us hold hands as he soothingly speaks of energy flows, the sounds of music, the colors of a rainbow. We are encour-aged to wrap ourselves in energy as we ease out of the séance and back into our ordinary lives. We sit silently in contemplation for what seems a long time until Magnus ends the session by saying, *Now I thank you—very much.* We stand, move slowly, and gradually emerge into the fully lighted anteroom and the kitchen where we chat amiably over coffee, cakes, cookies, and waffles loaded with preserves and whipped cream.

THE POLITICS OF SPIRITIST INSTITUTIONS

Until 1999 the two institutions, SRFI and SRSI, were almost entirely noncompetitive. In that year, however, Magnus relocated to larger quar-ters in a new four-story office building where part of the second floor is now owned rather than leased. The change of address was unimportant, since the new quarters remain close to where the old had been. What is truly different is an expanded and transformed agenda. Magnus now competes directly with the original society as he attempts to become "the" national society for spiritism, the true descendant of Einar Kvaran and the 19th-century Experimental Society. This sectarianism threatens to break up an institutional tranquillity that lasted for a century.

The spirit school and group séances continue unchanged in the new society. In addition, however, Magnus has engaged six mediums who meet with clients in private sittings, using rooms set aside for that purpose, and he would like to double that number. The fee for a sitting is 3,800 KR (about $45) and he claims that 1,300 medium visits took place in the preceding year and a half, which is all the mediums could handle. Another 1,300 clients are on a waiting list, he told me. Perhaps that is so.

To handle the various activities of the new center, a full-time office manager was hired. Her job is to take care of scheduling, payments, book-keeping, and so on. In short, the main functions of the old original society are now completely duplicated and even exceeded in the renegade new one.

The renegade has even taken over the respected old name itself. In the Reykjavik telephone directory a listing for *Sálarrannsóknarfélag Reykjavíkur* (SRFR, which is Magnus' new Spirit Research Society of Reykjavík) looks as though it ought to be a local branch of *Sálarrannsóknarfélag Islands* (the old Spirit Research Society of Iceland). Magnus has also listed his new organization simply as *Sálarrannsóknarfélagid* (The Spirit Research Society). Old clients, sup-porters, and donors of SRFI are said to sometimes call the new society and not realize, and also not be told, that they have made a mistake.

Gudmundur, still effectively in charge of SRFI, and Magnus, as pres-ident of the new SRFR, openly accuse one another of malfeasance in office, gross deception, outright lies, and spiritist heresy. I have no idea what really goes on behind the scenes and despair of coming to a judg-ment of who is right or wrong. However, it appears that there is enough demand to keep both organizations busy supplying mediumistic services in a busy spiritist marketplace. Magnus claims to have 3,600 members who pay a relatively small fee of 950 KR (about $10) a year in return for benefits similar to those of the old society. I have no way of confirming membership claims for either of these institutions.

What I find especially noteworthy, however, is that the new denomi-national spiritism has created small but intense secular congregations by bringing people together in classes and séances. Participants get acquainted and share their spirituality in these events and they socialize afterward in the kitchen. Whereas SRFI face-to-face meetings continue to be brief and ephemeral, those of the SRSI are periodic, repetitive, interactive, intimate, and enjoyable. And other venues for socializing have also evolved.

INFORMAL MEDITATION GROUPS

Siggi, the only medium I got to know at the Akureyri society, told me that seven people meet with him every Tuesday, all but one being women. The purpose is to help him develop, because even though he has had years of experience and is respected throughout Iceland for his skills, he still hopes to improve in accuracy and clarity. In those Tuesday evening sittings, he passes on messages from the spirit world to his sitters. The sitters help by providing spiritual energy that makes him more effective. They are just ordinary people. None besides Siggi is a medium, he told me, although several work as psychic healers.

When in England, Deborah does the same thing. She is developing as a physical medium that way, as I described in an earlier chapter. However, the practice is no longer common in Iceland, although Gudmundur of the Spirit Research Society told me it was in the recent past. *People used to meet once or twice a week for years with a developing medium. Now they just meet in spiritist circles.* I did not interpret that comment as a put-down for circles. On the contrary, he recalls his own experience in a circle of eight or nine people as one of spiritual growth.

Recalling that experience, Gudmundur laid emphasis on how it prepared him for his independent private devotions. *I meditated for a whole year. At first nothing happened. It took time. Each night on going to sleep I would ask for something to happen. I kept a paper and pen by the bed just in case, and at last it started. Part of the time I would try to go back and forth in time. Going into the past was easier than going into the future, which in theory is no problem, because you are traveling light, just in your mind.*

Our conversation then shifted to another topic, which was fine by me at the time, because we had that discussion quite early in my Icelandic fieldwork and I was groping for an overall orientation. Unfortunately, although I met Gudmundur a number of times over the next couple of years, I never remembered to ask for more details about his circle. However, I did get descriptions from others and I found all of them quite remarkable.

JÓHANNA'S SPIRITIST CIRCLE

I was fascinated to learn about this woman's spirit-filled life. You will recall that earlier I described how her grandparents were listening in on our conversation while we were in her front room. Later I wrote about a family party when the spirit of her deceased daughter showed up to greet everyone, another time, about visits with her deceased mother-in-law, and also about how she learned to heal by the laying on of hands. But Jóhanna was also the first to provide a somewhat more detailed description of a spiritist circle, and it is that I turn to now.

I first sat with my prayer circle about 10 years ago when I began to work more within the spirit. How did you become a member of that circle? *It was through the Spiritist Research Society of Iceland. I attended their meetings out of curiosity. One time a British medium was doing a demonstration and she picked out five of us, one couple, two men, and me, and said we should form a circle. We did, and we are still together, meeting twice a month on Wednesdays in the home of one of the men who is an old widower.* Do you meet all through the year? *No, not in the summer. We begin around the end of September or the first of October.*

Can you tell me what you do when you meet? *We pray to God. Sometimes in our meetings we all see colors with our eyes closed.* What do the colors signify? *Blue is the color of spirits and white, of lights, but I'm not good at what the colors mean. At other times we detect smells.* Smells? *Yes. For example, of tobacco,* whereupon she pointed to a portrait of her grandfather and said that when he is in the room she can smell his presence.

Jóhanna then explained that they do group healing. *Usually the spirits come when I am relaxing, sitting in the circle or in my kitchen. After the circle on a Wednesday I sit in my kitchen around 11 o'clock. We meet at 8:00 in the evening, but after going home we try to continue being together the hour before midnight, each in our own home. That's when we send healings to people who are sick.*

Whom do you heal that way? *It can be anybody.* Tell me about the last time you sent healing. *It was my father, who had an operation on his knee and had asked that his name be put in the book of those who need healing, so I entered his name in our circle book. It works better if all of us join to send healing.* Did your father get better as a result? *Oh yes. The next day he said, "I'm feeling better," and after a week he said, "I'm very, very good now."* So your circle sent healing energy to him? *Yes.* Do people know when you send healing? *Sometimes they know and sometimes they don't. In this case he knew.*

How are the spirits involved when you do healing? *I call the spirits my helpers. I think they are relatives, but I also have a French nun who comes to give me peace of mind. She also shows up in our circle. I was told that by a medium.*

Jóhanna meandered verbally here and there in telling me about the spiritist circle and at this point I realized that for her, the circle is just part of her daily involvement with the spirit world and not a container for it, so at one moment she was, in terms of my interests, off trail as she continued. *A different medium told me I have a lot of people close by who help me, including spirit doctors. They know what's wrong. They may be specialists in some way, and they come and cure people. I'm just the receiver. I do like this,* and she placed one hand on each leg as she sat, palms facing upward toward the sky. *I have the names and addresses of the sick in our prayer book and my helpers come to me through my head and then go to heal those who are sick. I sit in my chair at home and they go and do the healing. When I close my hands the spirits go away.*

Do you know who the spirit doctors are? *Not quite. I have not seen who comes to heal. I have seen my nun,* and then, apparently referring to the circle again, she continued. *Another lady with me may be the spirit of an American Indian. Other mediums say they have seen her. They have told me of Icelandic doctors too, but I don't know who they are. Also, there are different kinds of doctors from other countries. I know they are there. I feel them. I feel better when they are around me, but I can't see them. Not yet.*

MARTA'S SPIRITIST CIRCLE

When I transcribed my interview with Jóhanna, I realized that I had gotten more detail about the workings of a spiritist circle from her than I had teased out of Gudmundur, but I wanted still more. Marta, who has never met Jóhanna, became my key informant on this topic, beginning with our first encounter. As a 17-year-old waitress Marta had seen the ghost of a woman in Norway and more recently as a married woman was awakened by ghosts in a youth hostel in the north of Iceland. She is certain that spirits, including that of her grandmother, assist her in healing work. But those excerpts from her spiritual life do not do justice to the beauty and serenity she finds in working with the spirit world through what she refers to as meditation circles.

When she mentioned that she had seen the spirit of her grandmother I asked her to tell me more about that relationship. She explained, *When I was growing up as a 16- and 17-year-old we discovered that we had things in common, like an interest in history and philosophy or anything having to do with the spiritual. I had been interested in spiritual things from the age of 13, but it was several years before I realized that she was also interested.*

Their sharing of spiritual interests continued after death. *I was part of a meditation group that met to talk about psychological and spiritual things. I have seen spirits. I have seen people who have passed away. In this group we were developing this sensitivity, this ability that everyone has to connect with the spirit world if they are open to it. One day during a circle meeting, just before we were to take a break, the leader said, "We have the spirit of a former medium here." We were all excited as we went out for our customary break, thinking that someone in the group would have a chance to develop her skill.*

We were outside during the break, smoking and sipping coffee. Usually I enjoyed that time of camaraderie, but on that particular evening I felt really strange. I stood aside, uninvolved in the chatting, feeling strange in a way I can't really describe, except that I felt as if I had a hat on my head, a pointy hat, like a witch's hat. I felt ridiculous, awkward, and quite unable to really speak with the others.

Back in the room we returned to our places, but I still had this funny feeling, and the girls were looking at me. The leader was asking us all how we felt, and when she got to me she said, "You look a bit absentminded. What are you feeling?" I answered that I felt I had this stupid hat on my head and felt ridiculous. "Aha," she said. "Okay, and what else do you feel?" I said, "I feel this great warmth in my heart." I felt as though I was almost in tears, a sort of happy-sad feeling, an overwhelming feeling of happiness and sorrow. Instantly some person appeared, right in front of me at a distance of about a meter. I couldn't see the face very clearly, but I could feel the link and speak to her from my heart, or maybe it was from my forehead, but it was not with words. For some strange reason I sensed that this was my great-grandmother, but then the face cleared and I thought, "No, no, this is Helga, my father's mother. **She was telling me that she was with me, that I shouldn't doubt it, that she was there** [emphasis added]."

This unexpected appearance of her grandmother elicited powerful emotions. *I was overwhelmed with this feeling of warmth—and sorrow—and happiness—and I still had that silly hat on my head. There wasn't much communication with her, except that she was just making me realize, and, yes, confirming,* **that she was there** [emphasis in the original]. *I thanked her for coming and excused my confusion. I said I was sorry for being uncertain about her presence, because with my doubt I was probably almost pushing her away.*

Then a man appeared alongside of one of the other women in the group. He gave a name that didn't seem to have any meaning for that woman, and I didn't know him. I was aware that other spirits were present, but I only clearly saw my grandmother and this man. They were visible to me again and again during that evening. The leader of the circle said that the medium spirit had come to help me receive spirits, that he had not come to the others, and that was why only I could see my grandmother and the stranger.

That was a very powerful group, I said. *Oh, yes!* Do you still meet? *No. We had this course, which lasted 14 weeks,* and then she told me it had been organized by a branch of the Spirit Research Society of Iceland in a suburb of Reykjavík. *I got into this group because I went to see a medium there, the only time I have been to a medium. She said I was very sensitive, that I had this ability, and asked if I would like to join a group of others to develop these skills. "Yes," I said, so she rounded up some people. I chose the night, which was on Thursdays, the group met, and that was it.* How much did it cost? *Oh, not much. We paid 1,000 KR* (a bit over $10) *every time we met,* so it came to about $150 for the 14 weeks.

Then Marta described a typical evening. *We would begin with a bit of chanting together. Then we would talk about how we were feeling psychologically and spiritually. After that we linked ourselves together.* I interrupted to be sure I understood what she was saying, thinking of how we held hands to form a circle at the séances sponsored by the spirit school. *No, we didn't hold hands, we linked up by meditating as a group. As we meditated we relaxed and felt this drawing together. It was a grand feeling. We made ourselves huge, all coming together in a circle in which we could feel each other's energy flow. Our auras united.*

Aha, I thought, auras. I hated to interrupt the eloquent flow, but couldn't resist the temptation to ask, could you see the auras? *No, I didn't see them in those sessions, but I often see auras.* Then she picked up her narrative so gently that it washed over the interruption like a wave smoothing sand on a beach. *Together we gave energy, sent energy, beamed energy to people who had requested healing by having their names written in a book that we placed at the center of our circle. We turned our palms up and I always could feel these lines from each of us arching over to the center, and I could see this pillar of light over the book, very bright, very beautiful, in different colors and different patterns, but most of the time just a bright light. The energy flow from us sort of linked up and coalesced into this pillar of light. And I felt like there was a depression in the palm of my hand and I felt like a thick rope was being pulled out of my hand, feeling really warm and nice, and it was as though many ropes were being woven or plaited together. It was a grand feeling. I really felt that this was good.*

Do you know if people were healed? *Yeah, well, the feeling was we were all giving and someone was receiving and I—we—absolutely trusted that. And sometimes without asking people whose names I had put in our book—well—for example, my mother, I had put in her name, and she told me later that she had this feeling of "well-being" and "a strange feeling" exactly the night we were doing this. I felt a very strong emotional tie to my mother that evening and she had things clear up for her, so I felt that was a kind of physical confirmation, although I don't need that. Each of us could also think of people who were healed spiritually as well as physically, without our being egotistic about it.* Did you ever get feedback on somebody with cancer or some other serious disease? *No, we weren't looking for that. Maybe the person running the center might be able to tell you. She keeps these books with names and uses them for one group after another, so maybe she knows.*

Marta has an enviable ability to articulate her feelings and thoughts, and I was pleased when I got her to talk about what the meditation circle accomplished for her. *It combined three things for me, she explained. I work long hours and have a lot of responsibilities, and when I'm not working I go home to my husband and my girls and, really, I'm last on the list in terms of doing things for myself. So participating in the circle was a way for me to take one evening for myself. That was very important.*

In addition, the circle was like a hobby. It allowed me to practice something I'm interested in, anything having to do with the supernatural and with spiritual things, and it gave me a lot, doing what I am really interested in with other people.

Also, it was like a group session with a psychologist because we became so intimate. In this group I talked about things I have never discussed with anybody else. I got out of it what I would have gotten from a very good psychiatrist, and it was absolutely without commitment beyond those times together. We had no other links with each other. That freed you up? *Yes. Absolutely. We became very close, but just for Thursday nights. I haven't seen them since. I like that. We had a great time. The others often saw each other from week to week, but not me, in part because I don't live in their suburb.*

Tell me more about how you meditated. *I have meditated on my own quite often, quite a lot, and that's good. It's great. But to meditate with others in silence—nobody says anything—is a great experience. And also, it was another kind of meditation, when you visualize and there is one person leading the group. She was so connected, and she would take us somewhere.* As Marta spoke, I sensed a resemblance to what Magnus does when we are joined in a circle and he takes us on an imaginary journey. *She talked, like telling a story, and while in a deep meditational state we went along with her to different places, maybe out of this world, to some strange place, which she would describe.*

We sensed what she was describing and experienced all sorts of things while we were there. Often we would come back with something like colorful stars or strange pebbles, or something else that we would add to our spiritual kit. We would keep these [imagined] objects for ourselves and after the session we would talk about them.

She took us to an imagined lake, for example. One member of the circle would dive into the lake and see things under water. Others would puddle. Somebody else found a rock beside the lake and climbed up on it and looked into the lake. And what about yourself? *I puddled a bit, and then I found a rock that I climbed on to get a view over the lake, and I looked into the water.* What did that do for your spirit? *I always came back refreshed. I had seen a new place. I felt good there. I came back with a beautiful new place to visualize that was equal to a real place in my mind.*

Did you tell your family about it? *Yes, I tell them about it. But most importantly, I would bring calm. In those weekly sessions I learned to focus, to relax, to react in a different way, because in part it worked as a psychiatric treatment. If I had any problems, especially if I had big ones, I would bring them out in the sessions without deciding to do it before-hand. So I'd have a think about problems at work—they all have to do with communication, which I find is one of the most important things in life. Everything depends on how we communicate with each other.*

As a woman with other women could you share in a way different from how it is with men present? *I think so, yeah, but it also works with a mixed group, although I have never participated in a circle that included men. We could discuss things we would not have gotten into if men were there. Women together do talk about things they don't discuss with men.*

What kind of meditation do you practice? (Pause) Do you have a mantra? *No. I use what I learned in the beginning, which is just simple relaxation and breathing.* Were you taught how to breath? *Yeah, I learned by reading a book. I am self-taught in that way. I concentrate on the breathing and before I know it I'm in a state. I tend to go quite deep. Sometimes I lose myself, which is not positive. I go too deep. There is a feeling of pulsation, kind of inside and out, and my body moves,* which she demonstrated by rocking back and forth in her chair. *I lose control. It's like my body, the circulation of blood, is pumping. It's okay for a while. It's okay, and then I just come out of it. But I'm not as refreshed as at other times.*

CONCLUSION

Circles offer a well-established way in which people can experience and develop their spiritual capabilities. Believing that contact with spirits happens all the time provides an explanation; it postulates a mechanism that underwrites circle activities. Participants are able to make sense of what they experience because spirits are thought of as supernormal. However, quite apart from spiritism in that sense, these circles expand, elaborate, and deepen the mutuality I encountered in the spirit school séances, when we held hands in a circle, sent a spirit doctor off to heal people we cared about, and enjoyed one another afterward over coffee and waffles. It is an experience of spirituality, not to be confused with spirit contact as such.

It is difficult to articulate what I mean by spirituality. Gudmundur reminded me of that difficulty just days before the end of my first long visit, when I was preparing to return to California. *When we first met,* he told me, *you gave the impression you wanted to stay outside and look in at us without being involved. But now you have been involved and you know.* Yes, I have been very involved, I agreed, but what I know is still circumscribed, because in the end I am destined always to remain an outsider. Given that disclaimer, here is what I concluded.

Circles and group séances create moments of togetherness, what Victor Turner calls *communitas,* that allow participants to break out of the social constraints of daily life and the demands that normally dominate and confine self-awareness. They become what Turner would characterize as a kind of anti-structure. That is, they create moments when the usual demands of status and role fall away and an individual can experience the joy of being alive through a transcendence of self. One's sense of personal identity is modified in such a way that what is deeply personal becomes a shared sense of mutuality. One might call it love and compassion as the circle reaches out to heal the suffering of others. I call that spirituality. It requires no belief in the supernatural. However, it requires that one experience others in the circle as self and individuals beyond the circle as extensions of self and that is truly remarkable.

NEW AGE ELVES
AND FAIRIES

GLOBALIZATION AND SYNCRETISM

Until a few decades ago anthropologists tended to equate a culture with a society. For the most part, they wrote about the cultures of individual tribes or villages. Less commonly, they were challenged to describe the cultures of nations. Because a nation is shot through with ethnic, regional, and other kinds of diversity, it became good usage to speak of national character rather than national culture. The challenge was to identify central themes and characteristic practices, but increasingly after the mid-20th century it became clear that even tribes and villages were not as homogeneous as theorizing would suggest and the effort to describe national character was abandoned.

And if fuzzy boundaries rendered the equation of one culture for every society problematic half a century ago that fuzziness is even greater now as anthropologists deal with what is euphemistically referred to as the global village. Cultures seemed to lose whatever geographic and societal boundaries they may have had when communication became both worldwide and instantaneous as part of an amorphous process of globalization. The challenge for anthropology today is to describe cultures that are open to influences from all over the world. One of the most widespread spin-offs from this global process is New Age spirituality.

Many young people in the United States in the 1960s and 1970s were challenged by complex sociopolitical and economic changes that included the Vietnam War, which they saw as miscalculated and immoral. In questioning the war, the peace movement seemed to encourage and justify a youth rebellion against middle-class American culture in general, leading them to judge parents from World War II and the postwar period as being

153

Robert Anderson

The old and the new: McDonald's in central Reykjavík

too materialistic and narrow-minded. The civil rights movement added to this foment of cultural rebellion. The growing popularity of mind-altering drugs offered access to alternative realms of reality. Effective contraceptives and antibiotics favored sexual freedom. Worldwide transculturation challenged sacred religious beliefs.

In a fascinating reversal of the old acculturative drive that sent missionaries all over the world to convert so-called heathens to Christianity, Hindu and Buddhist gurus traveled to the West to offer their own missionizing alternatives to the Abramic religions. Freud was abandoned for humanistic psychology.

These complex and chaotic trends mushroomed into a global New Age counterculture that led many to abandon institutional religions in favor of personal transformation and spiritual growth (Levinson, 1996: 145–146).

Mixing different beliefs and practices to create stone soup for the soul, better known as syncretism, has always intrigued anthropologists, and they have described many societies in which one religion changed, not by replacement, as striven for by missionaries, but by adapting itself to another, as favored by heretics or colonized populations. Perhaps the best-known examples are those on the Caribbean islands and in South

America where African and Catholic rituals and myths amalgamated to become Santería, Candomblé, Umbanda, and other new religions.

The process is active in Iceland where Christianity, spiritism, and Icelandic elf lore have syncretized in at least a couple of instances. That process currently finds expression in a New Age school and in a New Age commune that on the surface seem quite bourgeois but, in fact, are totally dedicated to earth-friendly attitudes, open-minded values, and other-oriented spirituality.

ICELANDIC ELVES MEET THE BUDDHA

Erla Stefánsdóttir rents space for her school in an office building at the edge of the capital city. When I opened the door to her fourth story industrial suite, I found myself in a neat hallway sparingly furnished with a small side table and chair, fluorescent ceiling lights, white walls, and bare floor contrasting a row of framed pictures that were soft and warm. In the first picture, against a pale green background, two flowering plants looked as though they were responding to a fairy who was aiming her wand to enliven them. In the next, with a faint gray background, three winged angels drifting downward in long white robes seemed to be headed toward a brownish hillock surmounted by a yellow aura. Next hangs a pencil drawing made by Erla herself, colored in soft browns and blues. In it she brings into focus an otherwise invisible world of some two dozen identical little steep-roofed houses nestled against background mountains with a towering church to the side. The enormous church door is open, appearing to invite the community of elves into its warm yellow interior.

In all, a half dozen paintings of that nature invite perusal, but one painting is out-of-pattern both stylistically and thematically. In contrast to the softness of all of the others, that picture is geometric, printed in strong, saturated colors that are unsubtle and compelling. Centered on knights of the round table the subject is medieval rather than ethereal. Its message? An early sign that Erla's teachings are eclectic with no fear at all of synthesis or logical inconsistency.

Within moments I was invited into a room to the side where a table loaded with cookies and cakes stood next to the kitchen counter on which coffee would be brewed later in the evening. Six or eight people were adjusting costumes for later participation in a ritual, but the room itself promised we would eventually chat amiably with cups and cakes in hand. Someone explained, *Yes, we have coffee and cakes, and a lot of laughter, a lot of good friends, and a lot of questions. We wonder together.*

Erla reaching out as she directs circle activities

An old friend of Erla's led me through another door to brief me privately on what would be happening that evening. We chatted in the so-called prayer room in which soft green walls and ceiling-to-floor drapes set off a rather different collection of pictures and icons brought there from diverse parts of the world. Each was created in its own style, the totality portraying quite variable kinds of spirituality: Satya Sai Baba in India, an American Indian medicine man, Jesus Christ, the Nordic god Odin, a figurine of Buddha, and the triptych of a medieval Christian saint.

At last I entered the heart of the school, a sparsely decorated but surprisingly expansive hall in which portable chairs were arranged in a large circle so that the 25 or so enrolled participants could face each other. Erla sat with them at the far end with two old friends seated next to her, one on either side. But everyone in that room felt personally close to this rather plain-looking older woman who is able to see many inhabitants of the world who are completely invisible to nearly everyone else.

Classes convene every Wednesday evening throughout the winter. In addition, students break into small groups that meet separately once a week. Enrollees may also come to Erla's home on personal missions, as do many others who have become close friends over the years. Kristín and I did the same.

Spirits, Reincarnation, and God

The first time I met Erla was in her home where, as we got acquainted, she talked about that part of her invisible world that comprises the spirits of deceased loved ones. She was telling Kristín and me, with Kristín translating, that she sees her grandmother in her apartment every day. I wondered aloud, how do you know she is here? *I see her,* she responded. Well, do you see her bodily, or do you see the aura around her spirit body? *No,* she insisted, *I see her face and body.*

Now, that response was inconsistent with what she had said only 20 minutes earlier when she told us about her first encounter with spirits. *The first time was when I was 6 or 7 years old and was looking at pictures of my birthday party. I noticed that not all of the people who had been there were in the picture. I finally realized that people of the light were not there, because spirits cannot be photographed.* To clarify she added, *I see the light, the aura, from each person.* To further explain she added, *When I see my own children on TV or video I don't recognize them because cameras don't pick up auras.* Another time she told me that it is the same with hidden people and other elves. She doesn't see them as such. What she sees are their auras.

No matter. I'm an anthropologist, not a lawyer, and I didn't want to divert our intriguing conversation into what might become a semantic morass. Some of these inconsistencies may result from distortions that are inherent in translations. In all events, she was telling me about visits from her grandmother. *I see her face and body,* she said, adding that spirits look to her exactly like living people. *When I come into a room filled with a lot of people I can't be sure who is really there and who is there only as a spirit. Sometimes I greet a person whom nobody else can see, which can be quite startling to anyone who doesn't know me.*

Your grandmother was here this morning you said. *Yes.* Did she say anything to you? *No. She just walked through the room.* What did you feel when she went by? *Nothing. I'm so used to it.* Does it ever frighten you? *No,* was her instant response. Does it make you happy? *Hmm— well—yeah. You know, it's just part of life.* Do you feel that she watches over you like a guardian spirit? *Yes, that's part of it.*

Her most graphic story of being watched over did not involve her grandmother, however. *My car broke down on an isolated road one time,* she recalled. *I had a mechanic friend who had died 5 years earlier, so I contacted him and asked for help. When I tried again to start the motor again it worked. So, yes, **sometimes I get help from the other side*** [emphasis added].

Endless rebirth is central to Erla's cosmology. One day as I was asking her about the spirit world I made it personal to myself by asking, what will my life be like in the afterworld? *That's hard to answer,* she said, *because you choose your own life, here and in the afterlife. You make your own future both in this life and after.* Will I have a house to live in? *Yes.* Clothes to wear? *Yes.* Food to eat? *Yes.* A wife to live with? *Yes.* Children to raise? *Yes.* So life will be just like it is here. *Yes. And you will have conflicts between beliefs, too, in the afterlife,* and she laughed.

How about yourself? What will your life be like? *I don't think it will be any different from what it is today. Once I was interviewed on the radio and a priest asked why I believe in life after death. "It's so simple,"* I said, *"because I have died so many times and been reborn each time." Your body dies but your soul lives on and is reborn into this world, or perhaps another one. It may be 30 or 300 years between death and rebirth, but each lifetime is like one day in school. You don't learn everything in one life, so you have to come back to learn more.* Are other worlds at a higher level than ours? *Yes.* So, you work up to higher levels? Yes. Do you eventually end up in heaven? *I don't know. I believe paradise is in your heart.*

Since Erla is no longer young, even though she is not yet old, I thought it reasonable to ask what her lesson was for this life. *Patience,* she answered. Then I asked, do you know who you were the last time you incarnated? *I was Russian, a woman, and I played violin in an orchestra.* When was that? *1904 to 1935.* And what lesson did you learn that time? *I learned how to connect with people, acquiring skills in interpersonal relations. I also learned not to love too much. You create difficulties for yourself if you love your children, your family, too much. In the end you are nothing but your love, but you have to remember that you come alone into this world and you also leave alone, so you must not only love your family. What is important is to love all that exists.*

A month or two later I asked one of Erla's students, why did you decide to come to Erla's school? *We have been friends for a long time,* she answered. *I think everyone has their own inner time when they are ready to accept, and then they come. It is not a question of huge publicity.* I said, it seems that one source of comfort is knowing there is an afterlife. It takes away the fear of death. *I wouldn't say that learning about previous lives helped me overcome my fear of death. On the contrary, my reaction was to think, "Oh my God. Do I have to live so many more lives? I'm tired of it."* Fear of death? *I don't feel I had to overcome that because of knowing I had a previous life. It's more the fear of being alone. You lose loved ones. You are out there, lost.* Do your loved ones visit you? *I'm not like her. I don't have the third eye.* Can you sense the presence of spirits? *Yes,*

I trust they are there. I feel the warmth. **I feel that their love contin-ues** [emphasis added]. *That is clear to me.*

In contrast to that student, Erla attaches great importance to previous lives, but also to God. *Slowly I am learning to trust,* she told me. *To trust God more than I trust myself. I remember climaxes of my personal abilities [in previous lives], when I was at the top and was really successful. It gave me the feeling I can do everything. But there was more depth and humility that had to evolve, with more trusting in God. But at the same time, I had to learn not to let go of my personal way. It was a matter of finding the balance. That is who I am now.*

With God controlling you? I suggested. *No. I am in control.* But God influences your life. *Yes. He has trusted me with my life. So, what am I going to do with it? I want to do the best I can, by loving others.* And respecting others, I added. *Yes. To feel in harmony with everything that is around me; the life cycle, what's happening in the world, seeing the world.*

I like the idea of harmony, I added. You have used some important words: love, respect, harmony. But the word God doesn't fit. Does God really exist? *I don't look at him as up there,* she said, glancing toward the ceiling. *I know he is everywhere, but I feel him here,* and she pointed to her heart. *I'm trying to discover God here, in my heart.* I countered saying, I have trouble believing in this old man one a throne who is in charge. She suddenly seemed disappointed in me. *Who told you that?,* she demanded. *My church,* I answered, thinking of Revelation 4:1–11. *You have to question everything!,* was her instant response.

I then asked about heaven. She replied, *Doesn't it just come down to whether it makes you a better person or not? These are words we make up for things that are around us, whether we like it or not, whether we find words for it or not. It depends on how you interpret what is around us, and how you use it with others.* That seemed surprisingly pragmatic to me. I liked what I heard, even though her house is filled with elf dolls that I find hard to take seriously.

ELVES AND CHRISTIANITY

Spirits of the dead are a daily part of Erla's life, but her school and activities are much more about fairies, elves, and selves. You will recall that Erla conducts tours to the town of Hafnarfjördur to show people where invisible homes and communities can be found. She has produced maps with drawings of what they and their houses and churches look like and where they are located. She has even collaborated with a restauranteur so that in Hafnarfjördur a tourist can eat an elfin version of haute cuisine in the restaurant near the harbor known as Hansen's. Erla reports, by the way, that she puts porridge out once a year for her "house elf" (shades of Harry Potter). After he has consumed it, the porridge looks unchanged because he only takes its radiant energy. Those who eat at Hansen's restaurant leave empty plates, of course.

The purpose of Erla's school, however, is not to see spirits of the dead, elves, or auras. Rather, it is for participants to understand themselves better. *It teaches them to change their feelings, their mental states,* Erla told me one afternoon. *Each student will be different. Some need to change how they connect with other people, to learn respect for others. Others need to stop being so critical of a mate or friend and to start to love that person again, to be less negative and aggravated.*

In other words, I said, you emphasize positive thinking and love, right? *Yes. It's important, as the Bible says, to love another person like yourself, but you should do more than that. You should love everything, the whole environment, because it is all God's creation.*

Are you a Christian then? *Yes.* Is the Bible important to you? *Yes. I don't believe everything in the Bible, but I believe in God.* Do you go to church? *Yes, for Christmas and Easter.* And do you pray? *Every day.* To Jesus? *No, to God.* (In a different conversation she told me she also prays to angels.) Can you be a Christian and believe in auras and spirits? *Yes, of course.*

I asked a middle-aged woman what they do in the school. *We do exercises that she gives us. We talk. We meditate. It's very relaxed.* Can you give me an example of an exercise? *Last time we were trying to see the energy lines. We live in a material world, but she points out that there is no such thing as dead material. Everything is alive.* [Anthropologists refer to this belief as animism, which Edward Burnett Tylor postulated is the oldest and most widespread belief in the world. It antedates Christianity by many millennia (Hunter & Whitten 1976: 12).] *This material,* she continued, pointing to the cloth cover of a chair between to us, *you can see the energy.* Can you see the energy of that seat cover? *No, no. I can't, but she can. Oh, yes, she sees the auras.* Ah, you learn because she tells you what she sees. *Yes, but I don't consider myself a very good student,* and she laughed. But you benefit, don't you? *She's my friend. I think that's most important.*

Erla's goal is to increase certain kinds of sensitivity. Gudrun Bergman, who is now a New Age guru in her own right, recalled from her experience with Erla, *She teaches you to be more aware or to use your intuition in a different way. In the school she gives you a closed envelope and says, "Tell me what's in it." So you start trusting other elements in yourself. Your intuition becomes a lot stronger. Before I went to her school I didn't see as she sees but now I tell her, "I see this and this. Is that what you see too?" And she will say, "Yes." Maybe because she has been so psychic for so long, and because people trust her, you can learn. For me it has been very good to go to her for validation.*

Can you give me an example of how your ability has grown? *Yes. Near Grisavík there is a field of lava. I was talking about the special energy field you move into when you drive across that lava. It seems like it's gnome energy, from these little beings. So we were talking and I said, "It's so wonderful to be here because of all of the gnome energy," and she said, "Yeah, that's what you're feeling." So it's like a validation. Since studying with her I am able to trust myself more, because it's not as if I see with my eyes. I see with my intuition.*

Her husband Gully added, *We all have it, but we don't know how to use it. We are programmed from the beginning to close it off because we live in a so-called world of knowledge. But knowledge is not wisdom. We are filled with all kinds of knowledge, but only when we live our knowledge do we acquire wisdom, and wisdom is what we take with us when we pass on.*

A third woman, who is a professional masseuse, first met Erla 10 years earlier. *It was something I had heard about and I was real curious. I found that it is unique, because she can see on so many levels, something I have never personally been able to do.* Well, then, what have you experienced? *A lot through dreams. I did the weekend workshop in 1988 and I have been in the organization since 1992. I've been with her now for 6 years, but why I do so is hard to explain. It's mostly that I can sense the energy. But it's also like a link through education, connecting us with somewhere else.*

How is your life better because of that? *More love. More in relationship with other people. You learn to look at people differently, to understand, to see through some things, to become aware of what is behind appearances.*

Had you experienced contact with spirits of the dead before coming to Erla? *Yeah. It was open to me. I experienced their presence. But Erla doesn't talk much about people who have passed over. I know she can see them around you, but more important to me are the more developed beings or higher beings and the guidance they offer.* Elves? *No, elves are not higher beings.*

I asked yet another student what the school does for her. *It teaches everything of importance about one's life. It broadens your horizons in one way or another. In the beginning you feel a bit confused, because it is so big. The world is more alive and there is more to it than you realized, so it takes time to adjust. But the consequence is that you learn love. You feel more involved. You gain more respect for nature and the universe.* The key words seem to be love and respect, I said. *Exactly,* she agreed.

That evening at school, in addition to a slide talk, the big event was to perform class rituals. Dividing into four groups, each had created and practiced a ritual to express love, respect, and harmony in relation to one of the basic elements of medieval alchemy. Costumed imaginatively and yet simply, each cluster of men and women merged with the earth, water, fire, or air with such compelling movement and music that we all felt we had become one with the wholeness of Gaia, the Goddess Earth. Spirituality is about love. It is about experiencing others in Erla's circle as self and individuals beyond the circle as extensions of self. It is about loving Gaia, the living earth.

THE CENTER FOR PERSONAL GROWTH

The New Age center of Gudrun Bergman and her husband Gully is very similar to Erla's school insofar as both are dedicated to spiritual growth. That did not come as a surprise, since I knew that Gudrun once studied with Erla. But while Erla's school is decidedly urban, the center is rural and remote. It nestles against Snæfell, a dormant volcano thought by some to broadcast powerful beams of invisible energy in precise directions across Iceland and beyond. High above the volcano's glacier cap, the gigantic spectral body of a saga hero named Baldur stands high in the sky, enabling and protecting those who respect his presence. It is said that the most spirit-active terrain in the whole of Iceland is the peninsula that juts out from the foot of the mountain at the feet of Baldur. People say that clairvoyants have seen Baldur standing with his head in the clouds, as I learned from Gully during a beautiful fall day when Jósep Blöndal and his daughter Ida drove me to the spiritual retreat known as Snæfelsás.

It all started with Baldur Snæfelsás, Gully explained. *He was the pioneer who came here first when Vikings settled in Iceland more than a thousand years ago. His birthplace was northern Norway where the Sámi [Lapp] people live. His mother was Samish. Vikings often wanted Samish women because they had mystical powers. They could foresee and foretell.*

In that instant my thoughts retreated half a century to the winter of 1950 when George Nellemann and I, both ethnology students at the University of Copenhagen, traveled by train and bus to northern Sweden to collect artifacts for the collection of the Danish National Museum. The Sámi converted to Christianity in the 17th century, but every Nordic ethnologist knows that well into the 18th, Norwegians, Swedes, and Finns who had homesteaded in northern Fennoscandia feared the awesome powers of Sámi shamans. George and I were well acquainted with shaman drums and other ritual paraphernalia stored in the Danish museum and had stopped over in Stockholm to examine the Swedish collection. But my reverie was cut short as Gully continued.

Baldur inherited mystical powers from his mother, and he chose to settle on the Snæfell peninsula because it had mystical power. He could feel energy radiating from the mountain, lay lines they're called, the most powerful ever known. When it was time for him to die he did so by walking into the glacier. Gudrun picked up where Gully left off. *Baldur walked into the glacier, but no one succeeded in finding his body. It was magical, so people began to pray for his help.*

When Icelanders became Christians in the year 1000, some people thought it was hideous to call on Baldur, who had become known as Snæfelsás, "The God of the Snæfell Glacier." Yet, his power increased in response to people worshipping the energy of the mountain. Many still consider him the guardian of the glacier, and there is actually a huge guardian energy in this whole area as a result. That's why we settled here to build our commune.

In their younger days Gudrun and Gully were very successful in business, doing well enough to be able to devote the second part of their lives to spiritual pursuits. Those pursuits evolved in recent years into joining with three other families to establish a commune on farmland they acquired at a place called Hellnar on the Snæfell peninsula. Just a year before we arrived they finished construction of the first proper houses, which cluster around a communal building where they meet daily in a routine that begins with morning meditation and unites them periodically throughout the day to prepare and share meals.

Reaching out to others also eager for spiritual experience, they established the Center for Personal Growth that organizes workshops and personal consultations throughout the year. The program is continuous during the summer, when clients camp in the fields to learn from Gudrun, Gully, and others in the commune and, as they put it, *to understand that we who live here are also learning our lessons, and that we are on our way into the Light, just like everybody else.*

Back in Reykjavík a week later, Thorunn, who practices automatic writing to communicate with spirits of the dead, told me what it was like from her perspective. When I mentioned that I had just returned from Hellnar, she said, *I spent a spiritual weekend there 3 years ago. The energy in that place is so special. I stayed 2 nights in a tent and couldn't sleep, but I wasn't tired at all. I couldn't sleep because the energy is so powerful* [and perhaps also because the sun never really sets during an

Icelandic summer]. *Everybody was having great fun, with no alcohol, just children and grown-ups talking about things. There were also mediums. It was a wonderful weekend, and the power in my body lasted afterwards for weeks. When I got home I cleaned my whole house. That's how much energy I had. I don't know what it is, except that it comes from the glacier.*

SPIRITS OF THE DEAD

Yet, underlying the globalism of New Age spiritualism at Snæfelsás, one encounters a clear substratum of Icelandic ideas, including the concept of a spirit world, a belief in elves and fairies, Christian teachings, and Viking traditions. Not the least is the concept of a spirit world as seen in the practice of interacting with people who have passed away. For example, the Nordic god Baldur is thought of as the surviving spirit of a man who once was alive like the rest of us. Cloaked in myth, Baldur is appreciated in Snæfelsás as an adventurous Northman who acquired supernatural powers.

Gudrun told us that as a child she could see spirits of the dead, but such experiences play a much smaller role in her life now. *I don't see people so much who have passed away. I now seem to sense or see the hidden people or the spirit of this place rather than spirits of the dead.* Yet, shortly after making that statement, she told me that she is very aware of the closeness of her grandmother. *Oh,* she said, *she is with me a lot.* When was the last time? *Just 8 days ago when we were celebrating her 100th anniversary. She passed away in 1972.*

ELVES MORE IMPORTANT THAN SPIRITS

Gully, who had been restraining himself, could no longer hold back. *I am fed up with mediums!* Gudrun, accustomed to the emotional intensity of her husband's opinionated outbursts and his flair for theatricality, calmly put his provocation into perspective. *He may be fed up with mediums, but whenever anybody passes away in his family they come to him in dreams, which is a different way of being in touch.* You certainly find dream contact in the sagas, I interjected. *Yeah,* she agreed, but Gully took the floor again. *If I have any psychic abilities at all then it is with dreams, because dead people come to me and I talk with them just like I talk with you. I'm a Neptunized person, in the astrological sense of the word. I'm a Neptunized person, so I dream.* Then, somewhat indelicately, he added,

If I am in a dream but have to go to the toilet, I get up, go to the toilet, and then return to the dream where I left off. With that he shifted into a discussion of Helgi Pjeturss, remarking, *There are, of course, different kinds of dreams. In some I go to other planets,* which is not quite what Helgi taught.

By now geared up to maximally shock us, or at the least to command our full attention, Gully burst out with his condemnation of spirit mediums. *Have you gone to any of these mediums?* I nodded "yes," whereupon he voiced a parody of how they put petitioners in contact with dead loved ones. *She will say, there is somebody here for you, and then you have to find out by all this naming,* that is to say, in a dialogue with the medium you will speculate on who it might be. *Blah, blah, blah, and then all of a sudden, "Ah, yes, this is my grandmother," or whoever. Okay! Then your grandmother starts telling you that everything is okay and don't forget my grave, and as I listen I think, "Why in the hell are they so occupied with their graves." It's strange, all these delusions about nonsense. I do not deny that my father and mother and all of the others are in another world, because I know that no living creatures die. The body dies every minute. You know that as a doctor. So it's not a question of dying, it's a question of growing.* Aha, the cosmic university theme again.

That's the reason, he continued, *why Gudrun and others are just fed up with talking to these spirits who have merely passed over to the other side and have the same problems as we, although in a different way. What we want is to get closer to Mother Earth, to nature, to understand the beings, the energy, and to be one with the air, the sea, the storms, the Earth, the animals, trees, and flowers, to be one with them. So that's how it is when you understand this energy of the flowers, and the fairies, and dwarfs, or whatever, because they are in nature.*

NEW AGE CHANNELING

Fully wound up for his evangelistic oration, Gully zoomed into a monologue shaped by Icelandic beliefs in elves, trolls, dwarfs, hidden people, and other invisible inhabitants of the island, although he prefaced his disquisition with reference to a New Age form of spirit mediumship called channeling. *I went to a channeling workshop and I learned to channel,* he said. *And the only thing that really happened to me was that this person broke through. It was a little green man, very tiny, and he leaned forward in his chair to position his hand about a foot above the floor as he continued, in a green suit, with a hat and tight trousers rolled up at the cuff. He started hopping around and I could see that he was on a lawn. He said,*

"Hi! Why aren't you happy? What's wrong with you? You were always happy in the past. We love you because you love everything around you." And I started crying, Gully said, *and I cried and cried for 2 or 3 hours.*

The next day I came for channeling again and the little man came again. "Please be nice," he said. "Have fun like you used to." I said, "Who are you?" "Call me Síkki." "Who is Síkki?" "Well, I'm the one who takes care of the flowers and trees and the river. You were always nice, always smiling, because you were always thankful. Now we need your energy and happiness again. Please!" And then he laughed, "ha, ha, ha," and rolled over on the lawn, and when he did that, I started laughing.

Another time at a channeling session, Síkki came to me and said, "Tell your wife she has to return to thinking about the garden, because it's not nice that she isn't doing that anymore. She was so good about gardening. We and the flowers and trees are all waiting for her." Leaning forward in his chair he added, *Gudrun had been neglecting the garden for a long time and was thinking about it, so the very next day she returned to gardening. The reason I'm telling you this,* Gully explained, *is that there are these beings that want to be in contact with us. In the old days the American Indians and other nature people respected these beings. So I would say, if people are so far from understanding that there are these beings, if they don't believe that, then let them go to mediums. But when you have done that, then you can start going beyond spirits of the departed. Start getting information that you need. You don't need information that your mother or grandmother is doing this or that. We know what that would be, thank you. Good. But we need something more for growth, because we are here to do a fantastic task on Earth, in cooperation with everything that is.*

ON THE NATURE OF SPIRITUALITY

At this moment he clearly articulated his personal definition of spirituality. *When we become aware of this interconnectedness, conscious of it, that is spirituality, Bob. That's where it starts.* He then detailed a part of what he means by spirituality. *Whatever you say, whatever you do, whatever you think—and that is the most important thing, what you think, because most people believe you can think anything you wish. You know you can't say anything and you know you can't do anything, but you believe you can think anything you want because nobody knows what you think. But the thought is the most powerful energy on Earth. When you send a thought out, you can't take it back. So, if it's a thought filled with anger and fear, it gathers with thoughts of the same kind. Taking responsibility for our own thoughts is the most enormous task of all, and you know why, Bob? Because most of the time none of us is able to control what we think. If I start shouting at you, all kinds of thoughts will broadcast back from you, because you can't control it. To learn to control one's mind, to control what you think, is the most important task in the world today, because everything starts with a thought.*

How do you learn to control thought, I asked, knowing that it seems nearly impossible for most of us. *One way is probably to meditate, but there are other ways as well. We issue our magazine every 2 months. Gudrun is writing a book. I'm translating. We are doing all of these things. Of course, we are children of our society, our civilization, doing things, buying things, grasping. To get out of that is very difficult, but the energy we have here helps us to work at it. At the very least, we can walk out, see the northern lights, and be at peace.*

Tell me more about meditation. *If you go to a beach or sit at a cliff just to be there, you are meditating. When you listen to music, you are meditating, even though you don't know it. It is what's good for you. It calms you down, turns off the mind, stops you from thinking, but it is difficult.* My surgeon friend Jósep interjected, *It's close to Buddhism and to 12 steps. Yes,* Gully agreed. *It's all built on the same thing. We are always talking about love. But we are all afraid of love.* Gudrun added, *Gardening is a beautiful way of meditating because you can't really be gardening and planting trees and flowers and think about something else, because you are working in the soil and tending plants.* Gully added, *She has taught me to do that.*

Gudrun continued, *Buddhism is something I have recently studied. But to be in the Tao, to do what you are doing and love it, to be in the flow of the energy. You can put so much love into it. So often we are doing what we don't want to do, but you can put so much love into whatever you are doing and it can be beautiful. Gully, tell them what Buddha means,* she said. But before he could open his mouth, she spoke for him *Buddha means awake, conscious. Don't throw away feelings. You can't. So let them come. Feel the sorrow, the anger, and let it pass. Keep being who you are. You are bad and good and everything in between. Use the bad and the good, because we are part of everything. I love to make food, and I put a lot of love into the food.*

THE IMPORTANCE OF A GURU

Gully then told us about his "spiritual master," Amaram Michael Ivanow, a Bulgarian whom he has never met, but whose books he has read. *My master tells us that to make and eat food with love and care is more important than the food itself that you eat. A hamburger made with love by your grandmother is better for you than a vegetarian sandwich at a health food restaurant. Again, it's the energy. We have more energy in this place to emphasize what we want to do than we would have somewhere else.*

How did you come under the tutelage of a Bulgarian guru? The answer turned out to be magical. *How it came to me was very special. About 10 years ago I helped a young girl and her husband in Reykjavík. Suddenly one day she said, "I have a book for you. I was told to give you this book." Who told her? I don't know, but the book was called* Divine Magic, *written by Amaram Michael Ivanow. I was a businessman then, very busy, so I read it on the loo. That was the beginning. He taught that your personality is demanding, grasping, but you learn through it, and what you learn you take with you into the next life if it is wisdom. Wisdom? Yes, if you learned Greek, you don't take that into your next life, but wisdom and understanding, yes, those you keep.*

We are talking about love, here. It doesn't matter whether you know your guide, or whether your guide is an Indian or an Egyptian. All of that is rubbish. The important thing is to act in love, and that's difficult because of fear. Fear is always lurking in the world we live in. Our task is to conquer fear and to live together in harmony. Then we will have the Kingdom of God on Earth, and that's why we are here.

BECOMING A SHAMAN

There was a pause in Gully's monologue that permitted Gudrun to introduce a different New Age concept. *You have specifically been asking about spirits. I want to share with you that I do what I call spiritual healing.* I turned to her without comment, but silently reflected on the tendency of many to equate spirits with spirituality. It always struck me as an intellectual leap to make that connection, since one can be very spiritual by most definitions without being involved with spirits of the dead, celestial beings, angels, God, or whatever. But, Gully to the contrary, Gudrun was unaware of these thoughts and continued speaking.

I have studied quite a lot about shamanism, she said, explaining that several teachers had taught her the Harner Method of Shamanic Counseling. Was Michael Harner one of them, I asked. She said no, she had never met him, which gave me leave to brag about being a friend of Mike's from student days when he and I were both in the anthropology department at Berkeley. At mid-career Mike resigned as an anthropology professor and set up the Foundation for Shamanic Studies in order to teach people how to become practicing shamans. His program has so much appeal to those with New Age inclinations that his seminars and workshops are now taught by a staff of trainers who work out of his foundation in Mill Valley, California, very close to where I live and work.

What I especially do, Gudrun said, undeterred by my interruption, *is with people who have loved ones who have passed away—either recently or even as long as 20 years ago. I help them say good-bye to each other. It seems that even when people pass away, in an energy kind of way, through energy lines, their spirits appear to remain connected to us. Sometimes that spirit is in great sorrow or sadness, and the living survivor seems almost overshadowed by the spirit whose development is not taking place. The living person is also not developing much further.*

What I do in my work is to help people complete their separation in love. Once a person and a spirit have done that they both experience a tremendous feeling of freedom. Nodding in the direction of Ida, who was sitting near her, Gudrun elaborated. *It's like, if you can imagine Ida and me being linked together with endless threads of energy that are invisible to the human eye but are there nonetheless. We are connected to a lot of people in that way. If that connecting energy is anger, for example, it can be very destructive.*

How did you get into shamanic counseling? *It's not something that I advertise. It's just that people come to me and ask for help.* What else is incorporated into your program from shamanism? *Contact with the Earth. Contact with the spirit world by traveling in different dimensions.* Ah, you do soul travel? *I would say yes, I do.* Do you travel into a higher realm or a lower realm? *Actually, I do both. I travel to different levels in the form of an animal spirit or the shape of the animal. When I come to my destination the animal becomes my ally, a supporter. I feel I am moving in my body. Actually, I've just written a novel in which I use a lot of soul travel.* (By Christmas that year her latest novel was selling well in bookstores all over Iceland.)

Recalling what I had learned from Harner's book *The Way of the Shaman,* I asked, do you also do soul retrieval? According to Harner, a shaman may undertake a spirit journey to bring back a power animal, a guardian spirit, that his client has lost (1990: 69–89). Gudrun agreed that she had, but what she described was a metaphor rather than a soul as such. *I have on occasion. I think that soul retrieval is just bringing back the missing parts. Much of this comes out of my own soul retrieval, because I have had to bring back wounded parts of myself that I had left behind. You don't always learn from books. You also learn from what happens to you.*

Gudrun then told us about her experience a few years earlier when her father had major heart surgery. *After the surgery he didn't seem to be gaining consciousness again. It was a long time. I was at home, so I did a little shamanic ceremony and communicated with his spirit. I found his spirit above his body. He was very afraid of going back into his body because he hadn't expected it to be so painful. I had to remind his spirit that he had wanted this operation to improve and lengthen his life. Well, about 15 minutes after this ceremony, he regained consciousness. Sometimes people decide not to come back into their bodies, so they die, and part of that is that nobody communicated with their spirits.* This example left me confused, because the soul of her father was described as an entity rather than as a metaphor, so I was happy to have her continue.

I can give you another example. Last summer a couple had a little child with Down Syndrome. By the third week the child was seriously ill and in danger of dying. They were devastated. Two years earlier the mother had come for a consultation, so she called and we spoke on the phone. I said I would do a special ceremony and communicate with the child and find out what the child needs. I spoke with the spirit of the baby boy and asked what should be done for it to be healed. He said, I need to know that I am loved. I phoned back and could feel the wave of shock when I gave them that message. Later I learned that when the baby was born the father had totally rejected him, became angry, broke down emotionally, and didn't want to touch him. He knew he wasn't giving the baby the love he needed. Since then I think the father slowly he learned to love the child, slowly. The mother is very enthusiastic and wants to do her best. The key was just a little message from the baby saying, "I need to be loved." Hmm, I mused. Souls seem to be both metaphors and entities.

REINCARNATION AND KARMA

Gully then attempted to provide an explanation for why babies sometimes are born crippled, a puzzle with which Christian, Hindu, and all theologians struggle. It is the question of how God can allow bad things to happen to good people. *It could be an agreement, Gully suggested, to give these two parents a chance to grow. That may be the explanation if you don't believe in accidents. Why? It could it be that the Downs child agreed to be born as a contribution to the growth of the parents.* That explanation struck me as problematic, so I asked, what does it do for the child if that's the case? Gully's answer was, *It gets the experience of being a Down's child. It is also possible that the baby's soul had been bad to somebody who had been a Down's child or in some other way was crippled, and it is now learning, as a karma, to come into this body in order to live like that. Because there is always a reason. There is a reason, I think, for everything, if we can just see it. All of us have had something dreadful happen and then learned later that it was needed, and it was important that it happened.*

I find that concept impossible to accept, that everything has a reason and that everything is ultimately good. But I didn't attempt to dispute the point.

CHRISTIANITY REDEFINED

Gully continued his informal lecture. *We forget,* he said, *that God created us in his own image, with free will. We blame things on God, but he gave us free will. That means that anything that happens to us is by our own will.* Really? I was greatly tempted to get into an argument about this whole line of thinking. Now I wish I had, but instead I opted for filling in a blank on the list of questions I tried always to remember to ask.

Who is God, I said, remembering that I wanted to raise that question whenever the subject came up. *God, to me, is love. He is my father and mother and love and life.* I told them of my conversation with the bishop who said that God is not just some kind of energy because, in his view, God has a personality. *Yes,* Gully agreed, *God has a personality, if we want to call a personality God. But he is like you, Bob, much more than a personality. You are also energy. I could test your energy,* rising from his chair and moving to a far wall. *It reaches all the way to here. I have equipment to measure it.* Don't ask me what that is. It was never explained. Gully merely went on as though it were a given. *So, what are you? Are you Bob? Or, are you energy? You are both. God is personality. He is also energy. He is everything. We are sparkles of God. God experiences himself through us. We are parts of God. The only thing we are doing is to remember who we are.*

Curious to know more about God as a person, and feeling free to ask an outrageous question, I asked if God has a sex life, since that seemed rather improbable to me. Who would he have sex with? Himself? Gully said, *I'm sure God has a sex life, because we have sex. Also God has a lot of humor.* If that is true then he certainly is not talking about Jehovah. Perhaps he had Krishna in mind. As a child, Krishna was quite a trickster.

Gully continued, *I love God. It has been my privilege throughout life not to need a medium between me and God. I talk to God like I talk to you, and he always answers me. When you talk with God you are actually thinking, and before you can possibly think of the answer, you have it. It is God talking to you.*

All of this is rather unorthodox in Lutheran terms, so I asked, are you a Christian? *Yes, I'm a Christian.* But that was not a simple declarative sentence, because he went right on to say, *I am a Buddhist. I am a Muslim.* He listed a few more so fast that I didn't get them written down and they turned out to be inaudible on the camcorder. When he paused to catch his breath I interrupted to ask if he was a member of the Church of Iceland. *Yes, actually I am, but that is just because that is how it happens. I have nothing against Christians. What I have against Christianity is their arrogance in saying there is only one way to get to God, through Christ. Jesus never said that.*

Actually, it is said that he did in Acts 4:12, John 14:6, and elsewhere, but I was there to listen, not to argue biblical hermeneutics, so I let it go along with other unarticulated questions. Soon Gudrun interjected, *To me, God is spirit.* With a personality? I asked. *No, I don't perceive God as having a personality. God is more of a spirit.* What was clear to me was that Christianity for Gully and Gudrun is just one religion among many, and as such is not particularly influential in their lives.

ANCIENT WISDOM

Referring again to Harner, Gudrun said, *He has done tremendous good work. Learning about shamanism has also opened me to Icelandic shamanism, to the way people here used to sing or dance themselves into a trance. There is very little written about it in the sagas, because they were written after we became Christian, but you catch little glimpses of it here and there.* She then told the story of how Iceland accepted Christianity only after Thorgeir, who was probably a Sámi-influenced shaman, lay under a horsehide to get the spirit's approval for conversion.

I did a lot of work with old Viking mythology when I created a set of Icelandic divination cards, called Viking Cards. *Again, while working on my forthcoming novel I studied still more about the Norse and Sámi connection, which was very likely quite strong. If you look at where the settlers came from, the majority were from islands off the coast of Norway. They were good seafarers who sailed annually to Sámi territory to collect taxes. That resulted in marriages and many of those women were oracles. A lot of Northmen planning to migrate would go to a Sámi woman to have her foresee where they should claim land in Iceland.*

Showing me the beautifully crafted divination cards that offer an Icelandic variant of tarot reading, we looked at a picture of Odin, the god who is often portrayed as having a raven perched on each shoulder. Looking at that card together, Gudrun reminded me that every morning

Robert Anderson

A raven dive-bombed the window behind Gudrun.

Odin sent one raven to the earthly world and the other to the under-world, and each evening the birds returned to roost by his ears and tell him all that was happening in other worlds. When the settlers sailed to Iceland, they brought ravens with them in their boats.

It became a magical moment for us that afternoon at Snæfelsás, because as we were told about Odin an enormous black raven swooped out of the sky to dive-bomb the picture window. Magical to me, it was routine to the house. *Two years ago when we first came we lived in an old farmhouse. Every morning I placed raven food on a rock where the dogs couldn't get it. If their food wasn't there when they expected it they would fly over the house and call to us. They are telling us now that I must bring their food to the rock.* Alas, the message is not as interesting as when Odin's ravens flew to him, but it was dramatic, nonetheless, and it clear-ly evoked a memory of the old Nordic religion to have those black birds swoop down daily into their lives.

As the end of the afternoon drew near Gully and Gudrun shifted to talking about the importance of astrology in their thinking. There is no doubt in their minds that movements of the stars control people's des-tinies. In their view, the macrocosmic/microcosmic reality of human life is that people are souls who reincarnate in a quest for spiritual growth and cosmic achievement that takes many lifetimes.

But Bob, Gully concluded, *you can go into this magic, but what my teacher Amaram says is, get out of it. Start living in the world you live in.* Then, speaking for himself, *You can do magic, meditation, all these tricks, but what is important is to live in this world, to be in relationship with people and nature, to work with your emotions.* He emphasized that spirituality is more important than spiritism and invisible beings. I couldn't agree more.

CONCLUSION

During the first half of the 20th century, after two young priests brought modern spiritism from Copenhagen to Reykjavík, consorting with spirits of the dead caught on as a syncretism with Christianity that grew quite popular. Church authorities eventually rejected that easy relationship on biblical grounds, but it actually grew stronger and stronger as a popular a version of Christianity that was undeterred by theological dogma.

During the last third of the century, the openness to syncretism expanded in new directions identified as New Age spirituality. The counterculture movement was transformative for many people, especially young people. Of course, as William Fry points out, not everybody was enthusiastic about its virtues and some, although less so in Iceland than elsewhere, branded it a harbinger of the apocalypse, a movement empowered by Satan and his evil forces. But whether or not with approval, no one could fail to acknowledge that it brought about a revolution in "social customs, garb, artistic expression, communication, lifestyles, music, interpersonal interactions of many varieties, and religious practices" (Fry in Micozzi 2001: 289).

In the North Atlantic, New Age spirituality syncretized in a distinctively Icelandic way. Of course it was open to the same global influences as elsewhere, including Buddhist and Hindu spiritual practices, shamanism, humanistic ideologies of personal growth, ecological idealism, astrology, Earth visits by space aliens, tarot cards, mainstream spiritist activities, and versions of Christianity that are not even remotely derived from a literal reading of much of the Bible. Not the least, however, it drew on elf lore, including house elves, hidden people, dwarfs, gnomes, lovelings, light fairies, flower fairies, mountain spirits, and trolls (Stefánsdóttir 1993; Lacy 1998: 161–162). And just as Christianity has its institutionalized churches, and just as spiritism has its research societies, schools, and meditation groups, so also are New Age practices beginning to be institutionalized as in Erla Stefánsdóttir's school and in the Center for Personal Growth founded by Gudrun and Gully.

The Séance as Theater

A Basis for Skepticism

For an anthropologist, the idea of theater has served as a useful mirror for understanding how people interact as part of social life (Goffman 1959; Pegg 2001; Rappaport 1999: 37–46; Schechner 1985; Turner 1988). One can certainly adapt the theater metaphor to public séances featuring clairvoyants and trance mediums insofar as the room or auditorium serves as a stage for contacting the dead in the presence of a live audience.

The theater metaphor applies even more obviously when a transfiguration medium is possessed and supposedly has her face remodeled by the spirit to look the way the spirit did before death. Mediums claim that spirits accomplish this using "ectoplasm" as a kind of modeling clay that covers the medium's face. Since it is accomplished in the dark ambiance of a blackout room, illuminated only by a dim red lamp, it is more reasonable to assume that the effect is achieved by the way the medium sets her jaw or narrows her eyes. The effect is further enhanced by the use of dialect and changes in voice tonality, gestures, and body language. A transfiguration in that way can be said to effect the kind of transformation that is achieved on stage or in film by a professional actor who depends on makeup, costuming, and lighting for stage effects.

Analogously, a physical medium whose spirits move objects mysteriously in front of an audience is virtually impossible to distinguish from a skilled professional magician who also seems to perform small miracles on stage. Further, as is true for an actor playing a role and a magician demonstrating slight of hand, a transfiguration or psychokinetic performance is scripted and designed to be entertaining.

175

As an anthropologist trained to be open-minded and unbiased, am I entitled to make judgments of skepticism? Actually, I think it is unavoidable and necessary. When the spirit of someone who died is said to have come on stage to speak with an audience, how one makes sense of that performance will differ completely depending on whether it truly is a spirit or is merely a simulation or an illusion.

In his own way and more cautiously than I, James McClenon (1994) takes a comparable position when he writes of "alleged" or "apparent" psychokinesis, explaining that although he has witnessed various cases, he has to consider the possibility that he was deceived (p. 53). For example, in directly observing a Japanese medium who claimed that a spirit was bending the spoon he held in his fingers, McClenon cautioned that he had "never observed him perform under completely controlled conditions" (p. 203).

It is not enough to be skeptical of implausible claims, however. An anthropologist needs to assume a more holistic stance and ask why stage effects are taken seriously by the members of a society. If spirits are not actually present at performances, what is achieved for the audience? To answer that question, I take my lead from the work of E. E. Evans-Pritchard (1937) who described the practice of magic in Africa long ago. Although he acknowledged that witches did not really cause people to sicken and die and that oracles could not magically determine who was guilty or innocent, he found they were useful as metaphors for reality because they helped people resolve disputes and assuage anxieties. It is still true in Africa that the metaphor of witches and witchcraft satisfies deep needs in covert ways. Todd Sanders (2003) holds that "the African witch today provides Africans and Africanists alike with fertile conceptual terrain for constructing, considering, and contesting the multiple manifestations of modernity" (p. 339).

Analogously, I am prepared to argue that on an overt level the performance of a public séance represents skilled stagecraft, but on a covert or unconscious level it seems to reinforce social ties for a minimally institutionalized belief system and at the same time, simply and directly by the ritual act of coming together, apparently reaffirms the belief of all concerned that the dead really do live on in the afterlife (Rappaport 1999: 119–120).

TALES OF EMBODIMENT

It seems to me that the difference between possession and transfiguration is one of degree more than of kind, and that the boundary between the two is not sharply defined. I felt that Sesselja at spirit school séances approximated transfiguration when she assumed postures foreign to her

The medium's body and face appear to be controlled by the spirit who possesses her.

but congenial to the possessing spirit, when her body language, differing from what is usual for her, became that of the spirit, and above all, when her facial expressions changed along with her tone of voice. If instead of a lighted room she worked in darkness with only a dim red light for visibility, she might well have looked at times like a completely different person.

When witnessing a dimly illuminated medium in action, some observers are easily persuaded through the power of suggestion that they are witnessing paranormal transformations, a belief that is enhanced in retelling and no doubt also by the passage of time and the vagaries of memory. That is how I interpret the experience of Adalbjörg, the sixtyish office secretary whose son was attended to by a spirit doctor.

When I was 25 years old my girlfriend and I went to a small meeting with Einar of Einarstadur, who was well known during his lifetime. Only four or five of us were present that night, in addition to the two helpers who always sat next to him, one on each side. The lights were turned down low as we sat in a small circle and sang a psalm. He was sitting right across from me and very near, so near that when the spirits talked with me, his legs rubbed against mine and ruined my nylon stockings.

Although many people tell stories about this highly respected medium, I never it heard it said that he did transfiguration. But according to Adalbjörg, that night he demonstrated a pronounced bodily transformation. Her thoughts drifted back to that encounter, almost a half a century earlier, as she recalled, *You wouldn't believe it. The room was half dark. He sat close to me, and as I looked directly at him he got completely empty, like he had no bones. He collapsed with a hissing sound, like a balloon losing air.*

Before I witnessed a transfiguration for the first time Deborah explained what it could be like. She is a great story teller, and one of her tales of transfiguration began as follows. *This time last year one of my students said to me there's a young man in the spirit world called Collin who comes around. I said, well, I don't know Collin, but [he is] most welcome.*

The next day I gets a phone call from another medium asking me, could I do a transfiguration on the Saturday for a family. They had lost their son. Their son had been murdered only 7 weeks before. She said the family had come for a sittin'. Everyone had come through but the son. She said, but right at the end of the sittin' she said, "I saw your face." So she said to me, "I thought, right, I've got to ask Deborah to do a sittin'." So I said, "Yeah, I'll do it, but I can't say that that young man is going to come. I have no control over who's to come."

But on the Saturday morning I sat and meditated, and I say in my thoughts to the young man that if he possibly could come through, would he try for his parents' sake, and left it up to the spirit world. I go, meets the family. There's about a dozen people. Talking to them, and I says to them, what is the young man called? They said, Collin. "Oh, he came through on Wednesday night in the class—gave his name." I said, "Oh well, perhaps he's determined that he's coming through."

All his parents wanted to know, was he all right. There was his mother and father, then a sister, an aunt, and some other friends. First her mother's mother and father came through from the spirit world, built up [my face with ectoplasm to look like them], spoke to them, told them the son was with them, that they had been with him. This aunt, her husband came through singing. It seems he used to serenade her. He came through singing. He was using your voice, I suggested to Deborah. Of course it was her vocal cords, but she wanted me to know that they were under the control of the spirit, so she answered, *It was his voice, not mine. It was his voice what came through me.* Using your body? *Yeah, okay. He's showing himself,* whereupon she gestured with her hands around her face.

And then, right at the end, this young man came through. What he did, you don't just alter me face, gesturing around her face with her hands. *They alter the whole body, because I can grow very, very big,* stretching her arms out wide, *to being very small,* cupping her hands close together. *I can go from a child to a very big person, with a bull neck, and the whole lot.*

He said he always held out his hand to his mum, and he transfigured his hand over mine, so they saw his hand instead of mine. And he got hold of his mum's hand and he kissed it. I know when I come around, they were all crying. But all I can say, it was different parents what went out to what came in. They came out of there smiling, and his mum said, "I'm all right now. I can carry on. He's all right. I know he's all right now."

TRANSFIGURATION AS THEATER

Deborah speaks of appearing before an audience as doing a "demonstration." Her purpose is to exemplify how one spirit after another not only speaks through her but can change the appearance of her face and body. I obtained audiotapes of all three of the demonstrations she did in Reykjavík in 1998, two of which I attended myself and a third that was attended by a student who was taking a course from me.

What Deborah calls a demonstration I would call pure theater for a number of reasons. For example, as is customary for theatrical productions, an entrance fee is charged. She gave one free performance by invitation for only 20 guests of the sponsoring association, myself included. As another example of theatricality, performances were advertised in advance for set times and places, the times being the usual ones for matinee or evening theatrical performances and the places being facilities with public addresses.

As in live theater, the performer always faces the audience from a stage. For the small meeting at the spirit research center, the largest available room was a small one in what originally had been an apartment, rearranged so that Deborah sat in a corner with the audience seated in a semicircle facing her. The other performances took place in a classroom at the spirit school, with Deborah seated above the audience on a table that served as an improvised stage. Every performance required the same stage setting: an armchair in which Deborah sat, wearing a long-sleeved black pullover and black slacks with no jewelry. The costume leaves only her face and hands visible in the muted red light aimed at her from front and below. Windows and doors were always completely covered with opaque black material to eliminate even a glimmer of outside light.

Not the least, as in theater, the performance was scripted. This became clear in two ways. First, Deborah outlined the program for me

before I attended her first performance, unthinking of how such pre-
dictability contradicts her own insistence that she has no control over the
spirit world and that it is always up to them to decide what they will do.

In our first conversation she explained what transfiguration is, just as
I later heard her explain it to audiences. That explanation included the
dramatic story about Collin, one about a boy with a pet tarantula, and the
tale of the spirit of a lady who was still alive only hours before she
appeared in a sitting. Deborah told me that the first spirit to come
through would be "the Chinese gentleman." The second would be a spirit whose only function is always to demonstrate how big she can become
under his influence. She also told me to expect an old Yorkshire man and
a woman who sings out of tune. In addition to those set characters, her
demonstration would and did include spirits coming to visit with members of the audience, as is the case with all mediums.

THE START OF THE SHOW

The main evidence for theatrical scripting, however, comes from com-
paring the three so-called demonstrations to one another. All three began
with much the same introductory explanation of what we could expect
and what we in the audience would be required to do. The introduction
always started with a brief explanation of what the role of the medium
would be. In the first of the three performances, for example, she said, *It
is very nice to be able to demonstrate this gift to you. A medium never
knows what is going to happen, I have no say. I'm just going to go into a
sleep state, into an altered state of consciousness. The rest is up to the
spirit world and to you.*

In all three performances she also emphasized that it is necessary for
the audience to be actively involved. In one she put it this way, *The spirit
world is going to take energy from you. Your tummy may make funny
noises. Often the energy is coming from your solar plexus to me. You might
feel a bit sickly or headachy. You might start yawning. That also is energy.*

Her briefings included prompting the audience on what they were
going to see. I always say to people, she repeated in each of the three
demonstrations, *Could you mold your face without looking in a mirror?
I assure you I can't. Remember, the spirit world hasn't got a mirror, so
they may look a bit younger, or a bit older, or they may get it just right.*
In two of the demonstrations she added, *The last thing is the eyes, and it
will then look as though the eyes open and they are looking at you.*

Still speaking of molding the face she continued, *The spirit world is
going to take your energy and mine to form the ectoplasm. It comes from*

any orifice in my body: nose, eyes, mouth, ears. It looks like a silvery gray mix. Sometimes it has a smell, like damp earth.

She then explained that she can become very big, or very small, that she can acquire thick gray hair or end up bald, and that sometimes she will display jewelry in the form of *glittery stuff on the ears. And you may see animals. So it's not just built in the face. They actually can build hats, birds, all different things as well.*

The audiences were then told how they must behave. *You have a very important part in this type of demonstration, because your voice is energy. So, if you start to recognize somebody, do call him by name. Remember, I do not have an Icelandic mind, and just to tell you what level they get me in, last year in the far north, I came back out of sleep and everybody was quiet. I asked why,* and then she told the story of the woman who had only been dead for a few hours. *She spoke to them in Icelandic. They had a conversation. They must have got me in a very deep level, where they can completely cut my mind out.* Unfortunately, I only heard her talk about past meetings in which she claims to have spoken Icelandic or some other foreign language. She never spoke a foreign language in my presence. On the contrary, she cautioned, *Now, it's no use to ask, "Can you give us your name," because I've not got an Icelandic mind. Some of them will not speak, and some will. But by their mannerisms and the things that they do, even if they don't speak, you will know who it is. Just talk to them.*

It was clear from the start that a demonstration is supposed to take place with high good humor. It is meant to be fun, to be entertaining. Many in the audience take their seats knowing that lighthearted banter will be encouraged. *So, anyway, tonight let's have some laughter. Okay?* In her third and last performance Deborah encouraged good humor with this comment, *Now, last night we had a very good sitting. They were a good crowd, they laughed and took part, and really worked with the spirit world. So, really, it's up to you how much you get.*

In all three performances she told us who to expect as her helpers. *First, a Chinese gentleman. He is in control. He has a great sense of humor. You might see also a very, very big man. He is just a helper. He just shows you how big they can make me. Just to show you what they can do. Also a little lady called Alice. I just hope she doesn't sing. She can't carry a tune. She is absolutely tone deaf,* a remark that never failed to cause laughter. *There is also a very old gentleman from Yorkshire called Len. Ladies, watch yourselves, because he likes to chat with you. He has a great sense of humor.*

Finally, preparing us for spirits who would arrive to address members of the audience, she concluded by saying, *If you start to recognize someone, do speak to them. If you don't talk to them, they'll fade back and the next will come.* In one performance she added, *I did one yesterday and one woman said to me afterwards, "My father came into my eyes, but I didn't like speaking." What a shame. He made all that effort to come through for her and then she wouldn't talk to him. So, if you don't talk to them they'll just say, "Ah," for the next one to come.* With that she sank back into her chair, indicating in that way that a spirit was approaching.

THE CHINESE GENTLEMAN

After saying a prayer Deborah said, *See you all later,* after which she sank back quietly in her chair and closed her eyes. Taking that as their cue, since the routine was familiar to many in attendance, the audience sang a song. Then the room fell silent. Stage whispers could be heard during that quiet moment.

> Someone is coming.
> It's coming.

The appearance of Deborah's face began to change. She seemed to look somewhat Chinese as she peered at us through narrowed eyelids and a widened mouth. She, or, rather, I should say "he," spoke English in a higher, squeakier, more feminine voice than is normal for Deborah. It was distorted by a singsong accent and missing words, but demonstrated no true Chinese phonetics or tonal inflections.

Good evening. Ni hao. I welcome you, so you say, ni hao. The audience, in good humor, repeated back, *ni hao.* In the last of the three meetings one voice in the audience added an Icelandic equivalent, *"Godt kvöld,"* which led the spirit to say, *You have most funny language. Much easier to say ni hao.* The audience thought that was funny.

All of the standard characters are comedy figures, so the Chinese gentleman persisted in his amusing monologue. *And I say to you that medium is aware that I am talking to you. She very nosy lady.* Laughter. Deborah told me he would say that, and he did—every time. In one session he added, *All ladies are nosy.* More laughter, except from me, since I am well-bred from Berkeley and Mills College and would never encourage that kind of a male chauvinist remark, even given my respect for the dead.

As mentioned above, humorous repartee with members of the audience is encouraged. In the second performance, introduced with witticisms by Magnus who was serving as the spirit school host, Deborah's spirit guide added, *I am, uh, gentleman is in control of evening. Take no nonsense from this gentleman,* referring to Magnus. People laughed. *And I say to you, I have had much dealings with this gentleman before.* The spirit refers here to previous years when Magnus moderated Deborah's performances. *I say to you, I am boss.* Laughter.

That line came off better in the third performance when he prepared the audience by saying of Magnus, *He is, what you say, office boy. I am, what you say, boss.* But he only included the following in his middle presentation. *Good to have laughter, because laughter heals the soul.* Then, turning toward Magnus, *Very nice to come back and see you,* to which Magnus replied, *Nice to see you too.*

THE VERY BIG MAN

The Chinese gentleman soon faded away, leaving the medium to lapse into silence for a few minutes until the big man took over her body. In anticipation of the arrival of the spirit of a big man, I strained to see her face and body transform into his. I shifted my eyes back and forth between central and peripheral vision, all the while wishing I had infrared night vision glasses that might pierce the darkness. Why has the spirit world agreed to show itself, but only in the dark? Yet, it did seem that a big man was emerging, a man who in one session was said to be a Jewish gentleman. The man's torso seemed to rise much higher in the chair. The chest and shoulders widened. He held his right hand out like the pope offering his ring to be kissed, spreading fingers that seemed longer and thicker than before, perhaps because by reaching forward, the lighting shifted from shining on top of the fingers to backlighting from underneath. In the first demonstration the medium Vigdis, who was moderating that evening, said, *It's the big gentleman, for sure. Yeah, yeah,* several others agreed. It was much the same the other two times.

Questions addressed to the big man were answered with nods of "yes" and "no" or with an occasional arm gesture. The host asked, *Are you with us?* He nodded "yes," which stimulated Vigdis to utter a confirmatory, *You are.* Then Vigdis asked, *Are you coming from far away?* He shook his head in the negative. Vigdis was there to interrogate and translate, so she continued to verbalize the gestured responses, *No, you're not. Are you from Iceland? You are! Is your name Thor? Yes, it is.*

At that point in the second performance, Vigdis shifted to asking questions in Icelandic rather than English. The spirit continued to mime answers that were accepted by the audience as satisfactory, shifting, however, from nodding "yes" or "no" to full arm gestures that were quite ambiguous except for the final wave "good-bye," as the big man closed his eyes and Deborah slumped back into the chair, somewhat the way Adalbjörg saw Einar of Einarstadur collapse down into his chair.

A significant deviation from the big man routine occurred in the last performance. At the moment when he began to appear Magnus said, *Hello.* (Pause) *Good evening.* And as I watched, I could see the medium getting taller and wider, with the right hand held far out in front exactly as in the two preceding sittings. At that moment, however, some woman in the audience apparently didn't realize that this was the big man we were expecting. Instead, she thought she recognized a departed loved one, the spirit of a woman rather than a man. *Sigridur?* she asked, hesitantly. (Pause) *Are you my grandma?* The spirit nodded a strongly affirmative "yes." Accepting that it was her grandmother she asked, *Is Granddad there?* Again, the mimed answer was "yes." *Is he worried?* she asked. On receiving a shake of the head as "no," she then added, *I love you.* The spirit voiced a weak, squeaky response, *The same to you. Thanks,* said the woman, and that was the end of what was supposed to be the spirit of a Jewish man who always demonstrates how big he can become. What happened? Nobody asked and no explanation was offered.

STOCK CHARACTERS AS STAGE COMICS

A pause ensued. Some guesses wafted out from the audience about who was coming next, and in fact the program no longer followed a set sequence. Instead, each meeting offered a variable mix of two predictable kinds of spirits, one consisting of additional stock characters such as the Yorkshire man, Alice, and others who are not related to anyone in the audience, the second being spirits of relatives and friends of members of the audience.

Deborah told us we might encounter Len, the old Yorkshire man, and he did appear in two of the three sessions. His role is that of an amusing humorist whose banter with the audience incorporates sexual innuendo. He also conveys a serious message about the importance of loving people. I will present excerpts from the dialogue of the first followed by that of the second in order to document how he says the same lines every time, much like an actor on stage with a role to play.

THE YORKSHIRE MAN, FIRST PERFORMANCE

The audience was quiet, waiting expectantly. A voice said, *Is it Olaf?* and immediately answered itself. *No.* Another voice asked, *Olin Håkkensson?* Silence, then someone else whispered, *It's coming,* because we could hear heavy breathing, like that of an old man with chronic bronchitis or asthma. A voice in the audience faded away before it could finish asking, *Is it. . . ?* At that moment an old, husky voice from the stage said, *Howdy.*

Someone in the audience answered, *How do you do?* Vigdis added, *We are fine. Everything okay?* The Yorkshire man took note of Vigdis and said, *Nice to see you again.* She answered, *Thank you.* His rejoinder caused great laughter, *You've plenty of meat on ya. You're what we call "nice and* [unclear]." *What? Cuddly.* In good humor she shot back, *We don't help,* apparently meaning no way am I going to cuddle with you. It seemed funny to all of us.

I want to tell you how I died. I had these pains. I fell asleep. When I woke up this person told me I was dead. "Get off," I said. The audience howled with laughter. *How could I be dead when I'm sitting there wide awake? Then I realized people couldn't see me and I thought, "There must be something in it."* More laughter.

I'll tell you, you'd best learn your lessons here before coming over. Because I had to learn to love people—to like people. Turning to face Vigdis, *This lady here. Now I enjoy it. Nice to meet you, anyway. I think you are lovely.* Her laughing repartee was a jocular, *Behave! Behave!* Len responded in kind, *You didn't think you would get chatted tonight, did you? No,* she said.

Len then returned to the theme of learning to love. *But you know what? Religion's all* [unclear]. *All you really need is to love mankind. That's all you need.* Vigdis answered, *I know,* and he repeated, *That's all you need. You don't need the church. People come over here with some funny ideas, you know. They're in for a big shock,* a statement that caused people in the audience to laugh. Vigdis added, *I'll bet they are.*

After that, the Yorkshire man said, *Anyways, it was nice to meet you.* Vigdis responded by saying, *Thanks for coming through.* Len took his leave then in a way reminiscent of how the Chinese gentleman departed. *I'll teach you some Yorkshire. Good neet. Good neet,* the audience replied. *Good neet,* the Yorkshire man said, and then closed his eyes. The room fell silent.

THE YORKSHIRE MAN, SECOND PERFORMANCE

The second evening the audience sang the verse of a song each time they waited for the medium to be possessed by a newly arriving spirit. In anticipating the spirit who turned out to be the Yorkshire man, the host followed the brief song by saying, *Good evening,* adding, in a lighthearted, jesting tone, *You like the singing?*

Nay, the Yorkshire man said in a low, croaking voice that seemed funny to the audience, but after the laughter he became quite friendly and said, *Hello love. Hello,* the mistress of ceremonies replied. *Hello,* he repeated. *There're some bonny lasses here, ain't there?* Then his tone of voice turned serious. *Alice was telling me you wanted to know why, uh, about dying. You want to know?* "Yes."

When I was on the Earth I was a tramp. A man abroad, a self-characterization that struck many as quite funny. *I fell ill and I lay down in a field. I fell asleep. And then I felt all right. But there was this person kept telling me I was dead.* "*Get off!*" The audience burst into laughter. *I had never heard of life after death. When you were dead, you were dead.* "*Leave me alone,*" *I said till I realized people walking past me couldn't see me. I thought there must be something in it,* which caused a ripple of laughter. *So I decided I'd better listen to what was going on.*

Mind you, I had a lot to learn. Okay? So I took myself to a medium to learn. I didn't like people, you know, when I was on Earth. No time for 'em. You've got to learn, haven't yuh? You might as well learn your lessons here.

A man in the audience then asked, *What is the most difficult thing to learn when you're going over? You've all got different things to learn,* the Yorkshire man answered. *I had to learn to love, cause I didn't like people. I had no time for people when I was on Earth. So, I had to learn to love. Okay? Now, I took myself to a medium, and I've been learning with her, okay?* Then, with a second reference to one of the stock characters in Deborah's transfigurations, he said a surprising thing as concerns life on the other side. *Now I have children with Alice, and I love them. I'll show a picture of them,* he said as he seemed to be reaching into a coat pocket. *Here they are,* and with a wave of his hand supposedly holding pictures, he returned his hand to his pocket. That, by the way, was the only time I ever encountered a spirit who claimed to own a camera and carry photographs.

Scanning the audience from one side to the other, he stopped when he caught sight of a woman. *Hello, luv.* The hostess medium intervened in a smiling voice, *She's unmarried,* which led him to say, *What's her name? Mine's Len.*

Virtually without pause he then added, *Anyway, I'd better be going. I'll teach you a bit of Yorkshire. You say, "Good neet." "Good neet." "Good neet."* And with the last "good neet," he closed his eyes and the room once again fell silent.

PSYCHOKINESIS AT A GALA PERFORMANCE

Ninety years after Indridi Indridasson, mental mediums beyond number display their talents all over Iceland, but physical mediums are rare. Siggi did tell me that someone named Björgvin was a transfiguration medium,

Robert Anderson

Planning the gala celebration

but Björgvin lives in a small town in western Iceland and I was never able to arrange a meeting. No one said anything at all about physical mediums.

No one, that is, until winter 1998, when the Icelandic Society for Spirit Research began to sell tickets at 2,000 KR (about $30) for a grand gala to celebrate the 85th anniversary of the founding of the society. The president of the society, Gudmundur, told me they were planning a highly entertaining program and had billed an Englishman named Edwin as the featured attraction. "I haven't seen him myself," he told me, "but they say he plays wild circus music and makes trumpets fly around in a spectacular way." His wry smile and tone of voice were enigmatic. Did he have doubts about the role of spirits in this? Did he wonder if I had doubts? He seemed to be saying, we're celebrating an important anniversary and we want to have some fun doing it.

On a freezing cold December evening I presented my ticket and joined some 150 other people merging into the small theater that was engaged for the evening. Most of us were dressed rather formally, ladies in evening gowns and men in suits and ties. The atmosphere was festive. Wine and coffee were available at the intermission.

When it was time to begin, the house lights dimmed and spotlights brightened the stage. Dignitaries were introduced and honored. Two obligatory speakers recalled the past and celebrated the present in ways at once solemn and lighthearted. We were startled when a strange-look-ing lady in the front row suddenly approached the edge of the stage, where she looked up and began to harass the president of the society in the middle of his formal address. After the first sentence, as she contin-ued her loud criticism of what he was saying, she turned as though to say, "Don't you agree?" Good heavens, she was a wild woman. Her hair was tied back with a girl-like ribbon, her lipstick was too bright, her cheeks were too heavily rouged, and her schoolmarm gestures seemed inquisi-tional. She seemed a bit tipsy and yet spoke clearly.

The president acknowledged her with complete aplomb and made a wisecrack in return. By that time even I, the most naïve member of the audience, realized that she was a plant, a member of the society with thespian talent who had volunteered to speak up from the orchestra pit to enliven the speeches. This was to be an evening of music-hall theater, although it did get quite serious when Einar Kvaran, founder of the soci-ety and by then long since moldering in his grave, also addressed the audience.

We had been told in advance that his voice would be heard. I assumed he would speak by possessing a medium, which is what he did. However, the possession took place a day or so earlier at another location. A tape recording was made, so we heard his voice, but his stage presence was limited to two big black loudspeakers at either side of the stage.

After the speeches, three warm-up acts were put on by mediums, each of whom offered a somewhat different version of performance theater, each a virtuoso in demonstrating how her spirits could tell indi-viduals about themselves, give advice, and predict the future, all with great good humor.

From the start, Edwin, the physical medium, along with the hostess of the evening, the president of the society, and three mediums, was also on stage, sitting on a chair off to one side or standing at the edge of the curtain to the other side. He seemed to have no stage presence at all, leaning forward with his elbows on his knees, or standing with his pot belly on display, chewing gum furiously, occasionally sipping from a glass of water, staring vacantly into the audience, or taking in the performances of the three mediums, his tieless shirt rumpled and untidy.

During intermission, while the audience milled around with coffee and cakes, I hung back to chat with Edwin, who was busy adjusting his props and energizing the phosphorescent tape on his trumpet and three butterfly-tipped wands by holding them in front of a stage light, a routine task that freed him to turn to me and say, *Where are you from?* California, I said. *Deborah told me I would be meeting you.* From the tenor of those remarks I gathered that they saw me as a source of publicity, so our conversation was quite congenial. *She and I sit for each other,* he continued. *She once brought my son to me in transfiguration. I spoke with him for a few sentences and then I lost it. They were memorable moments.* Then he told me what he would be doing, anticipating what I later heard him say to the audience when he was back on stage. *My guide is a Zulu general, a young man who was executed in a cruel manner for sleeping with a woman in the harem. He is very powerful, very intelligent, with a good sense of humor.* As I left to get a cup of coffee I asked, *May I videotape this evening?* He said no, not during his demonstration, when only audiotaping is permitted, but it would be okay to videotape his introductory remarks, which I soon did.

Despite his unsophisticated appearance, he came to the gala with an enviable 30-year reputation that began when a highly esteemed English medium mentored him, which led early to stardom based on making a silver dolphin appear out of nowhere. For many years he gave up physical mediumship in favor of healing. I don't know why, but just months before arriving in Reykjavík he returned to demonstrating how spirits could cause trumpets and butterflies to swish around in pitch-black rooms.

His associate at the gala was Jan, a medium in her own right who accompanied him from England. Her assignment was to sit with the audience in the front row while he was on stage and supposedly out of awareness. She orchestrated the taped sequence of melodies by instructing the soundman over a walkie-talkie. She also acted as mistress of ceremonies while he did his demonstration. With her in place, the main event was ready to begin.

Standing at mid-stage behind the chair he would sit in for his performance, leaning on it in a casual way, Edwin introduced himself. He asked the audience to recite the Lord's Prayer, which they did, but seemed startled when the Icelandic mistress of ceremonies led the audience in singing a song. I guess they don't do that in England. *First of all I want to say, I'm very proud to come to Iceland. I've never been here before. I've learned four words of Icelandic, "hello," "goodbye," "no," and "yes."* The laughter was polite as he demonstrated his awkwardness with a foreign language. *That is the few words of Icelandic I already know.* Edwin could use a speechwriter, or perhaps he might consult with his friend Deborah, whose self-introduction prepares the audience in a similar manner but in a much more captivating way.

He explained that this was the first time he had performed for a seated audience. Usually he performs for no more than 30 people in a circle, and they are all people he knows can be trusted. In England his sister works as his assistant, but this evening it was Jan, *who I am not used to working with.* Jan, for her part, later wrote that she is quite used to working with him, a discrepancy of no great import, I suppose.

The demonstration I hope you will see is controlled by a guide of mine called Zambuli. He likes women. That was his downfall. Laughter. *Sometimes he does what I ask, but mostly he just does as he pleases.* More laughter. He then spoke of the duties of the audience, just as Deborah did. *The spirits get power from myself and from all of you good people. What you put in is what you get out.* I took that to mean that if you want to have something to laugh about you will have to laugh and if you want the trumpet and three butterflies to really dance you will need to clap and cheer and sing along, which is exactly what happened.

He went on to prepare us for what we would see and hear based on what he has been told by other audiences, since he insists that he is quite out of awareness while the spirits work through him. His demonstration would be enlivened with taped music. *The first tune is a hymn, "How Great Thou Art." The second one is sung by a group, which I don't know the words to. They help me relax and go to sleep, as I say. The other tunes are old Second World War and First World War songs. I don't know if many of you people know them, but if you don't know them, just go "la, la, la" or make a noise along with it.*

Holding up one of his trumpets, he continued, *This is of aluminium. It blows at the end* [sic]. *It writes backward to the spirit and forward to the people who can see it.* He was referring to the way in which he would communicate with the audience during his demonstration. He went on to say that we would see the phosphorescent trumpet write words in the air, stringing out a short sentence that can be read from the audience side. Jan would help by reading the words aloud over a microphone. (Since the spirit is invisible I fail to understand why the writing can't be from left to right in the usual way. Of course, if he or an assistant is doing the air writing, then backward would be required.)

Holding up yard-long sticks with wooden butterfly figures on the ends he explained, *These are just ordinary decorated butterflies. The circle I work with in England is known as the Butterfly Circle. Sometimes my guide will use my vocal cords, the thing I do not like him to do, because the next day I cannot speak very well.*

He concluded by looking at Jan. *Is there anything else I should say?* She shook her head, so he wound up his preliminary remarks. *Uh, perhaps at the end of the demonstration, Zambuli will want the last music on the tape to be played. It is called Greased Lightning.* A few people laughed softly. *Apparently this—because I've never seen the demonstration—I would want to see it one day—apparently this is the piece de resistance,* pronounced as though the words were English rather than

French, *where he demonstrates the power of spirit. This is the way I have been taught and this is the way it works, but please do not use any cameras, lighters, or torches. It's not good for me.* I have no doubt it would be very bad for him.

The demonstration proceeded exactly as predicted. At first, rather simple movements of the trumpets and wands moved about to the beat of the music. They began to move faster and to cover more space after a while. The trumpets did write a few comments in the air as the pace heated up, the hostess in the audience translating them over a microphone. We all laughed when none of us could make out what the words were and had to ask that the writer slow down. The trumpet showed frustration when people guessed incorrectly, vigorously shaking a "no" sign the way one might shake one's head. One word spelled out by the trumpet was William, which was easy enough. Then a "3." Someone in the audience shouted, "William the Third." Then the trumpet spelled out, "Has anyone found an old coin?" Aha, it must be an old coin with an image of William III on it.

As the excitement built up a woman sitting in the middle of the theater became agitated. She whispered to her companion that she felt ill and had to leave, but to leave the auditorium would precipitously end the show, because opening the door would admit light and harm Edwin, so her situation was desperate. Suddenly something fell into her lap. Zambuli had materialized a pendant made from an old William III coin, a rare and extraordinary achievement. She immediately felt better. The crisis transformed into a peak experience, and the audience went wild.

As predicted, Zambuli instructed Jan to turn up the volume on the music and have the soundman broadcast "Greased Lightning" from the musical *Grease.* Jan later wrote in a photocopied newsletter, *The trumpet and sticks went at amazing speeds and heights. Even I was surprised. But we had never done it in a theater before, only in rooms or small churches. It was,* she concluded, *a splendid demonstration of the power of spirit. We heard Zulu-style drums played at one point by the trumpet, but when the lights went up nothing was on stage except Edwin on his chair and a microphone on a stand, so how they managed we will never know.* The audience certainly seemed to have had a great time.

After the finale, the lights went up to reveal Edwin seated in the middle of the stage, exactly where he was before darkness concealed him. He looked tired from his great effort, and they made a big thing of slowly turning the lights back on in a way that helped him ease back into his body. After some moments of silence, he quietly asked, *How did it go?* Like Deborah when she did transfiguration, Edwin claimed to have been completely out of awareness. I doubt that they could pass polygraph tests on those claims.

Speakers and mediums returned to the stage for the final curtain call, when each was presented with a rose, including Edwin and the strange lady, who got her last laugh by miming egregious allure to the Englishman in his chair. While the hostess spoke over the microphone to bring the evening to a close, Edwin waved his hand at the woman who had discovered the materialized pendant on her lap, miming that they should meet at the back of the theater where he would give her his rose. The program ended. We shuffled slowly through the exits and into the cold blackness of a winter evening in Reykjavík.

CONCLUSION

William of Occam, a 14th-century English philosopher, offered a way to come down on the side of reason when confronted with supernatural explanations, such as in the gala when Edwin claimed that trumpets and wands floated all over the stage in the hands of invisible spirits, and in the transfiguration when spirits reputedly molded themselves on Deborah by using ectoplasm exuded from her bodily orifices. According to the rule of Occam's razor, when you must chose between two equally compelling (or uncertain) explanations, the one that is the simplest and which is most consistent with known realities is the one that most probably is correct. I submit that it is inherently preposterous to believe that invisible ghosts were willing to present themselves on stage for scheduled performances in which they would act out scripted performances for Deborah or would make phosphorescent aluminum stage props dance to heavy metal music for Edwin. The simpler and more compelling explanation is that Deborah and Edwin are skilled illusionists. They are theater magicians. On those evenings of theater, we were asked to sit in darkness and accept the claim that invisible living entities who could not tolerate light were performing for our enjoyment. By the rule of Occam's razor, I personally cannot be persuaded.

MISREPRESENTING THE DEAD

A REMINDER OF WHAT WE KNOW

To acknowledge ancestors who live on in an afterworld is very common and perhaps even universal, so I was not the least bit surprised to find that it occurs in Iceland (Levinson 1996: 3–6; Sheils 1975; Steadman, Palmer, & Tilley 1996). However, as I pointed out in Chapter 1, what caught me unawares was to discover that it is so meaningful to so many people that it can reasonably be described as the inconspicuous but pervasive unofficial religion of Iceland. How curious, I thought, because I would never say that about the other Nordic nations, even though they are all very similar in most ways. So I set out to explore the cultural contours of this difference, this quiet manifestation of a religion based on establishing contact with spirits of the dead.

I started out by identifying the menu of humanoid possibilities accessible in the Icelandic cultural repertoire and found there were ample opportunities to establish relationships with other paranormal personalities, especially with angels, space aliens, and elves. Yet the overwhelming preference is for the living dead. Why so?

An important part of the answer to the "why" question is generic to the human condition and explanatory for the apparent universality of belief in life after death. It is important for people worldwide to believe that they are in some way immortal. Since all of the Nordic peoples share in that desire, perhaps something additional in the history of Iceland may be explanatory.

In Chapter 3 I retell some very old ghost stories dating from the original discovery and settlement of the island, but the origin of contemporary spirit beliefs and practices turns out to be quite recent, having arrived about a century ago from Denmark. Why, then, is spiritism so much more developed in Iceland than in Denmark?

I can only speculate. Unlike Danes who lived in villages and towns, until the very recent past Icelanders survived freezing, dark, and stormy winters on isolated farmsteads where ghost stories were told and retold as part of one's life experience. Each family held out during those harsh months protected only by a damp sod hut half buried under snow and ice. They survived by providing care for one another. It should not surprise us, then, that many Icelanders feel that deceased members of their family continue to care about them and willingly use their prerogatives as inhabitants of the spirit world to provide guidance, transmit love, and ward off danger like guardian angels. The belief that love can survive death is inspirational in many ways, including that it inspires a desire to meet and talk with the dead. Contemporary spiritism offers a way to satisfy these yearnings. And, because the total population of the nation is quite small with lifeways that have been essentially uniform throughout, an orientation to contact with deceased family members apparently found easy acceptance as part of the cultural menu.

The "what" question is easier to answer. In Chapters 4, 5, and 6 I describe the ways in which mediums learn how to function as intermediaries with spirits, what they tell people and fail to tell about life in the hereafter, and how children and adolescents experience early contact with ghosts.

Those chapters led the way to a discussion of the sociology and politics of spiritism. The national church at first was hospitable but now is antagonistic, which returns to the "why" question. The social institutions that structure contact with the dead, and also with elves and fairies, appear to meet needs not adequately satisfied by the Lutheran church, in spite of the biblical injunction to love one's neighbor as oneself. Above all, in spirit circles and séances participants practice a contemporary ethic of mutuality based on caring and sharing, on a spirituality of love.

THE SKEPTICAL ANTHROPOLOGIST

Which brings me to this point. What is important about contact with the dead, I insist, is not whether the dead truly survive and contact people from the great beyond. What is important is the spirituality such beliefs inspire. When people say they receive messages from spirits, a person is entitled to be skeptical, because on intuitive grounds alone it seems highly improbable that the living can converse with the dead. The power of logic supports that intuition, as when, by the rule of Occam's razor in

Chapter 10, I concluded that the theatrical performances of ghosts can best be understood as contrived acts of illusion, mere legerdemain, vocal trickery, and stagecraft.

My efforts to observe and interact with spirit mediums can be called event ethnography (Bowen 2002: 80). By event ethnography I have in mind a specified practice of participant observation in which I carefully observed, recorded, and compared whole rituals, that is, complete séances, as theatrical performances Two such events were definitive for me, because they occurred as a kind of natural experiment. They were séances in which I supposedly conversed with my deceased father.

Those spirit encounters constituted a natural experiment insofar as they provided a unique opportunity to judge authenticity under conditions that resemble what is done in laboratory science. The theory under scrutiny is the claim that spirits pass on privileged information from the spirit world. If that theory is correct, then I would hypothesize that the spirit identified as my father would behave in ways consistent with the personality of my father as I knew him. As I shall demonstrate, that hypothesis failed. I would hypothesize that information about my family history would be accurate. That hypothesis failed. I would hypothesize that the spirit would provide information additional to what the medium already knew or could easily guess from talking with me. That hypothesis failed. In short, by these tests, the theory itself failed. In short, each of the two mediums got the facts and personality all wrong, convincing me beyond a doubt that both encounters were staged illusions.

As the following transcriptions demonstrate, each medium invoked a technique of calculated guessing known as cold reading. The guessing strategy includes eliciting clues by asking strategic questions in such a way that "the subject, anxious to hear from the dead, seldom realizes that he, not the medium or the departed, is supplying the answers" (Jaroff 2001: 52).

SITTING WITH CATHERINE

I will begin with the English medium who came to Iceland for the first time in 2000. Based on her solid reputation in England as a gifted clairvoyant, Catherine was invited to Reykjavík as a guest of the Icelandic Society for Spirit Research. While in Iceland she did sittings for a number of individual members of the society, all of whom were favorably impressed, thus ensuring that she would be invited to return annually. Halfway through that introductory visit, an informal gathering was arranged for several members of the board of directors and their guests, including me. It was an intimate meeting of nine people plus the medium.

The format was familiar to all of us except for one young woman who had never before encountered a medium. This kind of ritual or theatrical performance in Iceland may or may not begin and end with a prayer. In this instance, the prayer was omitted. After being introduced, Catherine spent about 10 minutes explaining how mediums communicate with spirits of the dead. *Spirits will always work with us if we just open ourselves to it. We guarantee nothing*, she said, insisting that she has no control over which spirits will come through, or even whether any will come at all. *We can't guarantee anything. But I know the spirits have never let me down*, which is to say that she can nonetheless virtually guarantee that spirits will appear.

She spoke of our obligation as an audience to ensure energetic inter-action with the spirits who come, an obligation Deborah and Edwin also emphasized whenever they initiated theatrical sittings to demonstrate transfiguration or psychokinesis. Catherine continued, *How they work is due to the sitters, because they work with energy. They use energy to com-municate, and that energy has to come from living people in the audience.*

She then gave her version of how one works as a clairvoyant medium. *In the spirit world there is no language. There are no people in the spirit world. We refer to them as people, but in actual fact it is wrong. People are of planet Earth. We are people now. But once we leave this Earth plane we return to our true environment, and that's a different level of consciousness. We don't have physical bodies. We don't need them. We don't have language. There is no physical body and no language.* It seemed to me that she was preparing us to be generous in excusing gaffs, since errors in transmission should not be interpreted as failure, but merely as diversions. *So when a medium works as I do, just bear with me. You'll hear me describe what I see. I don't see with these eyes. I see with my spiritual counterpart, my etheric eye, and I don't see physically, objectively. I see subjectively. So when a medium says she sees, that's how one sees. One doesn't see like these candles here, not very often, because there's no necessity to. We see spirit in our own way. And, of course, there is no language, so it is transparent thought—it's mind to mind—so I have to do translation of all forms of communication quickly, which is symbol-ism, words, pictures, everything. I have to transfer that and make it into a language* [which is very different from the way a trance medium works in permitting the spirit to use language and speak for itself]. *I am not con-scious when I do it.*

She went on to emphasize that the spirits who appear do so because they want to. *Some spirits are not willing to appear, and that is their free choice. They stay away. Some souls don't want to communicate. They are back there, away from this world, and they think, "Forget it." No soul is compelled to come back to Earth. The only reason they do come back is out of love. If they have loved ones here and for whatever reason want to be close to them, then they will make that effort. I've known people close to me who have never come back. Some say, "Oh, you shouldn't disturb these people." We don't disturb anyone. I can't command anyone to come to me. They come because they want to.*

Catherine's introductory remarks suddenly ended. It took a few moments for me to realize that she had precipitously begun to pass on messages from the spirit world. Her demeanor remained unchanged, even though she was supposedly functioning beyond her own consciousness. Her first two messages were to the wife of a member of the board of directors and then to the young woman who had never attended a séance before. She had just finished saying to the young woman, *You're giving out quite nice energies. Keep it like that,* when, unexpectedly, her very next words were directed to me.

I'm being given the name here, and it sounds to me like, and she paused before she turned to look directly at me, You said your name was Bob, didn't you? Who called you Bobby? I responded, Well, that was when I was a child. *Thank you, because I've got—actually it was earlier on. There was a lady giving me the name Bobby. I thought, no, not Bobby. Was it a grandmother that used to call you Bobby?* Oh, I said, everybody called me Bobby until I was about 12 years old.

It might seem simpleminded to problematize the connection between those two names, since it is well known that little boys are commonly called by the diminutive. In fact, it served a purpose in her cold reading. By making it seem unexpected and puzzling, it became available to her as a ploy to get me to offer information about a grandmother, but the ploy failed, so she tried another very different approach.

You don't have a Jewish connection, do you? No, I answered. *Your family wouldn't have anybody with a Jewish connection?* No. *Hmmm,* she said as she paused to ponder those denials, and no wonder. Who in Iceland or the United States does not have some Jewish "connection," be it to a Jewish identified doctor, teacher, friend, or fellow worker. And I didn't let her down because suddenly I reversed position and said, Oh, well, My daughter-in-law Debby—her mother Mary has some Jewish ancestry. *I wanted that Jewish link. And that's your son who is married to her?* Yes. *Do you get on well with her?* Oh, yes. *Yeah, because I'm being told here she is going through a little bit of a difficult time at the moment.* Well, she's an old lady, I replied. Everyone laughed when I said that. *Sorry?* She's an old lady. She has health problems. *Yes, and she's getting very disheartened about it.*

Note how manipulative this line of questioning was. It began with the question of whether I had a Jewish acquaintance or ancestor. That led to Mary, but her line of questioning no longer had anything to do with ancestry, Jewishness, or any such thing. Catherine suggested that Mary was experiencing a difficult time, a little bit, at the moment. Based on information I provided, our conversation moved from a slightly difficult time to one that is seriously difficult, from a momentary problem to one that has been long lasting, and the problem was not about family relationships, money worries, marital problems, ethnicity, or any of the other possible problem areas of life; it was about chronic pain, because I told her she had health problems. So, directed by the techniques of cold reading, the conversation was now about the health of one of my in-laws, based entirely on information I provided.

Catherine continued as though these non sequiturs had no importance at all. In cold reading you assume your audience will not notice or will forget the blind alleys you explored before finding your way to a topic of interest. In response to her saying, *she's getting very disheartened about it,* I said, Yes, she should be. She has serious health problems. *It's not going away,* Catherine responded, *You know that.* True, it isn't going away, I agreed, knowing that she had suffered from severe low back pain for decades. *What spirits say is that it would help if she had healing of some sort. It's not going to cure her.* No, I agreed. *Because this is part of her life experience* [part of what she is supposed to learn in this life], *this situation. And I don't know if she can understand that. Does she?* Well, I don't really know. I haven't talked with her about it from that point of view. But you know, in medicine, with chronic back problems that don't respond to therapy we always explain that even if we cannot cure it, we can help them live more effectively with the pain. *Yeah. And healing can help with the pain, you know.* Yes, absolutely.

What spirit is saying is, she could get more help than she is actually getting at the moment—by absentee healing even—it doesn't have to be a hands-on healer. Turning to look at the board member seated next to me she asked, *Do you have a healing book here?* He said that they did. Returning her gaze to me she continued, *Even if you* [just] *put her name in the healing book—if she gets absent healing—she's getting very exhausted—you know that!* Well, I'll have to talk with her about that. (The fact is, I almost never see her and I have never been briefed by her doctors.) Catherine continued, *She's getting very exhausted and she's getting—and it's almost as though she is giving up.* Yeah, well, I need to talk with her then. I wasn't aware of that.

At this point she apparently forgot that the Bob-as-Bobby ploy had dead-ended, because she inexplicably tried it again. *This lady who is call-*

ing you Bobby, she's very much instigated [sic] *in this, and I feel it is a grandmother, because she's coming on a very strong maternal energy. Was this your mother's mother?* They all called me Bobby, I reminded her, but she paid no attention. *I've definitely got a grandmother, but I think she is on your mother's side.* Yeah? *She's a very spiritual lady, or was. Very spiritually aware.* Yeah. *But a very good person, I wanted to say.*

With all due respect to the memory of that grandmother, I do not recall her as being "spiritual" or as a generous or caring person. I remember her as a divorced, bitter, chronically ill, self-centered complainer who never forgave my mother for leaving her to marry my father, whom she disliked intensely. But in response to Catherine, all I said was, Yeah.

I don't know that she was incredibly religious as such. No, she wasn't, I said. (But I was wrong. My brother recently discovered a letter she wrote when I was less than a year old. It was addressed *Til min kære lille Bob om Baptisterne og mit Hjem i Vejle.* She addressed me as Dear little Bob, not Bobby, and it was all about the family being born-again Baptist Christians in Vejle, Denmark! It would have been impressive if Catherine had given me that information, but I got it from Stan in a more mundane way.)

Catherine and I continued our conversation, unaware of Stan's discovery. *But she was a good person.* For some reason I responded by saying, she had premonitions [predictions revealed to her in dreams]. *Absolutely!* (What I neglected to add was that her predictions were often wrong and that she was mercifully off base when she cruelly told my pregnant young mother that I would be born deformed. In a cold reading, Catherine couldn't know that.) *Also, she said at that time you had to be very careful about what you said about upsetting people, if you spoke about things people didn't really want to talk about, anything that they didn't really understand.* (This makes no sense at all. I was still only a boy when that grandmother died.)

But she was a very psychic lady—very psychic. (I just told her that she had premonitions, so Catherine is just rephrasing what she learned from me.) *And she's very interested in this daughter-in-law of yours.* Oh? *Because she wants to help her.* Yeah? *She is saying that people on the Earth are doing all that they can but that's not quite enough, because they don't see what spirits see.* Yeah? *You know, spirits see the soul of this daughter-in-law.* Yeah? *And how exhausted she's getting fighting this situation. It's almost [that] she feels like just giving up.* Really? But it's her mother who has the chronic pain. My daughter-in-law Debby is young and healthy. (A well-executed cold reading requires keeping a lot of detailed factoids at one's fingertips, and Catherine slipped up on a major one here.)

So now Catherine had to reconstruct what she had just said by minimizing the error and carrying on as though nothing untoward had happened. *Yeah, but what I'm saying is, her mother is giving up. The daughter, I feel, has an inkling of this, but I don't know if she has actually said anything about it. Because it's almost as though she doesn't want to upset people. So there's a lot of things not being said, because people don't want to upset one another.* (Actually, Debby was seriously concerned and shared her concerns with her mother and brothers as well as with her husband Tom.)

Catherine continued, *Is she having surgery?* Oh, I don't think it's amenable to surgery. *No,* Catherine agreed, *because I was going to say, what spirit is saying is, that that would be out of the question.* Spirit has probably got it right, I agreed. *Because it's gone beyond that.*

Postscript: Shortly after that conversation Mary was operated on for sciatica (back pain radiating down the leg). The operation was a noteworthy success, and she is now pain free and able to exercise again. I was wrong to suggest that it was inoperable and Catherine (or the spirit) was equally wrong to repeat that back to me.

In these awful situations people say, oh, how can there be a God if people suffer like this, because they're only looking at it from the physical point of view, but from a spiritual point of view it's quite different. And it's not something that I don't know that she herself has ever looked at— the lady who is suffering—so do put her name on the healing list. I will, I said with good intentions, but I never got around to it. *Because I feel that will help her, and I also want to give you the name of Margaret.* All right, I said agreeably, accustomed by then to total incongruities in shifting from one subject to another.

Can you place the name of Margaret? Oh, oh, I see what you mean. No, not offhand I can't. Margaret, I said, and then paused. *I've been told here there's a connection with your parents.* Ah, it would have been Margrethe, a Danish cousin, and I laughed. *Foreign names again.* Yes. *She was connected with your parents?* Yes. She was a very important relative [from the generation before my parents]. It is mainly because of her that we still have close ties to Danish relatives on my father's side.

She was a very, very strong lady. She was, I agreed [although I have never met her]. *Yes.* She was ahead of her times, I added. She had been a buyer for a large department store in Copenhagen, which was an unusual achievement for a woman at that time. *Absolutely. When people met this lady they would never forget her. She used to make quite an impression on people. She was very strong. Very determined. She achieved quite a lot in her life.*

Maybe she did. Who knows? Catherine's descriptions were good guesses based on the information I gave her. She might well have been a very strong, very determined lady who made a lasting impression on people and achieved a lot in her lifetime. I didn't know enough about her to verify or falsify those claims, so it was a successful cold reading gambit that made a few trivial statements seem like true revelations.

Postscript: When Stan read this part of the manuscript he pointed out in his most sympathetic professorial manner that I had conflated two family stories. To put it bluntly, I was all wrong in what I told Catherine about the young Danish woman who was a buyer for a large department store. She was not Margrethe and was not even a relative. She was a buyer for the Emporium in San Francisco who frequently came over from Denmark. Back in Copenhagen she was a role model for Stella, who eventually traveled to California herself, where she met my father and, in due time, gave birth to Stan and me. Cousin Margrethe did visit the family in California, but that's another story. I unknowingly gave false information to Catherine, so, of course, the information she fed back was also false.

Catherine continued, *She [Margrethe] is very interested in what is happening around your family. She is saying also about yourself—what did you say? I've looked briefly at your business card. Are you a lecturer or something?* To clarify I explained that I'm a college professor. *Right. She's putting a book around you. Have you written a book?* Oh, yes, one is coming out just now from the Office of the Surgeon General [of Iceland]. I'll be talking with him about it tomorrow. *No,* she admonished me. *I would have told you that!* Everybody laughed as she implied that through a spirit contact she knew what was going to happen to me tomorrow. I couldn't tell whether she meant to be taken seriously on that point or not, but it has the ring of cold reading about it.

Catherine continued, *Because what she was saying about this book is that you were very inspired by spirit with that.* She then went on at length about how the spirit world was looking forward to the publication of my rather tedious monograph on a medical topic of quite limited interest even to its intended audience of health care professionals. With that, Catherine abandoned my cousin Margrethe who visited California just once when she was quite young.

And your father is extremely interested. Very, very interested. In response I reminded Ragnheidr, the office manager who was with us that evening, that I had a conversation with my father in this very building just 2 years earlier [with Vigdis]. It was the first time since before he died over 40 years earlier, I said. Remember? That caused laughter for some reason; maybe just because we were all in a good mood.

Also, still speaking of my father, she said, *he's actually acknowledging what you are achieving, and I think that takes quite a lot, actually.* I laughed and said, good for him. She continued without pause, *Because I don't find that he ever openly expressed those things to you, but he certainly does now. To say that he is proud of you is a physical term, but that is the energy that he has given me, that you have achieved.*

She seems to be referring to a common father and son issue here that was not part of the relationship. If anything, he and my mother were excessively proud of my brother and me, and never hesitated to tell us so. It is a common cold reading technique to describe spirits in ways that fit well-known stereotypes. She did it for Margrethe and here she is doing it for my father. She has a good likelihood of guessing correctly if she assumes that a father was unable to give voice to his love and admiration of a son, but in this case she was wrong.

Talking about pride and approval made me uncomfortable, so I decided to become politically correct. You know, I said, what's important to me is the love that's there. She instantly agreed. *Absolutely! As I said to you, that's why they come. They come in love. That's the only reason. They don't come for any other reason than love. What he is saying to you is, he's only a thought a way from you. He's only a thought away from you.*

With that, the subject shot off in still another unexpected direction. *He has also given me the month of November.* Hmm, I pondered. *Was that a day connected with him in any way?* Addressing her audience she added, gratuitously I thought, *Now, men are notoriously bad on dates, I know.* We all laughed at her sexual stereotyping, I along with the rest.

She was flat out wrong about November signifying something about my father, however, but I gave her a way out when I said, Well, I don't know, but November is when I will probably go back to Denmark. *Hold on to that, because it's going to be important. What he's saying to me is that he'll be there with you.* Good, I exclaimed. *Any doubts or anything, just ask.* We dropped that subject, but in my skepticism I took note of how November suddenly did not refer to my father at all, but to something totally unrelated, a date on my professional agenda. It was a deftly executed cold reading flip-flop.

He was a handsome looking man, your father. Oh, yes, I said emphatically. That caused laughter. *And also, he had a nice way with him as well. It wasn't just the looks.* That was true enough, I thought, so I said, he had a very nice personality. Catherine picked up on that, saying, *People! He was like a sponge. You know, people would gravitate towards him. He just had that way with him. He had beautiful energies with him, absolutely beautiful energy. He wasn't an angel by any mark of the imagination.* No, he wasn't. *He had his fine points and his weak points, but since he has been in spirit he sees things so differently.*

I was not very impressed with that characterization. He was definitely not a people sponge who attracted people in a charismatic way. Not at all. He was a very plain man, although he could easily exchange a few words with a stranger, who always left, still a stranger, usually never to be seen again. The cold reading assumption Catherine applied here got her in trouble because she was guessing at what my father was like based on what she knew about me. What threw her off was upward mobility. Victor was raised by an immigrant single mother in a hardscrabble working class neighborhood in East Oakland. He made his living as a house painter and barber. She described him as he might have been had he become, like his sons, a college-educated professional man. She was right about one thing, though. He was not an angel. What man is?

Without taking a breath, she suddenly and completely changed the subject. *And he said his eyes have been opened so much. He just wishes he had known all about this before. Because he used to dismiss things. He didn't delve into things too deeply in that respect. But I suppose at that time people didn't, terribly. But he is saying, this is an exciting time for you.*

That complex statement offered a couple of possible directions for further conversation. I picked up on the statement, *his eyes have been opened so much,* and acceded to the implied shift to what he now knew about the meaning of life, telling Catherine and those present that my father was deeply religious, whose social life centered on Sundays at the Baptist church. He believed he would go to heaven, I stated; I wonder where he is right now?

As is common when doing a cold reading, this comment offered Catherine the opportunity for a mini-lecture, leaving my father to languish for the moment. *You see, what people believe in, that's where they go.* Oh, I said out loud while making a mental note to give some thought to how I might want to conceptualize my own afterlife so I don't end up spending all of eternity playing a harp and singing hymns on a featureless cloud. Catherine continued her oration on what life is like in the spirit world. *You see, people say when you die, do you see God? I say, well, it's who you expected to see, because that's what we experience, is what we're conditioned to actually believe in. I mean, a Hindu or Muslim is not going to meet God, right? They're going to meet their own gods. It's not our idea of a Christian God or Jesus. The Catholic is going to meet the saints. So it's really what people believe in. Religion is an impediment because it holds us back. In fact, it denies us the ability to understand the true sense of our true selves. Religion just clouds the whole thing. It's not until we leave our physical bodies and we actually go to where we're going, that is, to the spirit world, that we actually see it. It's just a different level of consciousness.* That seemed consistent with what Magnus told me when I asked if spirits of the dead are still Christians, or Jews, or whatever. *Yes, they are,* he told me, *but their view enlarges so they understand all the other religions.*

Referring to the spirit world as a different level of consciousness, Catherine continued, *We do actually see it. Our truth is shown to us, whether or not souls accept it is another thing. People who have been very indoctrinated by religion find it very difficult to shake that off. It can take quite a number of years. Invariably they do. Because they are helped by spirit. But he's a thinker, your father.* Not even remotely true, I thought, but under the circumstances I just said, Oh yes. *He is an intelligent man, and he will work it out himself.*

The most amazing result when they leave their bodies is that they find they are still alive. That's what they find so amazing. We don't have these physical bodies, but we do have counterparts, because it would be too much for the soul to suddenly be without a body. So it has a spiritual counterpart made up of spiritual material. It is a replica of the physical body. We carry that with us for as long as we need it, but when we progress more we realize we don't need it and it goes. So it takes stages of experience and understanding before people can actually get rid of that and the religious dogma they were attached to while still on Earth. Organized religion is quite an impediment.

Inserting this lecture constituted a successful cold reading way to pass on a lot of information supposedly obtained from years of conversations with spirits of the dead. It could not be falsified by any of us present in that sitting. She claimed to know it by direct revelation. What did we know! It was rich enough in content to make her audience feel that they were learning what they would someday experience for themselves, but only after having passed over. By then, they would no longer be in a position to report back on her accuracy.

Finally she said this. *Your father has that awareness with him. He has the understanding that maybe religion was not all it was cracked up to be because of what he has experienced since he passed. That he is able to be with you has really shaken him.* She added, *He is very protective of you. Very, very protective.*

I'm sure he would be if he could. It made better sense than what Siggi told me. He insisted that it was my grandfather rather than my father who protected me. Magnus, for his part, said that personal guardians are not ancestors at all. So, the messages are inconsistent.

Suddenly the conversation took yet another unexpected and seemingly arbitrary detour. After saying, *He is very protective of you. Very, very protective,* she added, *And he's mentioning one of your legs. Have you had a problem with one of your legs?* No, I said, in no way at all. *Right. He's talking about one and it's circulatory. He's telling me—You don't smoke, do you?* No. *If you start to get quite a nagging sort of feel-*

ing in your leg, it's purely circulatory. I'm sorry to say, it's just the aging process. Again, ask for healing for yourself. You can do that.

My father was not able to tell her two things about my present health. She had to ask whether or not I had a leg problem and whether or not I smoked. Had I said yes to either one, a skilled cold reader would then feed that information back to me as a message from the spirits: my leg problem will get worse and smoking is bad for my health, or whatever.

Yet she predicted with confidence that I would have a leg problem as I get older. I am not impressed. Almost immediately she added, *But he's saying, at some point you're going to have to slow down and you won't be jet-setting as much as you do now.* Even I can predict that as a normal consequence of aging. I was not impressed. *But he's also saying you'll work until the day you, uh* [clearing her throat hesitantly], *go. Lots of love. Lots of love, okay?"* As a cold reading technique, these are exceedingly vague predictions she will never have to defend, because she will be long gone by that time.

SITTING WITH VIGDIS

Vigdis is very skilled in cold reading, as my sitting with her will demonstrate. Although they both share in the same spiritist culture, Vigdis enjoyed a big advantage over Catherine, because I had met with her several times in earlier months and had volunteered information about my work, my life, and my family. She was also privy to the conversations I had with others at the Icelandic Society for Spirit Research. She knew that I was a Danish American. Since Iceland was formerly a Danish colony and Icelanders still go to Denmark for graduate studies and professional schools or to work, she was, unlike Catherine, well informed about Danish culture.

Vigdis is so highly sought after that I had to wait a month before I could meet with her. When the time finally arrived, she greeted me in the waiting room to chat for a while before we moved into a private side room where the séance took place. Seated face to face, with Vigdis enthroned in her upholstered wing chair under a statuette of Jesus, we both became very quiet as she folded her hands in prayer and softly invoked the protection of God. *Father, in your hands I place us. I ask for the higher light, and to surround us, and those who come from the other side to help us, with love. Thank you very much.*

As she opened her eyes she said, *There are two ladies here. Another lady is very small.* Then she directed a question to me. *Your grandmother*

Mourners gather outside a church before going to the cemetery

*and grandfather on your father's side—they didn't live in the States?
Because they are taking me somewhere else.* They came to the United
States from Denmark, I answered. *They lived in Denmark for a while?*
Yes, I said, until they were around 30 years of age. (As a cold reading
technique, this was her way of starting off on a solid footing by making
my Danish ancestry seem like a discovery from the spirit world when in
fact it was information I had provided. Catherine started off in an equivalent way when she wondered who might have called me Bobby.)

She continued, *They are taking me to a rather small place in
Denmark. Not Copenhagen.* Yes, yes, I agree. I know just where it is, I
said, as my thoughts turned to Varde, the country town my father's
mother came from. (She could hardly go wrong on this cold reading
gambit, since every Dane in the 19th century had at least some relatives
who lived in rural villages. Many still do.)

*Okay. They are taking me to a rather small place, your father's father
and a Peter.* (With this her cold reading employed a very useful way of
getting the client involved. She identified a spirit by a name so common
that it inevitably should identify some acquaintance or relative. We all
know someone named Peter.) I volunteered that I didn't know who Peter
might be, but I told her that my grandfather's name was Jens Peder

Andersen, which she immediately accepted, saying, *Yes. That's it. Yeah, that's Peter.* (Thus, in a flash, instead of my grandfather being with a man whose name was Peter, he himself became Peter. I wondered whether we would continue to play verbal hopscotch in this way, but it appears to be common in a cold reading.)

I was unconvinced that the spirit called Peter was my grandfather as she claimed. He was never referred to or addressed as Peder, but always as Jens Peder or just Jens. Later, in the States, it was always just Jens. So I countered by saying that I had an uncle whose first name was Peder. Unabashedly, she abandoned her bold but mistaken assertion about my grandfather and replaced him with my Onkel Peder. *Was he skinny?* As she asked she placed the palms of her hands on her cheeks, pulling them together to make her face look narrow. He was small, I said. Yeah, I agreed, he was kind of thin faced [although, to be truthful, I couldn't really remember since the last time I saw him was in a village in Denmark more than 50 years ago]. *Okay,* she said, *that's him.*

Well, I thought to myself, that makes better sense, because Jens Peder was certainly not skinny. According to hospital records he was morbidly obese. The cold reading strategy that worked here was to appear to confirm the identification by adding a second clue, his physical appearance. She lucked out on that, because I agreed that he was a small man and maybe skinny.

So we transitioned to talking about my Uncle Peter, which is the Americanized name I always used. I voiced the observation that I had met him when I was living in Denmark as a student. Picking up on my having met him there, Vigdis clarified in an effective cold reading way where the spirits were located by saying, *Because I am in Denmark.* Yes, I agreed, he lived in Denmark. As soon as we had agreed on where she and they were, she hooked her thumbs under a pair of imaginary suspenders and puffed up her chest like a proud man, saying, *He says, "Denmark."*

This cold reading guess backfired on her. It is reasonable to believe that any Dane is proud of being Danish. But when she had him express himself the way she did, it seemed very unlike my Uncle Peter, who was a very quiet, soft-spoken, unassertive man, notable for being a devout Baptist, which is quite unusual for a farmer on the Peninsula of Jutland. He was not given to the sin of pride or the practice of boasting.

However, I didn't challenge her on that. Instead I simply stated that he was my mother's uncle. She took absolutely no notice of the fact that a grandfather on my father's side turned out to be an uncle on my mother's side, another instance of cold reading hopscotch. Instead, she shifted to a new cold reading "Guess who came?" line of inquiry.

After I said, That's my mother's uncle, she said, *He is also talking about Karía, Kári.* I asked, [could it be] Kaj? *Yeah,* she said, *Kaj, Kária.* In response I said, Kaj is a cousin on my father's side [in order to clarify, suddenly my mother's uncle is associated with my father's cousin, which seemed quite unlikely, since they would not have known each other]. Abruptly and with sublime assertiveness she continued, *He's there too!*

She consistently made strong declarative statements like that, which I see as a cold reading way to assert that she is absolutely certain about the accuracy of what she is transmitting. But in this case her certainty was premature, and suddenly she was put on the defensive by what I said next.

Is he? But he is not dead! I made that statement with the clear implication that he could not be present with us in that room as the spirit of a dead man if at that very moment he was still healthy and alive at his home in Randers, Denmark. Now, one would think that she would feel threatened or defeated by the piling up of inconsistencies, but on the contrary, she moved right on without batting an eyelash. *Well,* she insisted, *there is a Kaj here, whoever that is, so you'll have to find out.* I don't know, I countered. *So you'll have to find out,* she repeated, admonishing me with a wagging finger. I don't know, I repeated, truly unable to believe that I might conjure up any other Kaj in my family.

To this date, several years later, I still have not succeeded in that, but it was an effective cold reading achievement on her part. She attributed the gross error of saying he's there to my failure to identify a relative with the same name who was dead and buried. She reversed our positions. Now it was up to me to figure out who it had to be. She absolutely refused to acknowledge failure as she continued.

Because he is there, and also Jo, Jonas, Johan, Jo. Trying to be supportive, because I had not come with the intent of testing or tricking her, I said, Johan. *Yeah, Johan.* My great-great-great-grandfather was Johan Nielsen, I explained. *He's also here,* she said in her characteristically emphatic way. I didn't mention that once again we had changed kindreds, because old Johan, who lived in the early 1700s, was on my father's side, not my mother's, another example of cold reading gamesmanship. Instead I just said in an affirmative way, It seems that all of them are here.

She picked up on that, agreeing, *I see about 10 people.* Really? I countered, feeling both surprised and confused. *I see your father. I don't see him very well. It's like a little fog in front of him, because he wants your mother to come in for a little while.* As she made that statement, she moved her left hand as though signaling someone from behind her to come to the front. *He says, "I want your mother to come in for a while," and he is talking about Birket.* Birket? I queried, wondering if my old professor at the University of Copenhagen was making an appearance, Kaj Birket-Smith. But we weren't talking about university professors, we were discussing relatives. *"B," "B," something with "B." Your father lived in the States, right?* Right. *Could it be Becky? It's a lady with a "B" who is with your mother, that's for sure. She's standing next to her.* Well, I silently mused, Kaj Birket-Smith was definitely not a lady.

Out loud I replied, I can't think of who that could be. *And the house is a two-story house.* Where they lived in the States? I asked. *Yes, because I said, what kind of a house is it? Think on the house. He started to think about the house and now I see two stories. He said her name is, I think, Becky, or Bippie, or Bittie, or something. Anyway, she came in with your mother's mother and Maria, Maria, Mary.* I don't know, I responded, having absolutely no idea of who this might be. The names Becky and Maria, with variants, have nothing to do with dead members of our family. And I was totally uncomprehending of how we could be visualizing a house in America that somehow was present in a community in Denmark.

Instead, Vigdis moved on to put me in contact with my mother. *She's a very small lady—kind of a cute lady,* whereupon she made coquettish movements in her chair. *She walks like that,* miming a bouncy, perky walk, and she looks at me and she wants you to know, all of your neighbors are here! Oh, really, I replied, chuckling at what struck me as an incongruous possibility. *All your neighbors are here. "Your mother said to us, we can come, so we are not going to be a bother, but we decided we are going to come." So they kind of wave their hands and leave. They are in the background.*

Mistake was following upon mistake. True, Vigdis was right on target in seeing my mother as a very small lady, since she stood only 4' 11" in height before she started shrinking in old age. If Vigdis was merely guessing based on knowing me, she would surely have produced a bigger mother, since I stand 6 feet tall. However, to describe my mother as cute and to mime her as coquettish, perky, and bouncy is totally at odds with the constrained and rather stiff demeanor that was her way of being in the world. But perhaps one of her lessons in the afterlife was to overcome a lifetime of enormous social inhibitions.

Further, it is quite incomprehensible that our neighbors were present in a friendly and somewhat intimate way. My parents never had neighbors in any community in Denmark, because they met as adults in California where they lived for the rest of their lives. As to neighbors in the States, my parents hardly knew who lived nearby and certainly never socialized beyond saying "hello" when passing on the sidewalk or perhaps by exchanging a few words when meeting at the corner grocery store.

Edna Mitchell

A final resting place

They did chat briefly with acquaintances at our church, but that was in another part of town and those were also distant and uninvolved Sunday-only encounters. Certainly, not a single neighbor or church member had ever been invited into our house and my parents similarly were never in any of theirs. Working class people where I grew up in East Oakland didn't do things like that. The cold reading mind trap for Vigdis was to assume that the neighborliness of an old fashioned Danish village was replicated in an American inner city.

But to continue, Vigdis was telling me that our former neighbors were present with us at the moment, *So they kind of wave their hands and leave. They are in the background.* After which she immediately went on to say, *But your mother comes with a woman, a sister. Who's sister is that?* at which point she put her hand in her chin and gave me a quizzical look. *Wait a second,* and then, addressing the spirits by looking up and away from me she whispered, *Sister! Whose sister is that? Gai, Guh, nei, Guh.* Returning to address me she continued, *Your mother didn't have a sister who is gone?* My mother had no sister. Abandoning the possibility of a sister, Vigdis identified a brother, which was on target, but then she asked, *Did your mother have two brothers?*

She had one brother, I insisted. *She's talking about two brothers, but you are just an only brother.* This statement doesn't make sense. Was she referring to my mother having two sons, so that my brother and I can be said to be two brothers? So I asked, You say my mother had two brothers? Vigdis countered, *Did she have two brothers?* So I replied, saying, that's an interesting question. Vigdis interrupted, *Because she is talking about two brothers.*

I wanted to know more. What does she say about those brothers? Are they brothers that she knew? Here, Vigdis demonstrated her quickness of mind with a cold reading response based on my having told her there was only one brother, but she stated it tentatively, as though she is still struggling with what the spirits were telling her. *Possibly she knew one. I know. I know she knew one because she is taking the arm of one. But there is a distance between her and the other one.* I was happy to pick up on that in an affirmative way. You see, I told her, she was adopted, which led Vigdis to utter *Oh* with obvious relief. *That's the reason.* (In cold reading, miscarriages, abortions, and adoptions can all be used to account for nonexistent siblings or children.)

All right, Vigdis said. *I understand. I understand. Because she is shaking her head like this,* nodding her own head to indicate yes. *She also wants you to know she comes often to visit you,* adding, *so you must have children,* and she held up her hand with three fingers extended. Who me? I said, and then I said yes. Enigmatically, Vigdis, while still holding up three fingers, asked, *Do you have four?"* I countered by saying, I have six. *Why then is she showing three? And one?* Well, when I was first married I had three, and then I married Edna and she had three, so between us we have six. *Because she is showing me three,* Vigdis persisted. I suggested, Yeah, well that would be the three I had first. Note that "three" turned out to be a lucky guess, but "one" did not fit. Consistent with her sometimes reckless cold reading style, she found a way to keep "one" in play by saying, *then there is one who is kind of close to you.* That statement would probably work for many families, because favoritism does occur. However, it failed her this time.

She is showing me one kid who is very close to you. Especially one, she says. Especially one. That kid was very, very young when you were together. The youngest. Yes, I affirmed. Well, the youngest baby I had was Robin. (What I meant was that the first baby I had was Robin, but I stumbled over vocabulary. All babies are young when they are born.) *She's talking about him.* What is she saying about Robin? *She is telling me that he thinks about you a lot, about what you are doing, and why you are doing it.*

Being rather perplexed at all of this, since I have never favored one of the six over another, I sort of argued with Vigdis, saying, but Robin and I correspond regularly. *That's what she is saying. That's what she is saying* (the cold reading technique of feeding back what I had just told her).

I heard from her just this month, I said. *She says you are close to him, and she's going to tell you the reason for it.* What is it? I asked, with great curiosity. *The reason is, it's not your first life together.* (Reincarnation, like miscarriages and so on, can account for a lot in a cold reading.) With my daughter Robin, I said, making no big deal out of the fact that Robin is a daughter, not a son. Is that so? I added pensively.

Yeah, and also, whereupon she broke off that sentence and looked into space as she shifted to conversing directly with the spirits. *Energy. Yeah. The level of energy. Yeah. Yeah. Thank you.* Facing me again, and shifting without comment from Robin as him to Robin as her she said, *the energy of you and her is the same. It's the same energy level, and,* referring to my mother, *she puts her hands to her chest to indicate that both of you are at that level. And she wants you to know that. And she says that she often sits close to her, uh, she wants to, uh, she likes her. She says, "I feel so good around her."*

Just as favoritism is common in families, so is the experience of having a child who is or was difficult to raise and Vigdis took a gamble on that as still one more cold reading bit of gamesmanship. Finished with talking about Robin and my mother she said, without transitional comment, *But one of your own kids has a very strong will, and there's a problem. It's a boy I think, and there were a lot of problems with him for a while, and* she said he was trying to show off. *But now his position is a lot better.*

I uttered a noncommittal "oh," since our two sons were never in trouble of any kind and neither one was a show-off. *A lot better,* she concluded and then moved on to a totally different relationship.

I want to ask you, did your father have a brother? He had three brothers. *Did he have a brother who had an accident when he was younger? Around the time when he came to the States? Or maybe before?* No, not that I know of. *I see an accident.* In response I confirmed, Well, as an older man, yeah, one of his brothers had an accident. *Was there a young person with him in the car?* It wasn't that kind of an accident, I said. It was an accident at work as a carpenter. *I'm going to show you the picture I'm looking at. I see two people in a car. A car wreck. A very bad car wreck. I think one person died,* and she continued on in this vein. I could recall no such accident, and we seem to have wandered away from my father's brother having had an accident either in Denmark or while still young in United States.

Because this séance was very long, in recounting the rest of it I will cut out a lot that is not directly relevant to a discussion of cold reading.

Were you very connected with your father, she asked. Oh, yes, I said. Very close. I had a very loving father. *Because it was so unusual to see him back up and let your mom come through.* Well, they were very loving of one another. *So now he's closer here and he wants you to know he's very close to you. Always has been. He is showing me books. Did he read a lot?* No, I said, laughing, but he has books that I wrote. *Oh, is that what it is, because he's giving me the books. He said, "Here are the books. I want to hand them over to you,"* and as she made that statement she held out her hands toward me. *Here are the books. Okay. If he had books, then you must have them.*

This wasn't making much sense to me, but I said yes and she continued. *And there's one bigger book. Different. Not really to read. Really just pictures and something under each picture. Do you remember that?* Well, it would be hard for me to remember. *This one is brown and white.* I don't know. He didn't read books. I never saw him read a book in his whole life. Armed with that bit of information she shifted ground, *No, no, no. It was pictures. Do you have a book from Denmark about your people? Or a paper? He showed me that.*

Her cold reading misled her here, probably for the same reason that Catherine was misled by social mobility and the fact that my personal culture is very different from that of my father. He dropped out of school in the fifth grade, owned no books other than a rarely glanced at Bible, and, what I didn't remember at the time of this sitting with Vigdis, never possessed any of the books I have written because he died before the first one was published. We had no picture book of Denmark, since the illustrated book of Hans Christian Andersen's fairy tales would not fall into that category, but my mother did keep a black-covered photograph album of family pictures.

I interpret what Vigdis said about books as a total disconnect, and as a result, she was in trouble. So she loosened the net, effectively abandoning books for other kinds of paper artifacts. *I'll tell you why,* she continued, and with that we were now talking about a piece of paper, which underwent a third transformation to become a letter. My father was foretelling that I would receive a letter from Denmark.

He said, next winter you will get a piece of paper from someone in Denmark, or a person of Danish origin, maybe living in the States, I don't know. The person is Danish on both sides, and you will get a little invitation. You will have to fly a little to get there and you should go. When that invitation comes you will meet a lot of people, those you have never seen, so please remember it. I said I would and that I might well need to return to Denmark the following May. *Yes!* she said. I expect to be invited to speak at a conference in Odense. *Yes, that's it. He's telling you that. He says, "Go!" He wants you to go.*

As an aside, that was not the conference I discussed with Catherine, which occurred two years later. And it was not exactly an unknown future event, since I was already in correspondence on it. However, I responded to her prediction in a confirmatory way by saying, so he's saying it's going to happen and he's telling me it a good thing for me to do. *A ver-r-ry good thing. He says you will see a lot of people there. It's going to be very interesting for you. "If I were you, I would go," he says.* In retrospect I can confirm that I did go and it was a good thing to do.

Vigdis continued transmitting from my father. *Then he is showing me—his eyes kind of smile when he looks at me—I see his face very well. I don't see his height yet. I think, I'm not sure if he was tall. Maybe your size. Maybe a little smaller.* He was shorter, I affirmed. *But he's smiling and he says, "Do you know what? Everyone is going to come over here. No one can skip this place," he says.* I assumed that she was not referring to Denmark, so I chimed in, You mean, to pass over to the other side? She nodded and I said, Oh, yes, of course. *Yes, and he starts to laugh, "Everybody. That's the only thing we know."*

The give and take between Vigdis, my father, and me went on in this vein for another 15 minutes. None of it was very explicit or satisfying, which led to Vigdis saying, *well, anyhow, your father says he's very glad you came.* She closed her eyes and moved her face toward her lap, with her hands folded in prayer, she offered a mini-lecture much as Catherine had done. *And he wants you to know, "We are very close to you and we want you to know that when you dream you should write it down. Sometimes there is no meaning. We may just come to visit. But other times there is meaning. A dream can be very meaningful."*

In all, Vigdis skillfully used cold reading techniques of guessing based on the information she had or could elicit. She relied heavily on taking chances with name associations. Many of them seemed like revelations until they could be examined carefully and thoughtfully later in the printed transcript. She used knowledge of my ancestry to situate my parents in Denmark. Like Catherine, she offered stereotypic characterizations of my mother and father based on knowing me as a middle-class educated man. She characterized two of my children based on common family scenarios of difficult sons and loving daughters. She was able to salvage the statement that my mother had two brothers when I revealed that my mother was adopted. Not the least, she capitalized on ambiguities, as when a book became a paper that became a letter. As did Catherine, she ended with vague and unimpressive predictions, including that I should attend the planned meeting in Denmark because it would be good for me.

CONCLUSION

Two different mediums claimed to have put me in touch with my deceased father, and in each case the demonstration was completely unconvincing. Both encounters were full of errors and distorted characterizations because each was based on guesswork, the techniques of cold reading. The séances are best interpreted as theatrical performances played out on small stages. That conclusion is consistent with my characterization of the theatrical performances of transformation and physical mediums, which also are reasonably interpreted as no more than staged entertainment.

In terms of the scientific method, the existence of spirits living in an afterworld is not disconfirmed by these failures. From a logical point of view, as well as in the view of spiritists, these and the other failed séances I documented only prove that highly esteemed mediums do fail to live up to their claims at times. They do not prove that these same mediums, or others who mediate contact with the dead, might not be successful under other circumstances or with other clients. All that is required is one incontrovertible experience that is completely convincing, and the medium has the evidence to prove that while bodies may die and decompose, spirits live on, as immortal as the gods themselves. For that reason, it will never be possible to prove that gods and spirits do not exist. The most one will ever be able to achieve is to falsify the evidence that is provided at any one time.

In the field of medical anthropology, we often encounter alternative practitioners who accomplish absolutely nothing as far as curing diseases is concerned. Based on anatomic and physiologic evidence it can be stated categorically that in some cases they provide potions with no active ingredients. They perform manipulations that are ineffective or even contraindicated (Anderson & Klein 2004). They prescribe rituals that leave sinister pathologies unchanged (Anderson 1991). What is deeply worrisome is that they may actually cause harm. For example, in my own work I have witnessed the use of comfrey, a widely sold herb that can destroy the liver and cause death (Anderson 1992a). However, we do not therefore assume that alternative medicine cannot be valuable for other reasons. It may be highly effective for healing psychosomatic illness, for strengthening spirit, for alleviating suffering.

I want to argue a comparable benefit for spiritist efforts to make contact with the dead. I am personally prepared to dismiss all of the claims I have examined as unproven and merely speculative. I also think it is important to be alert to the possibility of giving advice that can lead to unintended harm. In my own experience, for example, when Catherine offered medical advice, saying *If you start to get quite a nagging sort of feeling in your leg, it's purely circulatory. I'm sorry to say, it's just the aging process,* she clearly did not consider the possibility that impaired circulation can be a sign of a serious disease that requires medical attention to avoid possible gangrene and amputation. That was bad advice. For Catherine to say that spinal surgery was out of the question for my in-law was irresponsible and, had Mary been aware of it, might conceivably have diverted her from the surgery she needed. A year or two earlier when Vigdis saw me for a healing she told me I should seek care from a chiropractor she knew. He takes X-rays, she told me, not realizing that I had examined his practice and determined that he routinely requires X-ray studies that unnecessarily expose his patients to the dangers of ionizing radiation and cancer (Anderson 2000: 42–43; Anderson 1992b: 165–166). That, too, was bad advice.

These conclusions do not mean that I am dismissive of spiritism. Quite the contrary. I was deeply touched by the love and compassion I encountered, the spirituality that is taught and shared. There is a healing power in the ideology of spirit communication that has a potential for alleviating suffering and bringing joy into people's lives. It is comforting to believe that loved ones are happy in an afterworld. An ideology of endless schooling that teaches how better to give oneself to others in unselfish love is truly inspiring. That is what spiritism is all about in Iceland, where the best-known ghosts of all are spirit doctors who make house calls to alleviate suffering and pain.

EPILOGUE

The Last Word

My fieldwork in Iceland led to two major conclusions. One is that efforts to contact the dead succeed quite well as theatrical performances but fail in their avowed purpose of channeling communication between the living and the dead, even though the mediums who make such claims appear to be sincere and well intentioned. The other conclusion is that the related ideology of spirituality is powerful and valuable in itself. It encourages personal growth in humanitarian values such as caring for the planet, loving both kith and kin, healing those who are sick, and nurturing the down-trodden.

I am deeply indebted to the many individuals and social groups who invited me to take part in their activities. I regret the disappointment it inevitably will cause when they realize that I have concluded that séances and public demonstrations of spirit contact are really no more than clever illusions. For that reason, I am happy to let them have the last word.

Time and again convinced spiritists told me that originally they were as skeptical as I about the reality of spirits. Without exception, every spiritist freely admits that not all sittings produce genuine contact with the dead. For each one, however, it is enough that at least once a spirit revealed information that only a spirit could know, which is enough to prove that life survives the grave.

Gudmundur advised me on this when he recalled his early experience with the Icelandic Society for Spirit Research, years before he became its president. *I started to test a medium in a private meeting. I tried to be negative, writing down a list of items to check out later. It disturbs the medium, though, if your attitude is, "Now I'm going to test you." It's better just to have a private meeting and listen.* Then, he told me that he became convinced of the reality of the spirit world when a medium put him in touch with his dead father, who talked with him just the way he used to when he was alive.

217

Thordis, a university student, offers a case in point as she described her first meeting with a medium and a spirit. It happened when she was breaking up with a boyfriend and was very troubled. On the advice of a girlfriend, she made an appointment with a woman who was said to be a good listener. *I thought it was a good idea because she was not involved in my life and it would be good to talk with somebody. I phoned. She invited me for a visit. Only after I got there did I learn she was a medium. She told me my granny was there with us, and she described her completely. My granny was there,* **watching over me and trying to help me** [emphasis added].

Elaborating on that visit, she recalled that the medium said her guide was an Indian woman, a medicine woman. *I find that interesting, but I'm not sure whether to believe it or not. The Indian woman said my granny was there along with my two grandfathers and a nun.* A nun? I exclaimed. *I suppose it was a Catholic nun. She said nuns tend to watch over people because they don't have children of their own, so they find people to watch over as though they were relatives.*

The medicine woman then told her about her past lives, one as an 11-year-old Jewish girl on whom Nazi doctors experimented and another when she was an Italian who died in 1960 at the age of 20. *I don't know whether or not to believe that,* she said. *But the fact that she really described my great-grandmother—I believe that. She described her and told me about her and, I mean, the medium couldn't have known anything about her, and that helped, to know that she was there with me. It made me feel better, less insecure.*

Adalbjörg, the sixtyish widow whose injured son was attended to by a spirit doctor and who has met with the spirits of her father and husband, got her first convincing verification when she was still a young woman. At that time she attended a public meeting in which, as she recalled, the medium said, *"There's a little boy here, about 2 years old. He's playing with his toys." My girlfriend knew immediately it was a little cousin of hers who by mistake had taken his grandmother's heart medicine. She told me it was not a child who was close to her, but she knew the family and they had this little boy, and that evening in the séance, the boy came. It's things like that, things the medium couldn't know. I'm quite definitely sure that we go on. I think that at first, especially, we stay around those we love, but later we distance ourselves. I'm sure we are born again. We have no recollection of previous lives, but we are born again and again.*

Persistent skepticism and discriminating belief tussle and turn in many life stories, including that of Adalbjörg. She is convinced that when she sat facing the famous medium, Einar of Einarstadur, he truly shrank into his body like a released balloon that hisses and collapses. He could not have faked it, she told me, because two individuals were sitting on either side of him, each holding one of his hands and she herself was sitting directly in front of him. *There were sobs and prayers. It was very dark,* she added, convinced in spite of the darkness that it was not an illusion. Yet, in her next breath she told me she could not believe that Deborah's transfigurations were genuine. *I think that's a fake,* she asserted, adding, *I know of a very good medium—my husband knew her. Somebody got her to fake something like that, and it ruined her completely.*

Vigdis gave me an example from early in her career as a medium of how she is absolutely positive that spirits communicate with her. *Sometimes I hear a voice,* she told me. *I will tell you a little story so you will understand. I was sitting in my bed with coffee and the paper one morning when I heard a voice say, "Come with me." I thought, I have coffee in my hand. I can't go anywhere. But then the voice came closer and repeated, "Come with me." So I put the coffee aside so it wouldn't spill and I followed the voice.*

Of course it was my soul that traveled, she explained. *In that way I went to a hospital where I saw a friend of mine. I knew she was very sick with cancer. I saw two people with her, one at each elbow, and I saw her in bed. I also saw her spirit.*

The voice said, "Follow them." So I followed. We came to a huge building and I thought it was strange. Walking around it I thought, "I'll never be able to get in. There are no doors." But the voice said, "Just follow," so I did, and then I realized we were floating, fast. I saw them take her into a big room. I noticed there were no windows, nothing, only flowers on the wall. There was a sweet smell. Light came from above rather than from the sides or from windows. I remember it as though it was just yesterday.

She looked at her friend in bed and at the two people who were with her. As she reflected on what she saw, the voice commanded her again, saying, "Come with me." And again, she obeyed. *This time I found myself in a huge hall with a lot of people hugging and kissing. Some were crying. I heard [my friend] say, "It's okay. I'm not going to be gone that long. It's okay." Then an elderly man and a young man took her. I followed them, because the voice said, "Follow them."*

Vigdis followed and realized she was on the north coast of Iceland. *I wondered where I was, and just like that I found myself in a small room where a woman was giving birth. I could smell it. Birth has a special smell. I heard the baby cry, and then I woke up, just like that.*

Back in her bedroom she found her coffee had spilled on her newspaper and she wondered where she had been. *It was important to know where I had been so I could telephone and find out if a baby had just been born.* But she had no idea where the birthing room was located, so she had to abandon that possibility.

However, her friend did provide proof of the reality of her soul travel. *I called [my friend's] brother and asked, "Has she passed away?" "No, no, no," he said. "I talked to her last night." I said, "Please check on it. You are her brother, so they will tell you. They won't tell me." Ten minutes later he phoned me back. "She passed away 15 minutes ago," he said. So I got proof of that, but I didn't get proof that the baby was born.*

Proof came to Halldór, the fisherman turned carpenter, in a different way when he had a sitting with a well-known medium. *I sat in front of him and he said, "It's better if you believe in what I'm going to do." I said I don't believe. Okay. He talked to me, and as he talked I fell asleep, and I stayed asleep for half an hour. When I awoke we went to the kitchen for coffee and to talk. He told me many things about myself. Later at home I asked my mother and we discovered that everything he told me was true.* Implicit in Halldór's account is the conviction that the medium could not possibly have known in advance about his personal life.

Halldór had a similar experience later, when just for fun, he and his wife were invited at the last minute to take part in a sitting. *This couple wanted to go with another couple, but we substituted for the other couple. I thought good, they expect the others and don't know us, so there is no time to collect information about us.* I asked, who appeared in that meeting? *First a friend of ours who drowned 2 years earlier. Then, strange to say, my mother's father. The description that was given fits a picture I have.* So it sounded convincing? *Yes.*

Ingi is a man in his early thirties, I would guess, whose parents are already both dead. He is very effeminate, very attractive, living in a long-standing marriage-like gay relationship. I was asking if he had visited with his parents since they had passed away and his answer was, *Yes, I have gotten messages in private séances. I was quite sure that my mother came. The medium described my mother quite well. She said, "There is a lady here who died recently. She has blood here,"* which he clarified for me by placing his hand over his chest. *My mother died when the artery from her heart burst. I'm quite sure it was my mother. I'm quite sure the medium didn't know. She thought she had a message from my grandmother, but it was my mother.*

What did your mother want you to know? *Well, there wasn't any clear message. The medium just described some things about her.* Did your father appear as well? *Yes, although it was not as strong.* Did he have a message for you? *Yes. Yes. I already knew what he told me that evening, but he had never said it to me directly when he was alive, never clearly.* What did he want you to know? Ingi hesitated, searching for the right words. *Well,* he said at last, *he told me that he liked me just the way I am. That came through the medium.* All of us who know Ingi feel the same way, but it obviously meant a lot to him that his father finally said it straight out and unequivocally.

Gudmundur, Thordis, Adalbjörg, Vigdis, Halldór, Ingi, and others who told similar stories all base their claims of certitude on one or a few experiences like these. They know of many cases in which utterances turn out to be wrong, but falsification is not taken as a test of the belief. On the contrary, it is universally acknowledged that mistakes are common. Siggi, the medium in northern Iceland, may or may not represent a common viewpoint on this issue, but he explained errors in this way. *When in a non-trance state and simply responding to spirits that happen to attract attention, a medium will usually only be about 15 percent correct. When doing a proper sitting with attention focused for spirit communication, one can expect to be 50 to 60 percent correct. When the medium is in a deep trance, correctness can reach 70 percent.* Siggi's goal is to achieve an accuracy of 70 percent. A failure rate of 30 to 50 percent is not taken as a reason to disbelieve.

Since early in the 20th century scientists have added their support in limited ways. What they can claim was summarized for me in a conversation with Iceland's eminent parapsychologist, Professor Erlendur Haraldsson, just before I left my post at the university. Based on decades of research that included formal experiments, he reminded me that there are solid arguments against the likelihood of survival after death, including evidence that memory and personality are dependent on the brain, which disintegrates. But then, shrugging his shoulders as though to acknowledge a lifetime of research that produced only limited results, he added, *I think there is something to speak for it, but I don't think we can be absolutely sure. Yet, there are many strange experiences which are in line with the theory that we survive beyond death.* Finally he added, *there are limits to what we can know and what we can understand.*

A VIBRANT SPIRITUALITY

In the end it really doesn't matter whether spirits of the dead truly exist or whether they are merely the imagined fictions of wishful thinking. What I found associated with efforts to interact with spirits was what I will refer to as a marvelous spirituality. There is a play on words in my use here of the idea of being spiritual. It has nothing to do with spirits of the dead. Rather, I would define spirituality as a way of living that makes it possible for an individual to be filled with love and respect for others, such that the fulfillment of self is acknowledged as being most fully achieved only when one invests oneself in the well-being and happiness of others.

The experiences of individuals, the seances of spirit mediums, and the activities of spirit circles structured spirituality in very effective ways. I think of Halldór, whose love of his father survived the grave. Of Jóhanna and Thordis who live with the surviving affection of a grandmother. Of Gully and Gudrun who love dogs, animals, and garden flowers. Of Erla who inspires the love of her students because she loves them so much in return. Of Catherine who assured her clients, *There's lots of love from spirit for both of you.* Of Marta, Thorunn, and Magnus who, with members of their meditation circles, send love and healing wishes to hundreds of people as the months and years go by. And from Vigdis, who in her opening prayer for a séance asks the heavenly father "to surround us . . . with love."

For most people, the heartfelt, meaningful religion of Iceland is not that of the official national Lutheran church, which is routinized and buried in scarcely attended churches overseen by a priesthood of civil servants. The true religion of Iceland is unnamed. It is not thought of as a "religion." It exists as the largely uninstitutionalized belief that life survives death in a spirit world, that one can converse with the dead across that funereal divide, that life and the afterlife are ways we all must travel until we graduate from that university of the cosmos in which the lesson we all ultimately must learn is that the meaning of life is to love one another and the planet that nurtures us. One can be a complete skeptic about ghosts and spirits and still adhere to the belief that life is like a school, in which the lesson is about loving. I was inspired by that. I hope you will be too.

References

Adalsteinsson, Jón Hnefill, 1978. *Under the Cloak.* Stockholm: Almquist & Wiksell.

Adalsteinsson, Jón Hnefill, 1987. Wrestling with a Ghost in Icelandic Popular Belief. *Scandinavian Yearbook of Folklore,* 43: 7–20.

Anderson, Robert, 1991. The Efficacy of Ethnomedicine: Research Methods in Trouble. *Medical Anthropology 13* (1–2): 1–17.

Anderson, Robert, 1992a. Comfrey in the Chinese Materia Medica. *Asian Medicine Newsletter 2* (new series): 7–11.

Anderson, Robert, 1992b. Standards for Interprofessional Relations. In *Chiropractic Standards of Practice and Quality of Care* (pp. 163–178), Herbert J. Vear, ed. Gaithersburg, MD: Aspen.

Anderson, Robert, 1996. *Magic, Science, and Health: The Aims and Achievements of Medical Anthropology.* Fort Worth, TX: Harcourt Brace.

Anderson, Robert, 2000. *Alternative and Conventional Medicine in Iceland: The Diagnosis and Treatment of Low Back Pain.* Public Health in Iceland. Supplement 2000 nr. 1. Reykjavík: Directorate of Health.

Anderson, Robert, 2003a. Defining the Supernatural in Iceland. *Anthropological Forum 13*(2): 125–130.

Anderson, Robert, 2003b. Constraint and Freedom in Icelandic Conversions. In *The Anthropology of Religious Conversion* (pp. 123–131), Andrew Buckser and Stephen D. Glazier, eds. Lanham, MD: Rowman & Littlefield.

Anderson, Robert and Barbara Gallatin Anderson, 1964. *The Vanishing Village: A Danish Maritime Community.* Seattle: University of Washington Press.

Anderson, Robert and Barbara Gallatin Anderson, 1965. *Bus Stop for Paris: The Transformation of a French Village.* Garden City, NY: Doubleday.

Anderson, Robert and Norman Klein, 2005. Two Ethnographers and One Bonesetter in Bali. In *Manipulating the Body: Bonesetting and Manual Medicine in Global Perspective* (pp. 1–19), Kathryn S. Oths and Servando Hinojosa, eds. Walnut Creek, CA: Altamira.

Bellah, Robert, 1964. Religious Evolution. *American Sociological Review,* 29: 358–374.

Benedict, Ruth, 1934. *Patterns of Culture.* Boston: Houghton Mifflin.

Bernstein, Alan E., 1993. *The Formation of Hell: Death and Retribution in the Ancient and Early Christian Worlds.* Ithaca, NY: Cornell University Press.

Bloch, Maurice, 1994. *Placing the Dead: Tombs, Ancestral Villages, and Kinship Organization in Madagascar.* Prospect Heights, IL: Waveland.

Bowen, John R., 2002. *Religions in Action: An Approach to the Anthropology of Religion,* 2nd ed. Boston: Allyn and Bacon.

Burkert, Walter, 1996. *Creation of the Sacred: Tracks of Biology in Early Religions.* Cambridge, MA: Harvard University Press.

Clifford, James, 1986. Introduction: Partial Truths. In *Writing Culture: The Poetics and Politics of Ethnography* (pp. 1–26), James Clifford and George E. Marcus, eds. Berkeley: University of California Press.

Cronk, Lee, 1999. *That Complex Whole: Culture and the Evolution of Human Behavior.* Boulder, CO: Westview.

Durkheim, Emile, 1915 [1912, original French edition]. *The Elementary Forms of the Religious Life.* J. W. Swain, tr. London: Allen & Unwin.

Edward, John, 2001. *Crossing Over: The Stories Behind the Stories.* New York: Princess.

Eriksen, Thomas Hylland, and Finn Sivert Nielsen, 2001. *A History of Anthropology.* London: Pluto.

Evans-Pritchard, E. E., 1937. *Witchcraft, Oracles, and Magic among the Azande.* Oxford: Clarendon.

Geertz, Clifford, 1973. Thick Description: Toward an Interpretive Theory of Culture. In *The Interpretation of Cultures: Selected Essays* (pp. 3–30). New York: Basic Books.

Goffman, Erving, 1959. *The Presentation of Self in Everyday Life.* Garden City, NY: Doubleday.

Greenfield, Sidney M., and André Droogers, eds., 2001. *Reinventing Religions: Syncretism and Transformation in Africa and the Americas.* Lanham, MD: Rowman & Littlefield.

Gudjonsson, Thorsteinn, 1976. *Astrobiology: The Science of the Universe.* Reykjavík: Bioradii.

Haraldsson, Elendur, 1988. Survey of Claimed Encounters with the Dead. *Omega* 19(2): 103–113.

Harner, Michael, 1990. *The Way of the Shaman,* 3rd ed. New York: HarperCollins.

Haviland, William W., 2002. *Cultural Anthropology,* 10th ed. Fort Worth, TX: Harcourt.

Heidegger, Martin, 1962. *Being and Time.* John Mcquarrie and Edward Robinson, tr. New York: Harper.

Hirschfeld, Lawrence A., 2002. Why Don't Anthropologists Like Children? *American Anthropologist* 104(2): 611–627.

Hostetler, John A., 1974. *Hutterite Society.* Baltimore: Johns Hopkins University Press.

Hreinsson, Vidar, Robert Cook, Terry Gunnell, Keneva Kunz, and Bernard Scudder, eds., 1997. *The Complete Sagas of Icelanders, Including 49 Tales,* vols. I–V. Reykjavík: Leifur Eiriksson.

Hufford, David J., 1982. *The Terror That Comes in the Night: An Experience-Centered Study of Supernatural Assault Traditions.* Philadelphia: University of Pennsylvania Press.

Hunter, David E., and Philip Whitten, 1976. *Encyclopedia of Anthropology.* New York: Harper & Row.

Jackson, Michael, 1989. *Paths Toward a Clearing: Radical Empiricism and Ethnographic Inquiry.* Bloomington: Indiana University Press.

Jaroff, Leon, 2001. Talking to the Dead. *Time,* March 5: 52.

Karlsson, Gunnar, 2000. *The History of Iceland.* Minneapolis: University of Minnesota Press.

Klass, Morton and Maxine Weisgrau, 1999. Introduction. In *Across Boundaries of Belief: Contemporary Issues in the Anthropology of Religion* (pp. 1–6), Morton Klass and Maxine Weisgrau, eds. Boulder, CO: Westview.

Kleinman, Arthur, 1980. *Patients and Healers in the Context of Culture: An Exploration of the Borderland between Anthropology, Medicine, and Psychiatry.* Berkeley: University of California Press.

Kluckhohn, Clyde, and William Kelly, 1945. The Concept of Culture. In *The Science of Man in the World Crisis,* Ralph Linton, ed. New York: Columbia University Press.

Lacy, Terry G., 1998. *Ring of Seasons: Iceland—Its Culture and History.* Ann Arbor: University of Michigan Press.

Landy, David, ed., 1977. *Culture, Disease, and Healing: Studies in Medical Anthropology.* New York: Macmillan.

Langness, L. L., and Gelya Frank, 1981. *Lives: An Anthropological Approach to Biography.* Novato, CA: Chandler & Sharp.

Le Goff, Jacques, 1984. *The Birth of Purgatory.* Arthur Goldhammer, tr. Chicago: University of Chicago Press.

Levinson, David, 1996. *Religion: A Cross Cultural Dictionary.* Oxford: Oxford University Press.

Lewis, Ioan M., 1986. *Religion in Context: Cults and Charisma.* Cambridge, UK: Cambridge University Press.

Linton, Ralph, 1937. *The Study of Man: An Introduction.* New York: Appleton-Century-Crofts.

McClenon, James, 1994. *Wondrous Events: Foundations of Religious Belief.* Philadelphia: University of Pennsylvania Press.

Mead, Margaret, 1928. *Coming of Age in Samoa.* New York: William Morrow.

Mead, Margaret, 1966. *New Lives for Old: Cultural Transformation—Manus, 1928–1953.* New York: Dell.

Merton, Robert K., 1957. *Social Theory and Social Structure.* Glencoe, IL: Free Press.

Micozzi, Marc S., ed., 2001. *Fundamentals of Complementary and Alternative Medicine,* 2nd ed. New York: Churchill Livingstone.

Miller, Barbara D., 2002. *Cultural Anthropology,* 2nd ed. Boston: Allyn and Bacon.

Park, Michael Alan, 2003. *Introducing Anthropology: An Integrated Approach,* 2nd ed. Boston: McGraw-Hill.

Pegg, Carole, 2001. *Mongolian Music, Dance, and Oral Narrative: Performing Diverse Identities*. Seattle: University of Washington Press.

Perry, Richard J., 2003. *Five Key Concepts in Anthropological Thinking*. Upper Saddle River, NJ: Prentice Hall.

Pike, Kenneth, 1954. *Language in Relation to a Unified Theory of the Structure of Human Behavior*, vol 1. Glendale, CA: Summer Institute of Linguistics.

Pjeturss, Helgi, 1919. Nýall: Nokkur Íslensk Drög til Heimsfræði og Lífeffræði. Reykjavík: Félagsprentsmidjan.

Polanyi, Michael, 1968. Life's Irreducible Structure. *Science 160:* 1308–1312.

Powell, Walter W. and Paul J. DiMaggio, 1991. Introduction. In *The New Institutionalism in Organizational Analysis* (pp. 1–38), Walter W. Powell and Paul J. DiMaggio, eds. Chicago: University of Chicago Press.

Rabinow, Paul, 1977. *Reflections on Fieldwork in Morocco*. Berkeley: University of California Press.

Rambo, Lewis R., 1993. *Understanding Religious Conversion*. New Haven, CT: Yale University Press.

Rappaport, Roy, 1999. *Ritual and Religion in the Making of Humanity*. Cambridge, UK: Cambridge University Press.

Redfield, Robert, 1955. *The Little Community*. Chicago: University of Chicago Press.

Rees, W. D., 1971. The Hallucinations of Widowhood. *British Medical Journal,* vol. 266: 209–221.

Roscoe, Paul, 2003. Margaret Mead, Reo Fortune, and Mountain Arapesh Warfare. *American Anthropologist 105*(3): 581–591.

Sanders, Todd, 2003. Reconsidering Witchcraft: Postcolonial Africa and Analytic (Un)Certainties. *American Anthropologist 105*(2): 338–352.

Schechner, Richard, 1985. Between Theater and Anthropology. Philadelphia: University of Pennsylvania Press.

Schouppe, F. X., 1984 [1893, original French edition]. *Purgatory: Explained by the Lives and Legends of the Saints*. Rockford, IL: Tan.

Sheils, Dean, 1975. Toward a Unified Theory of Ancestor Worship: A Cross-Cultural Study. *Social Forces 54:* 427–440.

Spencer, Frank, ed., 1982. *A History of Physical Anthropology*. New York: Academic Press.

Steadman, Lyle B., Craig T. Palmer, and Christopher F. Tilley, 1996. The Universality of Ancestor Worship. *Ethnology 35:* 63–76.

Stefánsdóttir, Erla, 1993. *Hafnarfjördur Hidden Worlds Map*. Published by the Hafnarfjördur Tourism Committee.

Strathern, Andrew, and Pamela J. Stewart, 1999. *Curing and Healing: Medical Anthropology in Global Perspective*. Durham, NC: Carolina Academic Press.

Stromberg, Peter G., 1986. *Symbols of Community: The Cultural System of a Swedish Church*. Tucson: University of Arizona Press.

Swatos, William H., Jr., and Loftur Reímar Gíssurarson, 1997. *Icelandic Spiritualism: Mediumship and Modernity in Iceland*. New Brunswick, NJ: Transaction.

Swidler, Ann, 1986. Culture in Action: Symbols and Strategies. *American Sociological Review 51:* 273–286.

Tomasson, Richard F., 2002. How Sweden Became So Secular. *Scandinavian Studies* 74(1): 61–88.

Turner, Alice K., 1993. *The History of Hell.* New York: Harcourt Brace.

Turner, Victor, 1967. *The Forest of Symbols: Aspects of Ndembu Ritual.* Ithaca, NY: Cornell University Press.

Turner, Victor, 1969. *The Ritual Process: Structure and Anti-Structure.* Ithaca, NY: Cornell University Press.

Turner, Victor, 1988. *The Anthropology of Performance.* New York: PAJ.

Tyler, Stephen A., 2004. Introduction to Cognitive Anthropology. In *Anthropological Theory: An Introductory History,* 3rd ed. (pp. 393–408), R. Jon McGee and Richard L. Warms, eds. Boston: McGraw-Hill.

Van Gennep, Arnold. 1960 [First published in 1909]. *The Rites of Passage.* M. Yizedom and G. Caffee, trs. Chicago: University of Chicago Press.

Weber, Max, 1947. *The Theory of Social and Economic Organization.* A. M. Henderson and Talcott Parsons, trs. New York: Free Press.

Willey, Gordon R., and Jeremy A. Sabloff, 1993. *A History of American Archaeology.* San Francisco: Freeman.

Index